Anthropology
and
Radical Humanism

Anthropology and Radical Humanism

Native and African American Narratives and the Myth of Race

Jack Glazier

MICHIGAN STATE UNIVERSITY PRESS | *East Lansing*

♾ The paper used in this publication meets the minimum requirements of
ANSI/NISO Z39.48-1992 (R 1997) (Permanence of Paper).

Michigan State University Press
East Lansing, Michigan 48823-5245

Printed and bound in the United States of America.

29 28 27 26 25 24 23 22 21 20   1 2 3 4 5 6 7 8 9 10

LIBRARY OF CONGRESS CATALOGING-IN-PUBLICATION DATA
Names: Glazier, Jack, author.
Title: Anthropology and radical humanism : native and
African American narratives and the myth of race / Jack Glazier.
Description: East Lansing, Michigan : Michigan State University Press, [2020]
| Includes bibliographical references and index.
Identifiers: LCCN 2019022078 | ISBN 9781611863505 (cloth) | ISBN 9781609176242 (pdf)
| ISBN 9781628963878 (kindle edition) | ISBN 9781628953862 (epub)
Subjects: LCSH: Radin, Paul, 1883-1959. | Humanism—United States.
| Winnebago Indians. | Slave narratives. | Anthropology—United States—History.
Classification: LCC GN21.R23 G53 2020 | DDC 306.3/62—dc23
LC record available at https://lccn.loc.gov/2019022078

Book design by Charlie Sharp, Sharp Designs, East Lansing, Michigan
Cover design by Erin Kirk New
Cover art by Kirsten Hinte | Adobe Stock

Michigan State University Press is a member of the Green Press Initiative and is committed to developing
and encouraging ecologically responsible publishing practices. For more information about the Green
Press Initiative and the use of recycled paper in book publishing, please visit www.greenpressinitiative.org.

Visit Michigan State University Press at *www.msupress.org*

✦

Remembering
Al, Bob, and Sam

✦

Contents

Preface

Paul Radin remains a distinctive figure in the history of anthropology, a virtuoso scholar whose catholic interests ranged across anthropology, linguistics, religion, literature, history, and philosophy. In relationship to his mentor, Franz Boas, and others within the Boas circle and beyond, Radin holds an eccentric position. He was unalterably opposed to natural-science models of culture, gravitating instead to the humanities. Early on as an anthropologist, he considered devoting himself exclusively to literature and history. Certainly brilliant, he could also be glib and inconsistent. Sociable and alienated, loved and deplored, he was a pure intellectual whose scholarly reputation lives in his prodigious publications on the ethnology and linguistics of native North America, particularly among the Winnebago and Ho-Chunk of Nebraska and Wisconsin.

In the 1980s, Mary Sacharoff Fast Wolf and Doris Woodward Radin, Paul Radin's widow, became close friends. At the time, Sacharoff Fast Wolf was an anthropology graduate student at San Francisco State University, where she wrote several papers on Radin, including her master's thesis, "Paul Radin: New Perspectives on Ethnology," submitted to the anthropology department in 1989. Captivated by her subject, she planned to write an intellectual biography of Radin. Doris Radin provided Sacharoff Fast Wolf with considerable help, including access to the Radin papers in her possession. She also told Sacharoff Fast Wolf about less well-known, undocumented aspects of Radin's career. Seeking additional material—particularly the recollections of those who knew him—Sacharoff Fast Wolf embarked on a vast effort to contact Radin's colleagues, friends, relatives, former students, both in Europe and the United States; archivists here and abroad; and even children of his Winnebago and Ho-Chunk informants. Explaining her project in each lengthy letter, she received numerous cooperative, often detailed replies, sometimes establishing continuing exchanges and epistolary friendships. Limited funds for travel prevented her from conducting extensive face-to-face interviews. Still, she amassed a remarkable set of letters that, together with her reading of Radin's published and unpublished work, would form the core of her projected book. Since the letters date from the 1980s, most of Sacharoff Fast Wolf's correspondents have passed away, and with them, except for her documentation, their memories of Paul Radin.

It is a great sadness that Mary Sacharoff Fast Wolf did not live to complete her admirable project. Sacharoff Fast Wolf and her husband, Calvin Fast Wolf, had made no provision for the disposition of their property, including the array of documents and Radin papers in her possession. At Calvin's subsequent death, the contents of the Fast Wolf apartment in San Francisco were cleared away by their landlord. Only through the alert and devoted efforts of Sacharoff Fast Wolf's friend, anthropologist Helene Hagan, were the Radin papers rescued from a trash bin. Hagan typed up some of Radin's handwritten pages before eventually arranging with her friend Mark Thiel, archivist at Marquette University, for the curation of the retrieved papers at that institution.

The unpublished Radin manuscript "Souls Piled Like Timber: The Religious Experience of the Prewar Negro" was part of Sacharoff Fast Wolf's document collection. "Souls" derived from Radin's work as research professor of anthropology at Fisk University from 1927 to 1930. He and graduate student Andrew Polk Watson, working in Nashville, collected narratives from elderly African Americans, either former slaves or those born shortly after the Civil War. That work represents Radin's least known fieldwork and his only research among African Americans.

In 2017, I began an examination of digitized copies of the documents Mary Sacharoff Fast Wolf had compiled. Having spent some years in research and writing on African American history and culture in the upper South, I was well aware of Radin's work in Nashville. The "Souls" manuscript, albeit with three missing chapters, therefore held considerable interest for me. It represented Radin's only statement about his African American research. I thought there was some small possibility of publishing it, despite the missing segments. With its many marginal notes, emendations, and odd, nonsequential, or missing pagination, it was a long way from publishable quality. That some of the narratives in "Souls" had already appeared, published by Fisk University in 1945 and by a Christian printer in 1968, presented yet another obstacle. After writing a lengthy editor's introduction and imposing some order on the surviving chapters, I tried to interest a publisher. My doubts about the viability of the manuscript were confirmed when several presses reported that they had no interest in the publication I proposed.

Consequently, with access to the Sacharoff Fast Wolf collection in the Marquette Archives, I decided to write the book at hand, incorporating heretofore unknown aspects of Radin's Nashville work into a fresh consideration of his overall career. The Radin-Watson collaboration yielded landmark first-person narrations as exceptional as they were rare. As this study shows, they evince some remarkable parallels to the spiritual world Radin documented among the Winnebago twenty years before. Elderly African Americans, survivors of slavery whose thoughts and emotions were generally denigrated in America of 1930, confided their stories to two men who recognized their profound import. As this country is only now facing the pernicious residue of slavery and the broken promise of postbellum civil rights, the Radin-Watson texts compel attention. They lay bare the intellectual and emotional resources that African Americans mustered to assert their human dignity and value in the face of unremitting scorn and defamation that continued into their old age.

In sum, this book joins biography, culture theory, and history to assess the many implications of Radin's self-defined goal of "finding the native," whether in Nashville or on the American prairie, effectively establishing the complex, human-centered quality of his unique legacy and, at the same time, that of the people who confided their stories to him.

Acknowledgments

Thanks are due several individuals and institutions for their help in the preparation of this book. Mark Thiel, archivist at Marquette University, kindly responded to my requests for digital copies of letters and manuscripts in the Radin collection. I appreciate the great convenience this afforded me in the conduct of my research. I am grateful to DeLisa Harris, reference librarian at the Fisk University Library, for making the papers of Charles S. Johnson available to me. I thank the Brandeis University Archives for providing a copy of Max Radin's reflections on the Radin family in Lodz, Poland. The American Philosophical Society has done a great service to scholars interested in Franz Boas by putting the Boas Papers online. Some of the Boas correspondence judged sensitive has been held back until their content could be vetted. I appreciate the responsiveness of the APS to my requests for the early release of particular letters. Once again I thank the splendid staff of the Mary Church Terrell Main Library of Oberlin College for assistance with multiple matters. I called on various colleagues regarding several ideas developed in this book, and with gratitude acknowledge the comments of Herb Lewis, Alice Kehoe, Grant Arndt, and Richard Werbner. Early on, as I contemplated this book, I benefited from conversations with late friends and esteemed associates Nancy Lurie and Erika Bourguignon. A completed draft of the manuscript received positive evaluations from two anonymous press readers, whom I thank for their constructive suggestions. It was my great pleasure to learn more about Paul Radin's Fisk collaborator Andrew Polk Watson, and his career at Wiley College through discussions by phone or in person with his surviving sons, Andrew Polk Watson Jr. and Bransford Watson. Finally, I thank Julie Loehr, Kristine Blakeslee, and Amanda Frost of Michigan State University Press for their advice and assistance.

A Note on Tribal Nomenclature

The Winnebago constitute two federally recognized American Indian tribes residing in Wisconsin and Nebraska. The Wisconsin segment identifies itself as "Ho-Chunk" in keeping with their historic self-designation. The Nebraska segment continues to utilize the more familiar Algonquin term "Winnebago" adopted by white settlers. Paul Radin conducted fieldwork in Wisconsin and Nebraska among people he collectively referred to as "Winnebago." To avoid confusion, I retain for the most part Radin's usage in his various books and articles. Occasional references in the text to the Wisconsin community as "Ho-Chunk" reflect the tribal name as it appears in recent publications or in contemporary usage.

Introduction

The publication of Paul Radin's *The Racial Myth* in 1934 marked the first sustained anthropological critique of the foundational racial theory of the newly ascendant Third Reich. *The Racial Myth* expressed the author's personal and professional values while at the same time showing the irrelevance of racial factors to any empirical understanding of historical or social questions. A moral, humanistic vision guided Radin in unmasking "the unrelieved stupidity and cruelty to which a racial and nationalistic myth can be pushed."[1] He asserted that in "the crisis of civilization through which we are now passing, no thinking and feeling man can long remain untouched and unaffected." Radin argued with great faith in reason that an awareness of the influence of diverse peoples in the development of human civilization would render erroneous all assertions of racial superiority.[2] Moreover, he thought that ethnological and historical evidence could expose racial fictions, whether in Germany or the United States, and that a liberating anthropology built on that evidence would ultimately free people from the heavy burden, sometimes catastrophic, of their own deep-rooted prejudices. Reason alone, however, proved insufficient as substantial numbers of people in Europe and the United States throughout the 1930s and beyond continued to embrace illusory beliefs and the destructive actions they motivated. Even with the defeat of fascism, other versions of the racial fantasy persisted, usually on the margins, but they are now rhetorically and violently resurgent in the United States and Europe as these words are written. It is utterly dispiriting that the admonitions in the worn pages of *The Racial Myth* again resonate in a world where political inspiration can still be found in the incitement of "blood and soil."

Radin's message was especially welcome among African Americans, who were particularly attuned to his reasoned arguments in support of racial equality. Although the rise of Nazism and the delusions of the Nordic myth within Europe motivated the book, its relevance extended well beyond events in Germany. Black Americans were day by day living with the malignant consequences of similarly vicious racial fantasies, both home-grown and borrowed. Radin exposed historical distortions positing race as the explanatory key to understanding culture, progress, and the human career worldwide.

Accordingly, *The Racial Myth* elicited particularly strong notices in the African American press. The *Pittsburgh Courier,* for example, headlined its review "California U Scientist Lauds Negro Culture." Stating that "Dr. Paul Radin, Anthropologist, Claims That No Race Is Fundamentally Superior to Another," the *Courier* observed that Radin studied the contributions of multiple races to human civilization and concluded that "all races have combined in the building of modern culture."

The newspaper, quoting Radin, praised his recognition in East and West Africa of "a rich artistic development, an amazing prose and poetry, and a complex religious development" as indices of "a great and advanced civilization."[3] Radin criticized the "strange and thoroughly reprehensible artistic obscurantism that would extol the poetry, wisdom, and religiosity of the psalms and not give a high measure of praise" to a Yoruba hymn celebrating nature and the benevolence and justice of the high God.[4] Answering eugenicists' claims of Negro inferiority, Radin, the *Courier* pointed out, showed that in the United States, under the severest conditions, enslaved Africans over the course of three centuries created an original literature and music. By contrast, "it took Northern Europe, under infinitely more favorable conditions, at least twice as long to absorb Graeco-Roman civilization and do anything with it."[5] To those skeptical of the terms "literature" or "literary" applied to dark-skinned people without writing, Radin later wrote, "Every anthropologist knows, or should know, that there is no inherent correlation between literacy and artistic and literary ability or craftsmanship."[6] In attributing "civilization" to African-derived peoples, Radin stood against the broadest spectrum of academic and public opinion in the 1930s.

In the United States of the early 1930s, Radin's observations about African and African American achievement were nothing short of radical. On matters of race and racism, Radin was the most outspoken critic among the first generation of Franz Boas's students. Equally disturbed by the twin dangers of racism and an extreme, xenophobic nationalism, both men confronted popular thinking that rationalized the segregated and socially unequal character of American society. Misrepresentation and disparagement, often in the guise of science, suffused portrayals of the African American experience both in slavery and the postbellum years of American apartheid. African American writers and scholars were of course especially critical of academic and popular racial myths and thus shared common ground with an emergent American anthropology, substantially shaped by Franz Boas and his critique of the biopolitics of race.

In the same vein, the sociologist Charles S. Johnson attacked racism rationalized through faulty social science. Prior to his 1928 appointment at Fisk University, where he was chair of the Social Science Institute during Radin's three-year research stay (1927–1930), Johnson edited the influential journal *Opportunity,* sponsored by the National Urban League. Besides its promotion of the Harlem Renaissance, the journal also confronted biological explanations of social questions. Johnson pointed out, for example, that a Harvard professor declared "that the brains of Negro children cease to function after the age of fourteen." That occurred in a classroom where some Negro students excelled "his supernally endowed Nordics." A Columbia professor, Johnson continued, asserted that the Army Intelligence Tests indicated that the innate capacity of Negroes did not exceed that of white children. Likewise, Princeton classes heard of an unalterable inferiority of black people in relationship to Nordics.[7]

Academic racism in various disciplines across the humanities and social sciences joined popular versions through the 1940s. Captive to the unexamined racial stereotypes of the time, historians for the most part shared the assumptions of the dominant Jim Crow pattern of the country, thereby disfiguring their representations of the lives and experiences of African Americans. By contrast, a genuine, objective focus on black history was the almost exclusive province of African American scholars, such as the historians Carter Woodson and W. E. B. Du Bois. Black sociologists, including Johnson, E. Franklin Frazier, and Du Bois, who was equally at home in sociology and history, faced a less recalcitrant profession. Black sociologists, despite the lingering racism within their discipline, did not part company with their white colleagues by forming a professional association separate from the American

Sociological Society. Black historians, however, joined together in the Association for the Study of Negro Life and History, established in 1915 through the efforts of Carter Woodson. Within a year, Woodson launched the *Journal of Negro History* as an outlet for research by black scholars writing black history free of the intellectually crippling suppositions of mainstream American historical scholarship. Johnson, Du Bois, Woodson, and other black sociologists and historians found support in American anthropology, unencumbered as it was by specious ideas about race embedded within the sociological and historical professions.

At the same time, anthropology as a discipline was confronting the much larger and seemingly intractable issue of racism in the American political and social order. Boasian anthropology asked fundamental questions about the human species, at once part of the natural world and transcending it through learned and variable cultural traditions. Biology neither determined nor explained those traditions, proceeding as they did independently of the physical differences characterizing human populations. In other words, the major task of a reconfigured anthropology as practiced by Boas and his students was the replacement of biological race by culture as the behavioral and cognitive wellspring of a universal humanity.

Summoning the findings of anthropology and history, Radin negated erroneous views of African peoples, including those in the diaspora, as naturally incapable of adding even the smallest measure of value to the long record of human achievement. People of African origin, in the conventional view, might be elevated or redeemed, but only through exposure to Christianity that slavery had made possible. Yet they would forever suffer the imagined liabilities of racial inferiority that nature had allegedly imposed.

For Radin, the radical humanist, not even centuries of enslavement of African peoples in the New World could stifle cultural achievement and the creation of literary and musical art uniquely their own. Shortly before publication of *The Racial Myth,* he also explored the ways in which enslaved Africans and their descendants transformed Christianity into a distinctive cosmology that they integrated into black tradition. That creative transformation captured Radin's attention in one of his least-known scholarly endeavors as research professor of anthropology at Fisk, where he and Andrew Polk Watson, an accomplished anthropology graduate student, collected the narratives of former slaves.

Radin's observations about African peoples enslaved in the United States are particularly significant in recognizing a characteristic American black culture prior to the landmark 1941 publication of Melville J. Herskovits's *The Myth of the Negro*

Past. Herskovits found African cultural resonances in black life in the New World despite centuries of slavery. Established opinion had posited a complete effacement of Africanisms in the United States, while granting the survival of African cultural patterns in the Caribbean and Latin America, particularly Brazil. Radin's view of an indigenous black culture, however, was not predicated on African survivals in the New World; it was rather self-generated, built on an indefatigable human resourcefulness that reinterpreted, under brutal conditions, the new universe of European cultural elements surrounding them. However different their emphases, Radin and Herskovits in the Boas tradition opposed ubiquitous scholarly and popular views of New World Africans as inferior people with neither a history nor a culture worthy of the name.

In the 1970s, when interest in African American culture was intensifying, Sidney Mintz remained agnostic about the provenance but not the reality of a characteristic African American culture. It was quite clear by that time that some of Herskovits's claims for an African origin of certain African American practices depended on very thin evidence. But ultimately that did not negate the reality of a distinctive African American culture in the United States. Accordingly, Mintz observed, in the manner of Radin, that "the content of Afro-American cultures in this Hemisphere takes on its significance in what those who are Afro-Americans have done with it, not in whether its origins are demonstrably African."[8] At about the same time, the historian Lawrence W. Levine also thought that the preoccupation with origins was overdrawn as the key legitimating factor in identifying an authentic African American culture.

> We have only gradually come to recognize not merely the sheer complexity of the question of origins but also its irrelevancy for an understanding of consciousness. It is not necessary for a people to originate or invent all or even most of the elements of their culture. It is necessary only that these components become their own, embedded in their traditions, expressive of their worldview and life style.[9]

Aside from the analytical, historical, and sociological questions about the relationship between Africa and the New World, those issues have remained emotionally charged since they also concern the continuing African American quest for cultural dignity and individual and collective self-esteem.

On the social dimension of race beyond its physical manifestations, the dominant social-science perspective of the 1920s and 1930s centered in the discipline of sociology, particularly under the influence of Robert E. Park of the University of Chicago. Park and others, including his African American students, the distinguished black sociologists E. Franklin Frazier and Charles S. Johnson, argued the conventional view that the experience of slavery had sundered all connections to Africa. African Americans, thus bereft of a distinctive African past, were instead shaped and influenced exclusively by their American experience of white domination, first through centuries of slavery and then segregation in virtually every area of social life. Americans of African descent, in the dominant sociological view, were a people who had undergone cultural if not social assimilation in the United States.

Herskovits's early foray into research on African Americans aligned him with Park's prevailing sociological view emphasizing the nearly complete obliteration of African cultural beliefs and practices among black Americans. Contributing to Alain Locke's *The New Negro,* a book celebrating the Harlem Renaissance, Herskovits in "The Negro's Americanism" observed nothing resembling a distinct Negro culture in Harlem. And regarding the transatlantic movement of cultural traits carried by slaves, he says simply, "Of African culture, not a trace."[10] Instead, he considered the social life of Harlem typical of the American institutional pattern, including jobs, businesses, recreation, and the like, distinguished only by race.[11] In the context of Locke's landmark volume, Herskovits's paper was stunningly out of step with many of the chapters. Locke and his contributors were emphasizing a new, confident, and dynamic spirit among black Americans manifesting itself in the arts and other domains of American life. The new Negro was anything but a reproduction of the white American. By 1935, with the publication of a *New Republic* article identifying Africanisms in the United States, Herskovits had reversed course, culminating six years later in *The Myth of the Negro Past.*[12]

When Radin published *The Racial Myth,* the color bar and social inequality were vigorously maintained by law and custom, questioned only by African Americans and a few white allies. The rise of Nazism and its assumption of political power in Germany in 1933 were regarded approvingly by many Americans who believed in black inferiority and the alleged dangers posed by colored peoples, Jews, and other non-Aryans. Displays of Nazi emblems in the United States, open expressions of anti-Semitism, admiration of the Third Reich, even by heroic public figures such as Charles Lindbergh, were not unusual during that decade and up to the eve of American entry into World War II. Just months before Nazi forces invaded Poland, more than twenty thousand people rallied in Madison Square

Garden, many in German-style uniforms, to hear the anti-Semitic blather of Fritz Kuhn, head of the German-American Bund. Thousands of other like-minded people across the United States were indeed "Hitler's American friends" in the words of Bradley W. Hart.[13] Influential figures in the United States, such as Madison Grant, alarmist patrician author of the racist screed *The Passing of the Great Race,* owed their fame to the promotion of eugenics and race theory that rationalized restricting the growth of nonwhite populations in the United States. Refracting history through the distorted lens of race, they argued for the strict separation of white people from all others to avoid race mixing and ultimately miscegenation, believed to portend the doom of biologically ordained white domination. Aryan ideology was not simply a pernicious European development. Nazi scientists early on also looked to the United States as a model for establishing eugenics as a national program. American eugenicists in turn borrowed considerably from Nazi race theorists.[14]

Very sympathetic to race-based eugenics, Congress in 1921 severely curtailed the immigration of allegedly inferior eastern and southern Europeans and in 1924 enacted even more draconian restrictions. For the previous four decades, other efforts aimed to restrict the arrival of Italians, Slavs, and Jews, so different from the old stock of Anglo-American Protestants who, for all their alleged biological vigor, were believed vulnerable to certain decline should race mixing occur. Through the 1930s, eugenics continued to be a powerful cudgel in the hands of American racists determined to resist the "passing of the great race."

Strenuously opposing Nazi racial doctrines and equally grotesque domestic manifestations was a small group of anthropologists who had studied with Boas. Radin and others were providing the empirical and theoretical armature against popular and academic support of racialized public policy. Over the first four decades of the twentieth century, they established modern four-field American anthropology with the concept of culture, or the nongenetic heritage of humankind, at the very center of the new discipline. Biology was no longer destiny, race no longer the measure of human achievement, Western society no longer the pinnacle of the human career on earth. They proved that race, language, and culture are fully independent phenomena. History, not the germ plasm, accounts for any recurrent associations between them.

Nevertheless, intellectual disagreements were common within the Boas circle beginning with the earliest student cohort and continuing into the subsequent generations. For example, in *The Method and Theory of Ethnology,* Radin sharply criticized Boas's diffusionist studies and, more moderately, those of his good friend and fellow Boas alumnus Robert Lowie, to whom he dedicated the book. Others also engaged their teacher and each other over various issues, such as the role of the individual in culture; the place of psychology in anthropology; the relationship between language, culture, and thought; the nature of historical as opposed to scientific explanations; and the like. A. L. Kroeber aptly observed that there was never anything resembling a "Boas school," or a strict protocol directing research along particular lines.[15] Kroeber made his remarks in an article setting forth his own eccentric view of history that managed to exclude the lion's share of Boas's work conventionally regarded as culture history.[16] Responding, Boas asserted "my complete disagreement with his interpretation."[17] Nonetheless, as Leslie White demonstrated, Kroeber and others, beginning with Radin, Lowie, and Edward Sapir, whether or not they denied the reality of a "Boas school," continued to use the term.[18] Hostile to Boasian anthropology in general, White went much further; he criticized Boas not only as a scholar but also as "the head of a cult," the charismatic leader of worshipful followers.[19]

Controversy lay outside the mutual respect and warm personal feelings between Boas and Kroeber. Contemplating his retirement, Boas without success hoped to persuade Kroeber to leave Berkeley and come to Columbia as his successor. An equally cherished but unrealized hope was that Sapir, then at Yale, might join Kroeber in accepting an offer from Columbia.[20] By contrast Radin, although he held his mentor in high intellectual esteem despite serious theoretical disagreements, sometimes sent accusatory letters to Boas over failures to gain grants administered by his mentor or concerning personal criticism that Radin felt was unfair. The affectionate personal feelings that marked Boas's relationship to Kroeber, Lowie, and Sapir and extended to later students, including Benedict, Mead, Hurston, Klineberg, and others, were altogether missing regarding Radin.

But however much intellectual dispute or even interpersonal conflict divided the anthropologists who studied with Boas, none dissented from his transformational contributions to American anthropology, to scientific knowledge, and ultimately to American intellectual thought. Quite the contrary. They sustained and promulgated Boas's scientific argument that biological race, language, and culture bore no essential or inevitable substantive relationship to each other, and that, consequently, race constituted an explanatory cul-de-sac in efforts to understand human history, behavior, or cultural differences. Their undertaking was formidable since biological explanations of human behavior pervaded popular thinking; moreover, those views had a strong grip on the academic world, including those physical anthropologists espousing remnants of pre-Boasian race theory in the United States.

Radin's claim in *The Racial Myth* that racial superiority is imaginary and unfounded was a credo of those who studied with Boas. It thus comes as no surprise that African American observers, such as the *Pittsburgh Courier* reviewer previously noted, would find not only much to admire intellectually but also much to celebrate. Radin undermined the entire rationale of any political order built on racial hierarchy. He remained throughout his life an outspoken critic of racial segregation, real estate covenants, and all other exclusions defined by race. These were radical positions in the United States during Radin's career, and his forthright anti-racism attracted intrusive FBI scrutiny. Over several years, the FBI compiled a substantial Radin dossier on his associations, his speaking engagements, and his support of civil rights. Until the end of his life, his various academic appointments were only temporary, certainly related to questions about his personal reliability and probity. But Radin's radical politics may very well have diminished his chances of securing a continuing academic appointment.

As to his research, few field encounters can rival the longevity of the relationship between Paul Radin and the Winnebago of Nebraska and Wisconsin. His extensive writings ranged from his first Winnebago publication in 1911 to his last two in 1956, three years before his death. During a long professional life, Radin wove his Winnebago research into much of his published work set in an ethnographic present prior to sustained contact with the expansionist American state. Over the course of his field studies, Radin gained a high level of competence in the language, and his writing ranged widely across a spectrum of institutions and practices, reconstructed for the most part from his informants' descriptions. He wrote on social organization, linguistics, religion, ritual, narratives (including folklore), and other aspects of expressive culture. His collection of the life history of Crashing Thunder established native autobiography as a lasting contribution to anthropological method and set the stage for his collection of autobiographies among aged former slaves in Nashville.

Radin also wrote on the linguistics and the culture history of other Indian groups in the United States, Canada, Mexico, and South America. Of the linguistics scholars among Franz Boas's many accomplished students, Radin ranked high, although none rivalled the gifted Edward Sapir in the range and scope of his linguistic work. Radin also commanded a remarkably broad range of ethnographic literature, evidenced by his scholarly absorption in indigenous philosophy and religion among the peoples of North America, Africa, Asia, and the Pacific.

Yet Radin was curiously silent in print, lectures, and conversation about his three-year research appointment at Fisk beginning in 1927.[21] Although he produced a manuscript, it did not reach publication; nor did he publish any analytic papers on the materials he and Andrew Polk Watson, a Fisk graduate student, assembled. Consequently, anthropologists and others interested in the African American experience know little beyond the fact that Radin held a research position at Fisk. Living in Nashville, he and Watson each collected African American autobiographies narrated by former slaves. Under Radin's supervision but without his professor's regular participation, Watson also recorded accounts of religious conversion among this same population. Although brief, Radin's work at Fisk is nonetheless a notable chapter in American anthropology, pointing up its singularity among academic disciplines in sharing the methodological and interpretive goals of the black history movement. Consistent with Woodson, Du Bois, and others, Radin portrayed African Americans as worthy subjects of history and authoritative interpreters of their own experience. His work is yet another corrective to various misplaced charges characterizing anthropology as a colonial endeavor that objectifies people as an exotic, ahistorical Other.[22]

Given the paucity of his published work on African Americans, Radin's research at Fisk appears incidental to his worldwide fame as an independently minded scholar concentrating on native North America and author of some seventeen books. He did not live to see the publication in his honor of a long-planned *Festschrift* of nearly one thousand pages edited by his friend and Brandeis colleague Stanley Diamond. Comprised of more than fifty papers, the *Festschrift* ranged over numerous topics, aptly reflecting Radin's own unbounded interests and contributions to his profession.[23] Yet that paean to Radin's career barely mentions his Fisk years, containing as it does only a three-sentence reference by Cora Du Bois, who mistakenly observed that his Fisk narratives had never reached publication.[24] Additionally, a noteworthy collection of two decades later appropriately featured Radin as one of the "key figures in the history of anthropology," but with only a passing reference to his stay in Nashville.[25] Finally, a recent book on Boas and his students contains a chapter on Radin yet fails to mention his African American collection.[26]

These various omissions are understandable since Radin did not live to complete his manuscript "Souls Piled Like Timber: The Religious Experience of the

Pre-War Negro," which would have brought his Fisk research to a wide audience. As it stands, he left few traces of his Fisk appointment, where the archives contain only some unpublished narratives from the Radin-Watson collaboration as well as a partial printing of *God Struck Me Dead: Religious Conversion Experiences and Autobiographies of Negro Ex-Slaves*, published by Fisk University in 1945.[27] The latter publication contains a selection of some of the autobiographies and conversion narratives of the Radin-Watson collaboration, but without analysis, except for a brief introductory essay by Radin.

Understanding the significance of Radin's Fisk interlude requires close attention to several factors marking the much larger, highly racialized climate in which it occurred. The critique of popular and academic thinking about race from approximately 1900 to 1945 was in process, and American anthropology pointed the way to a more enlightened vision. Radin's work among African Americans in the late 1920s is a case in point, exemplifying the unique role of anthropology among the academic disciplines in confronting and refuting the biopolitics of race.

The continuing critique of racism that defined American anthropology was primarily scientific, built on empirical and statistical research inspired by Boas. It was also driven by the anti-racist human values of Radin and others within the Boas circle. Boas, particularly, acted on his personal commitment to the cause of social equality and justice, as his many unselfish efforts on behalf of black students, scholars, and institutions attest. Owing to their minority and/or immigrant status, many of Boas's graduate students were, like himself, "marginal natives" outside of the normative Anglo-Protestant mainstream. In the first four turbulent decades of the twentieth century, they were assuredly not "one hundred percent American," a measure of worth and belonging lampooned by Ralph Linton in 1937.[28] Like all effective satire, Linton's brief send-up exposed absurdity, which in this case focused on cheap patriotism and claims of cultural purity. He drew back the thin veil covering the xenophobia, ignorance, and complacency of those who considered themselves real Americans. Many of Boas's students were Jewish immigrants like himself or second-generation American Jews. Kroeber, although not Jewish, was the son of German immigrants and spoke German as his first language. Boas's close mentorship also included large numbers of non-Jewish anthropologists sharing his viewpoint on race. Moreover, anthropology among academic fields, at least that part centered in New York around Boas and at Berkeley under Kroeber's stewardship, was particularly attractive to women, both Jewish (e.g., Ruth Landes, Gene Weltfish, Ruth Bunzel, Amelia Susman, Esther Goldfrank) and non-Jewish (e.g., Ruth Benedict,

Margaret Mead, Ella Deloria, Gladys Reichard, Zora Neale Hurston); they were, in comparison to their presence in other disciplines, relatively well represented in anthropology. Quite out of keeping with the administrative leadership and the prevailing pattern in other disciplines, Boas at retirement as department head at Columbia recommended Ruth Benedict as his successor. He was overruled by the president of the university.[29] As a black woman, Hurston brought her own unique experiences of marginalization to her anthropological studies in which she enjoyed the strong support of Boas, whom she affectionately referred to as the "king of kings." Never patronizing, he demanded of her and all others their best work.[30] Amelia Susman, interested in studying for a graduate degree in psychology, was advised that "only the Department of Anthropology at Columbia University under Franz Boas willingly accepted women into its graduate program." Most other disciplines were strictly men only. Susman was accepted at Columbia in 1935."[31]

In looking at the United States, these anthropologists—as individuals straddling two worlds through gender, race, or religion—could thus be "close at a distance." They were well-positioned to expose ill-conceived racial beliefs as American cultural artifacts, or ethnocentric reflections of local tradition, in this case the American race obsession, rather than the universal findings of science. Yet scientifically groundless beliefs persisted, exercising their most enduring and damaging influence on statutory law and public policy regarding African Americans. Immigrants as well, including Jews, Slavs, Italians, and others from heavily Catholic eastern and southern Europe, did not fit the Anglo-Protestant template and ran afoul of highly discriminatory public policies. Boas and those he mentored thus had a special stake in laying bare the biopolitics of race that impeded not only their own life chances but also those of so many people with whom they identified.

When Radin arrived at Fisk, Charles S. Johnson was about to head the department of social sciences, where he assembled a multiracial group of scholars focused on empirical studies of race relations. Radin's collaboration with his student Andrew Polk Watson occurred in that unique research setting. Johnson and his colleagues aimed to put black people at the center of research projects as subjects rather than objects. Their research documented the lived experience of black people, who were given wide latitude to narrate their life stories. Radin brought to Fisk his long experience of collecting Winnebago narratives and instructed Watson in the procedures that he had successfully employed in Nebraska and Wisconsin.

Johnson created a research center that rivaled the department of his mentor, Robert Park at the University of Chicago. He maintained a wide network of professional relationships with not only sociologists but also prominent anthropologists, including Radin and Boas as well as Melville Herskovits and Bronislaw Malinowski. Beyond his administrative duties, Johnson as a scholar undertook innovative field research that will be considered subsequently.

Radin's interest in the collection of African American narratives of enslavement, liberation, and spiritual rebirth complemented both Johnson's interests and, especially, an oral history project already underway when Radin arrived at Fisk. Ophelia Settle Egypt of the Social Science Institute was engaged in the collection of narratives of former slaves. Those narratives were eventually published by Fisk in 1945 along with the Radin-Watson compilation.[32] Together, these two projects constitute the earliest systematically collected corpus of life stories of former slaves. It is of course significant that these two programs were conceived and carried out, apart from Radin, by black scholars at a black institution. Radin's project extended his highly original life-history work to the American South and marks the first planned research effort by a white scholar to tap the memories of people born into slavery. The two Fisk collections began nearly a decade before the Works Progress Administration (WPA) project—the most extensive and well-known collection of narratives of former slaves—conducted predominantly by white researchers in seventeen states. The Fisk appointment enabled Radin in partnership with Andrew Polk Watson to turn his humanistic interest in texts and narratives, up to that time focused on native peoples of the Americas, to a community of elderly survivors of slavery and the demise of Reconstruction in and around Nashville.

The present study now revisits Radin's career, looking closely at the distinctive ethnological orientation that marked his research among both the Winnebago and African Americans. A new but long overdue examination of the Radin-Watson collaboration at Fisk is now possible owing to the survival of the partial manuscript "Souls Piled Like Timber: The Religious Experience of the Pre-War Negro." "Souls" contains Radin's only extended commentary and analysis of the narratives in addition to much of the previously published collection. Moreover, up to now, very little was known about the collecting process or the very important relationship between Radin and Watson on which the success of the entire project depended. This study will thus expand understanding of a heretofore little-known chapter in the professional life of an original and controversial figure in the history of anthropology. At the same time, the Fisk research provides an important example of the American anthropological engagement with African American life, likewise pursued by Boas's other students, including Melville Herskovits, Louis King, and

Zora Neale Hurston, as well as by anthropologists who did not study with Boas, such as Hortense Powdermaker, Allison Davis, and St. Clair Drake. While Radin's mid-career work at Fisk represents a clear ethnographic break from his Winnebago fieldwork, his humanistic, actor-oriented focus unites those two endeavors. They were emblematic of the ways that unique historical individuals across diverse societies engage in philosophical and existential reflection. This theme recurred throughout Radin's acclaimed book *Primitive Man as Philosopher,* published shortly before his Fisk appointment.

Radin was a singular anthropologist in many respects, including his choice of research sites. He was the only major figure in anthropology to work both with American Indians and, in very unusual circumstances, African Americans. Those field endeavors during the period of Boasian dominance of anthropology speak, at least indirectly, to Lee D. Baker's highly ambivalent view of Boas and his influence. Boasian anthropology in Baker's critical view was indifferent to race as a social category or cultural feature among African Americans, concentrating instead on race as an imprecise biological category. At the same time, Boas and his students were committed to documenting the cultures of American Indians. Baker objects to that bifurcation.[33] He is not the only critic of Boas's extended examination of the biology of race. A decade before, an extreme, reactionary claim alleged that the Boasian biological focus on race actually helped promote scientific racism.[34] Baker's response was at best equivocal, somehow managing to agree with the latter view as well as the compelling counterargument centered on Boas's anti-racism offered by Herbert S. Lewis.[35]

Baker of course recognized Boas's position against racism, acknowledging that his "initial scientific move was important in terms of promulgating public policy, bolstering court decisions, and forcing many Americans to rethink notions of inferiority."[36] But one must point out that despite Boas's untiring efforts and successes in separating biological race from culture, he remained deeply pessimistic up to the moment of his death about weakening the grip of racism and biopolitics. A wide segment of American public opinion in the 1930s believed that black civil rights and social equality were contrary to the natural order. In other words, Boas's scientific mission of uncoupling biological race from behavior was much more formidable than his latter-day critics acknowledge. Moreover, it was precisely the socioeconomic and political dimensions of race that caused Boas's despair at the stubbornness of bigotry against an entire class—American Negroes, numbering some 13 million people in 1940.

In the lives of former slaves recorded by Radin, the biopolitical uses of race cannot be exaggerated. To be sure, Radin did not undertake a study of African American culture, or race-specific social and political behavior. Instead, his task as an anthropologist was even more fundamental than charting the way of life of a particular African American group. He and his Fisk colleagues were documenting how elderly African Americans were proclaiming their very humanity, reviled and debased by the nearly insuperable force of race science and popular bigotry.

Thus, Radin's placement of African Americans at the center of their own stories as thoughtful, reflective adults exemplified the scientific, humanistic, and moral vision of American anthropology under Boas's commanding influence. Radin's African American research did not stand apart from his long-standing professional engagement and field experience among the Winnebago. In Nashville as well as Nebraska and Wisconsin, Radin sought in first-person narratives the subjective understandings of personal experience, often traumatic, endured by unique individuals. Turning the perspective he honed among the Winnebago to the world conceived by elderly former slaves, Radin emphasized the ways in which individuals meet a universal need to find meaning and psychological adjustment in their lives. That perspective accounts for the sweeping departure of his Fisk project from contemporaneous but racially tainted portrayals of slavery by most white writers. At the same time, Radin's humanistic, empirical anthropology dovetailed with the research and writing of African American scholars. Although the Fisk research is the only project he ever conducted among African Americans, it is of a piece with his entire career, defined as it is by the same profound human-centeredness that marked his more widely known research in native North America.

CHAPTER 1

The Unsettled Career of a Radical Humanist

The literary, historical, and philosophical allusions pervading Paul Radin's publications attest to the humanistic character of his thinking. With great passion, he eschewed the use of scientific models to explain culture, a position he elaborated in his 1933 critique of Boasian anthropology, *The Method and Theory of Ethnology.* Accordingly, Radin found interpretive inspiration in history and literature rather than in explanatory models focused on the natural world.

The critic and poet Mark Van Doren begins his foreword to Radin's book on the Winnebago Medicine Dance, *The Road of Life and Death,* by quoting the author: "The problem then resolves itself into finding the native."[1] This can well be taken as the rationale for all Radin's research. Van Doren states that while he lacks the expertise to comment on the religion and ethnophilosophy of the Winnebago, he has observed Radin's "human character," which enabled him to gain the trust and confidence of Jasper Blowsnake and his brother, Sam Blowsnake, or Crashing Thunder, whose autobiography collected by Radin became a landmark in the history of anthropology.

Van Doren observes that Crashing Thunder disclosed all facets of his life experience to Radin, the ethnographer who brought to research his human character that "made Negroes, Japanese, and Chinese confide their life stories to him, and that makes all of Mr. Radin's friends so much at home with him."[2] The allusion to the other groups refers to Radin's subsequent work at Fisk, followed by research among ethnic minorities in Depression-era San Francisco for the California State Emergency Relief Administration (SERA), part of the WPA.[3] That his work invited the attention of a critic of Van Doren's stature was undoubtedly related to Radin's devotion to the collection and explication of native texts, including myths, autobiography, accounts of rituals, and the like. Other luminaries of the literary world, including Kenneth Burke and John Crowe Ransom, Radin's one-time colleague at Kenyon, admired his work. Ransom perhaps found inspiration for "The Idea of a Literary Anthropologist" from Radin's perspective on literature.[4]

Personal and Intellectual Influences

Paul Radin, the youngest of three brothers, was born in 1883 in Lodz, a Polish city then part of imperial Russia. The family came to the United States in 1884, settling in Elmira, New York, where Paul's father, Rabbi Adolph Radin, served as a spiritual leader of a local synagogue before the family moved to New York City, where the elder Radin again headed a synagogue. Radin left no commentary about his family's origins in eastern Europe, and at the point of immigration he was too young to remember any of it. His eldest brother, Herman, became a physician in New York City. His second brother, Max, a distinguished legal scholar and professor of law at the University of California, wrote a brief memoir of life in Lodz.

Rabbi Radin had studied in German universities and in orthodox seminaries in Russia, becoming a learned Talmudist respected by other rabbis in Lodz. Nonetheless, he adopted the nascent religious reforms that had begun in Germany and were loosening the strictures of orthodoxy that had long defined Jewish life in the town. Max Radin wrote that on his father's return to Russia-Poland he boldly set about "the hopeless task of organizing a reformed Jewish congregation in Lodz." The reforms were modest, but the entire effort was doomed from the outset, and the family set off for the United States after the congregation failed.[5] As to familial influence on Paul Radin, one can infer the self-possessed character of his father, confident and inner-directed, an independently minded reformer amid an unmovable orthodox community. Above all, Paul Radin, in dedicating *The Racial Myth* "to the memory of my father," praises the humanistic commitment of the elder Radin, "who was always in the vanguard of liberal movements and who understood, as he exemplified in his life, the dictum of the great Greek: *'Tis not in hate, but love, that men unite themselves.'"* To the humanism linking father and son, one can also add an abiding and defiant idealism.

Of his more intellectual influences, Radin drew some diffuse inspiration from the extreme presentist writings of Benedetto Croce.[6] He argued that "all history is contemporary history" as distinct from "dead chronicle" that has no bearing on contemporary lives.[7] History is thus an active engagement in the present. For Radin, history was embedded in the life experiences of singular individuals and therefore either in field research or in assessing its results, he would also discover a living history:

> The task . . . is always the same: a description of a specific period, and as much of the past and as much of the contacts with other cultures as is necessary for the elucidation of the particular period. . . . This can be done only by an intensive and continuous study of a tribe, a thorough knowledge of the language, and an adequate body of texts.[8]

George W. Stocking Jr. has aptly characterized Radin's historicism as having "at best an imperfect temporal dimension."[9] That is, Radin's vision of history paradoxically is undynamic, indifferent to the transformative processes characterizing temporal change.

Radin found more immediate value in the work of the historian James Harvey Robinson—the father of his first wife, Rose Robinson—and John Dewey. Both Robinson and Dewey taught Radin at Columbia. Like many famed academicians educated in the latter years of the nineteenth century, Robinson studied in Germany. A prodigious scholar and accomplished writer, his many publications were part of a movement known as the "new history," also promoted by his renowned Columbia colleague Charles Beard. The "new history" expanded scholarly vision, looking to social and economic analysis and the insights of the emerging social sciences. For Robinson, this movement explicitly reacted against narratives of the past—"dead chronicle" in Croce's terms—that were divorced from contemporary concerns. He and Dewey were allies of Boas in various progressive causes, and, like Boas, had each reached the pinnacle of his profession. In Dewey's case, his reputation extended well beyond the academic world of philosophy and psychology to progressive education. Like Boas, Dewey was a well-known public intellectual.

Boas and Dewey, both influenced by pragmatism, agreed that their respective disciplines ought to begin with lived experience. They each reacted against research that began with abstract theory, whether cultural evolutionism insufficiently attuned to ethnographic and historical reality or closed philosophical systems divorced from human action.[10] Radin certainly was grounded in this perspective.

Paying homage to his three former teachers, Radin's *Primitive Man as Philosopher,* published in 1927, entered new territory in its portrayal of "primitive man" as intellectually individuated. That is, up to that time the ethnographic literature by and large represented people in undifferentiated terms, each person accepting without question the dictates of "corporate consciousness" and behaving accordingly.[11] Writers in that vein, lacking fieldwork experience and thus sustained contact with the people in non-Western societies, succumbed to conventional academic theorizing about the "primitive" world. Included here was a certain belief that doubt and intellectual questioning were alien in those settings. For Radin, a genuine individualism permitted people "real freedom from the shackles of group tyranny" (a phrase reminiscent of Boas's critique of tradition and Robinson's views about the burden of history).[12]

In his foreword, Dewey predicted that Radin, in "fixing attention upon phases of the culture of primitive man, which are usually passed over lightly, if they are not overtly denied," would provoke "debate and heated controversy" among anthropologists. But as a nonspecialist, he chose not to enter the likely controversies. Instead, as a philosopher, Dewey found the book important, requiring from philosophers either an "authoritative refutation or else a pretty thoroughgoing revision of notions which have become current."[13]

Indebted more substantively to Robinson, who had written on the intellectual classes of western Europe, Radin posited the radical notion that an intellectual class existed in every society known to anthropology. This was a point that Dewey also found important and original. Closely surveying the anthropological literature detailing vast cultural differences across the world, and drawing on his own field research among the Winnebago, Radin asserted that "among primitive peoples there exists the same distribution of temperament and ability as among us."[14] Unlike contemporaneous historians and sociologists, he used the term "temperament" to denote a nonbiological, psychological disposition.

Radin described two such psychological dispositions or types. One, "the man of action," numerically dominant, thinks in practical terms and outcomes, unconcerned with internal states or ruminations about existential questions. The other, "the thinker," while not oblivious to practical matters, is more given to reflection, analysis, and meditative consideration of subjective states.[15] Regna Darnell identifies Jung as the source of Radin's thinking about individuals oriented either to practicality or philosophical concerns.[16] Pushing the source further back, one can see that Jung's identification of psychological types relied heavily on the work of William James.[17] Radin's "thinker" anticipates by several decades consideration by anthropologists of the special qualities of their prime informants, often analytically minded native intellectuals.[18]

Writing from the Napostkovo Museum of Prague in 1905, where he was studying a collection of South American hunting technologies, Radin, with youthful exuberance at age twenty-two and some arrogance, commented on his courses with Robinson.[19] His letter begins, "Dear Bob"—undoubtedly written to his lifelong friend Robert Lowie, whom he knew as an undergraduate at City College of New York—and describes his enthusiasm for historical study.

> The kind of history that I'm interested in, the kind of historical problems that awake my enthusiasm are rarely taught or suggested at the European or for that matter at the American Universities either. Robinson was the only man who suggested some and even he did so, in such an indefinite manner that I have the firm impression that although his alert mind perceived the possibilities inherent in his suggestions, he himself was too lazy mentally to take full advantage of them. That is Robinson's great merit and his striking defect—the possibilities of historical interpretation are suggested and there he stops. What I intend to study, make my life's work is neither history nor ethnology, but both.[20]

Radin realized his goal, however unconventional his views of history and ethnology proved to be within the developing framework of Boasian anthropology.

Robinson shared Boas's concerns about the shibboleths of thought, of stultifying patterns of mind leading to intellectual complacency and the acceptance of injustice. Robinson's diffuse skepticism about what had heretofore been taken for granted resonated with Radin's own questioning of unexamined, conventional understandings. Robinson's new history reconceptualized the past, not simply as the minutiae of dynastic succession, or aristocratic familial relationships, or the recitation of facts with no relationship to the present. Rather, Robinson proposed that a new kind of history ought to provide insight and understanding of contemporary circumstances. Asserting that all the problems of the present have their origins in the past, Robinson as a true progressive believed it incumbent on historians to discern prior folly and error in order to ameliorate the present and future.[21] Toward that end, he looked to the insights that anthropology and the other social sciences could offer to history in coming to grips with modern problems. He fully embraced the idea of human progress, a possibility if only people would cease their uncritical veneration of the past for its own sake and begin to ask how it bears on contemporary issues.[22] For Robinson, "History alone can explain the present and in this lies its most unmistakable value."[23] Enthralled by it, historians who do not look beyond the past, Robinson believed, will fail to identify the certain connections between prior events and the errors and misconceptions of the world in which they live.

Informally, Robinson encapsulated this attitude in a letter to Boas, concluding,

> I am sorry that we do not see one another anymore. I owe a great deal to you and the men you have trained. But there is no hope of finding out much in one's short life time when he has to spend most of his time getting over the fool ideas in which he was bred.[24]

For Robinson and Boas, tradition held people captive to ways of thinking that perpetuated irrationality and error. Robinson, the historian, also found the tyranny of tradition residing in historical writing. Radin's rejection of the self-imposed constraints on academic thought resonated with the fundamental professional critique of traditional history offered by Robinson. Thus, Radin in 1934 imagined a world order succeeding Nazism and taking on the form of a "new cooperative state" that "must be based upon a world that has broken with its past," despite what would be considerable opposition to that transformation. For Radin, following his mentors, Robinson and Boas, resistance to that change derives from "the obsessive and irrational hold daily habits of the mind and of the heart have upon us."[25]

Radin's Distinctive Place in Anthropology

Radin's empathic humanism focused on unique individuals and the events, practices, and beliefs they conveyed in their narrations of life. Wherever Radin found such distinctive individuals—in his own fieldwork or in the ethnographic literature—they were no different from himself or other people in their cognition, potential, or capacity for doubt or affirmation. They were part of the stream of humanity, unsegmented by natural qualities that could be judged as superior or inferior. In no sense was their reasoning and mentality faulty, prelogical, or unreflective—qualitatively different from modern thought, as argued by Lévy-Bruhl and his many followers. Sustaining his critique of Lévy-Bruhl in *Primitive Man as Philosopher*, Radin was, in the words of literary critic Kenneth Burke, "righting an ethnologic wrong."[26] Radin's informant-collaborators were his coevals, fully contemporary individuals. They were not people representative of an earlier period, temporally immobilized in an arrested evolutionary stage. Radin and others in the Boas circle rejected that idea out of hand, having mustered wide-ranging ethnographic evidence discrediting cultural evolutionary progression and its corollary, increasing human rationality at each stage of social development.

Radin's most extended statement on anthropology appears in *The Method and Theory of Ethnology*. In that volume, he sets himself against Boas and his most prominent students, declaring a kind of intellectual independence from the group. Essentially, Radin insisted that anthropology, more commonly referred to in the volume as "ethnology," is situated within the humanities, not the sciences.

> In science we stand beside or . . . above the facts. We are not a part of them. But we are a part of the cultural facts we are describing in a very real way. The moment we stand beside or above them, we do them injury; we transvaluate and make them facts of another order. In short, they are reduced to facts of the physical world. The disadvantages attendant upon being an integral part of the phenomena we are describing must seem a fatal defect to the scientific mind. Unquestionably it is. But it is inherent in cultural phenomena and nothing can very well be done about it.[27]

Consequently, portraying other lives across a vast cultural and linguistic chasm could be impossible, "but although it couldn't be done, you have to do it anyway."[28]

Alienation was an integral part of Radin's character and intellectual life. If he was to understand in any depth the people in the societies he studied, either in the literature or through fieldwork among the Winnebago or aged African Americans, it was essential that he come to grips with often unacknowledged sources of observer bias. This was no less true of other anthropologists. Particularly relevant were preconceptions built into the Western intellectual tradition, including anthropology itself, which Radin came to comprehend through his extensive knowledge of Western history and philosophy. He had to stand at a distance, to be alienated from the tradition he knew best, to avoid its distorting influence. Arthur Vidich put the issue as follows:

> It appeared to him that the values of social science itself frequently were only reflections of the dominant social, political, and economic currents peculiar to the civilization in which they existed. To the extent that this was the case he saw that studies of primitive life continuously face the risk of reflecting ourselves and the established framework of Western thought, rather than reflecting the inner dimensions of primitive society.[29]

This attitude partly reflects the teaching of James Harvey Robinson. Yet Robinson was referring to home-grown cultural presuppositions of the past, not to the profound epistemological differences between western and non-western peoples.

Recognizing the likelihood of cultural bias in research, Radin nonetheless pressed on, concentrating throughout his career on the self-representation of his informants. He wanted to know Winnebago and African American subjects through their own words, exemplifying their own thinking and their own experience as the best check on the imposition of western bias. But as a research strategy informant self-representation paradoxically is itself mediated and thus subject to the anthropologist's implicit preconceptions and expectations. In numerous ways, especially in his Winnebago field research, the claim of self-representation could mask Radin's interpersonal involvements, their effect on native depictions of their own lives, and the choices he made in accumulating and publishing the gathered texts. Several scholars, including Arnold Krupat and Michelle Burnham, have explored these complications from a literary point of view.[30]

Given his strongly held views about anthropological method and intrinsic biases, Radin reserved his sharpest criticism for those who did not conform to his strictures. Margaret Mead's work in Samoa and Manus is a case in point. Praising her for rejecting conjectural history—a designation usually referring to then discredited reconstructions of nineteenth-century evolutionists—he argues that Mead is not thereby justified in rejecting historical study altogether. In his critique, Radin provides a view of history that depends on the actions of real, that is to say, named historical individuals. In claiming that Mead is "entirely unhistorical," Radin explains, "I mean what every historian means: the description of a culture in such a way that we feel we are dealing with real and specific men and women, with real and specific situations, and with a real and specific tradition." Mead, Radin asserts, deals not with "specific individuals or situations but with generalized ones." Moreover, Radin was skeptical of the information that Mead claimed to have obtained in a year or less; he thought that it would instead require "an intensive study of a lifetime" and added, "I seriously doubt whether an outsider can ever obtain it."

However well-organized Mead's work and methods, they were not adequate qualifications for making her findings authoritative, "which only a long and protracted residence and a complete command of the language can bestow."[31] Radin's commitment to Winnebago ethnology, including field research, extensive writing over many years, and remarkable control of the language, set the highest standard for text-focused fieldwork that very few could match.[32]

The Method and Theory of Ethnology also forcefully criticizes others in American anthropology who fall victim to the errors of positivist and quantitative approaches to cultural data. Defining ethnology as simply "the study of aboriginal cultures," he argues that descriptive adequacy must include as much history as can be ascertained. That position, he believed, was unexceptionable among American anthropologists. Most of his colleagues, however, posited a role for ethnology beyond basic, historically informed description. That added function entailed an analysis of "historical processes and cultural dynamics," aiming to produce laws of culture. Radin bristled at the suggestion, asserting that "little warrant exists for thus extending its meaning and that . . . confusion and mischief have followed in its wake." Ethnology, then, for Radin entailed no purpose beyond providing a detailed account of a specific culture through sustained presentations of individual informant narratives. Kroeber, too, in ignoring the individual, also invited Radin's criticism, which was generously forthcoming. Still, Kroeber reviewed *The Method and Theory of Ethnology* favorably, admiring its fairness and candor while feeling himself to be "one of those who has pieces of his professional hide stripped from him time and again."[33]

Radin's charge against Kroeber curiously avoids extensive discussion of his famous formulation of the superorganic, or culture as a distinct reality divorced from organic phenomena. The latter was represented by individual psychology, biology, or race. For Kroeber, no factors at the organic level could provide an adequate explanation of a cultural phenomenon, which was a distinct reality, sui generis; invoking psychology, biology, or race to explain culture was reductionist.[34] Thus for Kroeber, an appropriate explanation of any aspect of culture lies within the stream of culture itself. If Radin's distinct, idiosyncratic individual had a theoretical antipode, it was certainly Kroeber's superorganic in which "the personal or individual has no historical value save as illustration."[35]

Radin's most pointed commentary on method and theory focused on Boas's work, criticized as a continuation of Boas's early training in science. His interest in diffusion was merely a repackaging of generalizing scientific concerns of the nineteenth century wherein, Radin argued, Boas treated cultural data as if they existed in the realm of nature. Insisting that ethnology deals with phenomena created by people rather than natural forces, Radin believed that in imposing natural-science methods on human-centered issues, Boas distorted the object of study. Radin, however, ignored the tension that had existed in Boas's thinking. Since very early in his career, Boas recognized the opposition between generalizing scientific study in a quest for laws and the study of phenomena for their own sake, a contrast he laid out as early as 1887 in "The Study of Geography."[36] Claiming that Boas never set aside his training in science, Radin argued that Boas's interest in culture areas and the diffusion of fragmented cultural components within those areas misdirected field research. There was no connection to actual individuals, the creators of those components, and the methods used were more appropriate to science. Consequently, Radin opposed inferring time sequences, or history, from the distribution of scattered cultural traits, a practice followed at one time or another by Boas, Kroeber, Sapir, and Wissler.[37]

Radin's blueprint for ethnology entailed an understanding of a local community through the medium of the native language and a body of texts created by singular, historical individuals, not composite figures. One comes to see that a person who has undergone a particular ritual is unique, both as an individual and as a ritual participant. It will not do to consider him representative of a larger social body, or of a class of phenomena that might yield a generalization. Arising of course is the question, never satisfactorily answered by Radin, of how he derived his statements about "Winnebago culture" or that of any other community from the actions and beliefs of idiosyncratic, historically unique persons.

A political radical, Radin attracted FBI attention in the 1930s and was identified as a Communist. His political inclinations were not, however, manifest in his ethnographic research. Marxist concerns with political economy, infrastructure, modes of production, and other materialist features of social life yield to Radin's predominant interest in individual experience, philosophical outlook, and religious belief and practice. He occasionally invoked material factors in order to compare industrial society with so-called primitive societies—the kinds of smaller, less differentiated polities and economies that anthropologists normally studied. In observing the differences between industrial and precapitalist political economies and focusing particularly on the relationship of the individual to the collective in each social formation, he rejected all efforts, Marxism included, to order societies hierarchically or temporally.

Above all and consistently, Radin argued that preindustrial societies gave wide latitude to the speculations and meditations of native intellectuals, a minority of the population in every kind of society.[38] Their role in precapitalist societies was poorly understood, obscured in Radin's view by an ethnological literature that emphasized "generalized men and women who . . . serve as a kind of academic cement for vague ideas and still vaguer emotions." Instead, in recognizing the ubiquity of individualism, Radin viewed religion or other symbolic contrivances as expressions of distinctive human personalities.[39] In his fieldwork, consequently, he proceeded more as documentarian than participant observer.

This becomes abundantly clear in his discussion of the narratives of the Winnebago, whether in autobiography or in extended disclosures of the intricacies of the Medicine Dance. Likewise, among former slaves, Radin took their narrations at face value, representing deeply thoughtful and therefore authentic representations in their own right of personal religious experience. Radin had too much respect for the elderly African Americans with whom he spoke to gainsay their intimate testimony by recourse to Marxist notions of false consciousness, mystification, and the like.

Yet his *Primitive Religion* (1937) devotes an entire chapter to the economic context of religion. The relationship of socioeconomic factors to religious behavior was one of the rationales Radin offered for writing the book, and represented a marked departure from Boas's philosophical idealism. Although Radin esteemed *The Mind of Primitive Man,* he criticized Boas for indifference to material factors in the historical process. Radin believed that Boas was too steeped in the neo-Kantian emphasis on ideas to consider economic factors of greater value than any other cultural feature.[40] Radin, however, recognized that religion, particularly in settled agricultural communities with some wealth and power differentials, could serve the aggrandizing interests of ritual or sacerdotal figures, especially when they were allied to chiefs.

For example, taking the classic anthropological cases of the Nupe of Nigeria and Azande of the Sudan, Radin pointed to the uses of witchcraft in each society to support the power of the economically and politically privileged.[41] In many other societies, Radin argued that fear of the shaman does not simply emerge from a complex of cosmological beliefs, but rather depends on an alliance between the shaman and the chief. While emphasizing the importance of understanding how economy may affect the shape and practice of religion, Radin, however, disavowed any tendency to reduce religion to a veiled expression of material interest.

> Let me state that I am fully aware of the danger that lurks in any over-emphasis of the economic side of religion and magic; I know how easy it is to minimize the importance of their actual content and of the multiple and often independent aspects religion and magic have taken on. I do wish to stress, however, that no correct understanding of the fluctuations either in their content or in their form is possible unless this interrelationship with economic forces is fully recognized. Religious beliefs and attitudes were assuredly not created either by methods of food production or by some mechanism of exchange. But they did grow up together with them, and it was the economic system that made certain constituents and certain forms of religion relevant at one period and others relevant at another. . . . The elaborations and superstructures religion has developed in its own right . . . also constitute an essential part of its study.[42]

His acknowledgment of the "economic side" of religion notwithstanding, Radin in the main explored the spiritual experience of individuals independently of a substrate of material factors.[43]

Although focused for decades on the Winnebago, Radin also wrote extensively on American Indian linguistics, religion, folklore, narrative, worldview, and anthropological method. The focal point of his multifaceted research was consistently the unique individual rather than culture abstracted from its human agents. Radin wished "to allow natives to talk for themselves, interpreting their thoughts only in those cases where explanation seemed necessary and of value."[44] What Radin considered "necessary and of value" in offering his own gloss on the native perspective is not always clear, well-defined, or consistent.

Two Crows, Radin, and Sapir

The earliest monographs produced by the first generation of American ethnologists, particularly those associated with the Bureau of American Ethnology, founded in 1879, suffered from several weaknesses. Radin observed that the urgency of salvage ethnography in the face of the rapid transformation of traditional societies led to an uncritical view of the sources of information. Given the palpable presence of material culture and the relative ease of gathering information about it, Bureau monographs were weighted in that direction. Before formalized training in anthropology had developed, the research by individuals coming from a number of different professions or vocations tended to resemble antiquarianism, clearly disdained by Radin and others trained by Boas.

Conventional histories of American anthropology tend to begin with Boas, emphasizing a sharp departure from the immediate past without regard for the achievements of notable nineteenth-century figures associated with museums or the Bureau. Regna Darnell, particularly, has concerned herself with the pre-Boasian record of American anthropology, emphasizing continuities that link Boas to his American predecessors.[45] Herbert Lewis, on the other hand, regards Boas's intellectual impact as a radical departure from the anthropology practiced by Bureau researchers. He identifies a number of Boas's achievements marking the break with the past, including his rejection of cultural evolutionism and his critique of racial formalism dominant at the time of his settlement in the United States.[46] Moreover, the organizing framework of Bureau research was cultural evolutionism, as Darnell has pointed out. Boas's thoroughgoing demolition of evolutionary theory in 1896 by itself would have precipitated an intellectual schism.[47] In other respects as well, Boas was estranged from Washington-centered anthropologists over the direction of the profession.[48]

As to continuity in American anthropology, Radin managed to find it, but only in the work of J. O. Dorsey, author of *Omaha Sociology*. Otherwise, Radin had little regard for the ethnography presented by Bureau fieldworkers and certainly regarded his own work as discontinuous with theirs. According to Radin, Dorsey was "one of the best ethnologists the United States ever produced." He admired Dorsey for his competence in the southern Siouan language of the Omaha and for maintaining the coherence of the data he collected by not mingling it with interpretation.

Radin thus believed that interpretation should always remain a distinct and separate feature of any monograph in order to preserve the integrity of ethnographic data.[49] Just as archives utilized in historical research must remain inviolate, so too the primary data of the anthropologist. In his preface to *The Winnebago Tribe*, completed in 1916 but not published until 1923 by the Bureau, he wrote:

> It has been the aim of the author to separate as definitely as possible his own comments from the actual data obtained, and for that reason every chapter, with

the exception of those on history, archeology, and material culture, is divided into
two parts, a discussion of the data and the data itself.[50]

Radin praised Boas for presenting data in the manner Dorsey established.
But "in spite of the great influence Boas has wielded . . . there are very few
ethnologists besides himself who have conformed to this simple requirement, and
only one, as far as I know who has secured all of his information in text."[51] Radin
modestly asks the reader to infer the identity of the latter figure. Earlier, he gratefully
acknowledged Professor Franz Boas "for directing him to the Winnebago, for the
methods of research inculcated in him . . . and particularly for impressing upon him
the necessity of obtaining as much information as possible in text."[52]

Yet one goes too far if no interpretations follow the primary data. Radin criticized Boas on this point. In his books on the Kwakiutl and Tsimshian, Boas offers the
"bare facts" without interpretation. He provides no information on his informants,
nor does he comment on the actual data gathered. Instead, Radin argued that Boas
believed the data would speak for themselves, an arguable expectation in the natural
sciences but certainly untenable in the study of cultural facts, which "do not speak
for themselves."[53] Radin once again suggested that the historical dimension of Boas's
work gave way to his fundamental natural-science orientation.

Dorsey's monograph portrays Two Crows as a dissenter from what seems to
be general opinion, or what might be called "the cultural norm." In numerous
instances, Dorsey registers the disagreement Two Crows expresses with Dorsey's
other informants. For example, Dorsey quotes an informant identified as "a servant
for the Elk people." The latter explains that "at the conclusion of this ceremony
the rain always ceases, and the Bear people return to their homes." Dorsey then
continues, "But this is denied by Joseph La Flèche and Two Crows, who say, 'How
is it possible for them to stop the rain?'" Or, in another instance of inconsistency,
an informant says, "At that time [the creation] there were no gentes [unilineal
descent groups]; all people were in one gens. Joseph La Flèche and Two Crows
never heard of this." Or, following Dorsey's description of the role of servants in
bringing food and water to assemblies of the gens, "La Flèche and Two Crows
said there were no servants of this sort in any of the gentes."[54] La Flèche was the
Omaha chief who also served as a key informant for Dorsey. Were it not for Edward
Sapir, the naysaying Two Crows would likely have remained a long-forgotten
native figure in a Bureau monograph. Dorsey had ignored the problem of internal
variation and disagreement among informants, preferring instead, according to

Sapir, simply to pass the anomaly on to readers who would then somehow manage the inconsistency.

But as a student, Sapir took note of Two Crows's commentaries and later wrote about it in connection with his developing interest in intracultural variation, culture and personality, and the role of psychiatry and psychology in exploring the relationship of the individual to culture. Like Radin but for different reasons, Sapir admired Dorsey as an anthropologist well in advance of his time.

> Living as he did in close touch with the Omaha Indians, he knew that he was dealing, not with a society nor with a specimen of primitive man nor with a cross-section of the history of primitive culture, but with a finite, though indefinite, number of human beings, who gave themselves the privilege of differing from each other not only in matters generally considered as "one's own business" but even on questions which clearly transcended the private individual's concern and were . . . implied in the conception of a definitely delimited society with a definitely discoverable culture.[55]

Sapir raised the question of "whether a completely impersonal anthropological description and analysis of custom in terms which tacitly assumed the unimportance of individual needs and preferences is . . . truly possible for a social discipline."[56]

It was certainly important to Sapir as psychological questions continued to inform and then dominate his work. Ultimately, issues of internal cultural variation, differing individual views, the relationship of individuals to the larger collective, and the like would take their place in the developing field of psychological anthropology. But despite understanding the meaning of history and the importance of actual individuals in writing history, Sapir, in Radin's critical view, continued to posit "an intuited generic man," instead of real, historical individuals of varying opinions and beliefs. Sapir was certainly not alone, as others continued to ignore actual persons.[57]

By contrast, Radin offers the example of John Rave, a key Winnebago informant on peyotism, who provided a singular narrative describing conversion to the peyote cult and his role in introducing it to the Nebraska community. It prompted Radin again to emphasize the importance of distinctive individuals in anthropological research and thus to set himself apart from others in the Boas circle:

> I hope I have made clear by this commentary and exegesis how illuminating a document may become, how specific and how vivid are the multiple interrelations

between an old culture and a newly introduced cult, and what reality some of the intangible and unformalized aspects of culture assume when seen through the mirror of an actual man's heart and brain and not through the artificial heart and brain of the marionettes with which Boas and Sapir and Kroeber operate.

Radin concludes by underscoring the value of the document he provided, even if his interpretations are rejected, for "there still remains the document for them to interpret better and more profoundly."[58]

In the context of Radin's voluminous work and his view of history in all its specificity, it would be erroneous to posit any single individual as the prototypical Radin informant. For that reason, the naysaying Two Crows would have as much claim to authority as any "thinker" or "man of action" within Radin's framework. The Two Crows phenomenon created a methodological and theoretical dilemma for Sapir, moving him toward psychological anthropology and Radin's interest in real persons.

An individual, such as Two Crows, dissenting from the opinions of others was not an issue for Radin, who would have subscribed to Sapir's observation that "we shall have to admit that in some sense Two Crows is never wrong."[59] Radin resisted generalization. His view of culture was amorphous, neither a systematic synthesis of the texts he collected nor a disembodied consensus of generic individuals against which dissent might be defined.

The Paradox of the "Primitive"

The continued use of the term "primitive" by those who were among the harshest critics of its cultural evolutionary implications—Radin, Lowie, Kroeber, Benedict, Mead, and Boas himself—strikes a particularly discordant note. It of course undercut their critique of evolutionary theory since "primitive" implied its opposite—"advanced," "developed," "civilized"—and therefore implicitly acknowledged orthogenetic cultural development. Radin's books include *Primitive Man as Philosopher, Primitive Religion,* and *The World of Primitive Man;* Lowie wrote *Primitive Society* and *Primitive Religion;* Mead's Melanesian research culminated in *Growing Up in New Guinea: A Comparative Study of Primitive Education;* and of course, there is Boas's seminal *The Mind of Primitive Man.* Darnell has observed that Radin without comment substituted "aboriginal," a term frequently used in his writing, for the pejorative "primitive" in "Methods of Approach," a new section appearing in the 1957 reprint of *Primitive Man as Philosopher.*[60] The substitution did not, however, signal a modification of his original views.

For Radin, the concept of the primitive spoke to the kind of social order that anthropologists most frequently examined. The subject matter of ethnology is "the culture of aboriginal peoples, more specifically those aborigines with whom the Europeans have come into contact since the fifteenth century."[61] "Primitive" did not refer to a higher or lower mentality or to the imperfect development of rationality and intelligence among people in those societies. Radin's recurrent use of "primitive man" persisted, but that designation did not belie his egalitarian humanism. Rather, for Radin the implicit referents of "primitive" were to social and economic landscapes, not to inherent limitations of mind. People were "primitive" because they lived in "primitive" societies, which to be sure, presented their own distinctive challenges to how indigenes understood their world. Specifically, those landscapes included nonindustrial technologies and economies along with stateless segmentary political organizations, particularly based on unilineal descent groups, such as the clan, or chiefships and other more centralized polities exemplified by the Nupe and Azande. Radin also addressed the role of writing and machine technology in enlarging the scope of human activity and transforming "primitive" society.[62] Still, the persistence of the term in the Boasian lexicon has led to much confusion.

In *The World of Primitive Man,* Radin sought to overcome the ubiquitous but false attribution of negative characteristics to the so-called primitive world. Scholars and laymen alike tended to regard the people of that world as creatures of instinct, motivated only by fear and emotion. They also regarded the great civilizations of Egypt, Babylonia, India, China, Greece, and Rome, on the other hand, as predicates of a social and economic system that nurtured human rationality and objective thinking. Radin, however, pointed out that such civilizations frequently faced economic instability and crisis that in turn led to otherworldly preoccupations promising greater satisfactions after death. Radin, the secular humanist and rabbi's son, expressed greater admiration for those "primitive" societies, such as the Winnebago, where religion attended to earthly concerns.

In Radin's view, objective thinking and rationality were not dependent on a particular socioeconomic order but emerged worldwide in what he called, interchangeably, "primitive civilization" or "aboriginal civilization."[63] Eliding the very significant ethnographic differences among these societies, Radin in a romantic vein portrayed life in those cultures as close to sublime, not very different from the folk society in Robert Redfield's rhapsodic formulation.[64] In Radin's words, primitive civilizations were "semi-ideal" or "semi-perfect," also resembling in some ways Sapir's view of "genuine culture," embodying social harmony, spiritual fulfillment, and respect for the dignity and integrity of the individual.[65] Radin's depiction of the civilizations of the ethnographic world emphasized respect for men and women, old and young; a high level of social and political integration ensuring personal security; an absence of the alienation characteristic of industrial society; and economic stability that did not distort social arrangements as instability did in the classic civilizations. And because life on earth was satisfying and valued, aboriginal religions developed only rudimentary ideas of the afterlife, preferring instead to conceptualize a return to earth.[66]

Without mention, this latter observation was likely Radin's encomium to the Winnebago, whose customary belief in reincarnation was fundamental to their worldview. Despite Radin's continued use of the word "primitive," its connotations were altogether different from the rudeness, ignorance, and irrationality cultural evolutionists smugly attributed to the societies he most admired. Radin's usage sentimentalized the term, providing a perfect counterpoint for expressing his own alienation from the most inhumane dimensions of modern life, including racism and worker exploitation.

Professional Relationships and the Itinerant Life

After completing his PhD in 1911 following his initial research among the Winnebago, Radin worked briefly at the Bureau of American Ethnology until allegations of impropriety regarding his expense account resulted in dismissal.[67] Writing to Boas, Radin explained that he had heard that the actual reason for his termination "was due to my being one of your students."[68] That claim was likely true, at least in part. Boas's unpopularity in Washington at that time anticipated the palpable regional tensions within anthropology that erupted when Boas famously denounced those who used the cover of anthropology to spy during World War I.[69]

Shortly after leaving the Bureau of American Ethnology, Radin joined Sapir at the Geological Survey of Canada in a non-continuing capacity until mid-1912. With Boas's assistance, he received grants providing a year of study in Mexico, where he focused on Zapotec linguistics. Radin's chronic financial problems were well known to his various colleagues, who continued to support his efforts to find employment. In 1912, when Boas recommended Alexander Goldenweiser to Kroeber for an available position, he asked, "Can you do anything for Radin? I want very much that he could be provided for. He is a very industrious and skillful fieldworker."[70] Although Boas had a genuine interest in and even a continuing sense of obligation to his students, those feelings toward Radin sometimes reached their limit owing to Radin's growing reputation for irresponsibility. It deeply offended Boas's own keen sense of personal and professional rectitude. More than any of his colleagues and friends, Sapir stood by Radin but not uncritically, regarding his scholarship and personal style. Radin was certainly the least favored among Boas's first group of distinguished students, including Kroeber, Lowie, Sapir, and Goldenweiser.

However trying and petulant Radin could be, his prodigious fieldwork and linguistic abilities garnered critical respect among his peers. Radin also had a lively, sometimes whimsical manner and an eccentric charm. In one way or another, his professional friends and colleagues seemed to feel a responsibility to assist Radin in spite of himself. Goldenweiser, for example, facing his own employment and financial insecurities in early 1912, nonetheless hoped that Boas might assist Radin, whose Winnebago research he praised with superlatives.

> Radin is leaving soon for a prolonged stay among the Canadian Ojibway [sponsored by the Canadian Geological Survey]. I feel very sorry for him. On several occasions we have talked over his field results somewhat in detail, and in my opinion his contribution to Winnebago ethnology will be the best monograph ever written about an American Indian tribe, in volume, character of material, and abundance of points of theoretical interest. Have you heard of any possible opening for him? If there are any I think he deserves the warmest recommendation notwithstanding his well-known "faults."[71]

In a similar vein, following Radin's short stay at the Bureau of American Ethnology, Sapir joined Boas in trying to help Radin, writing to Kroeber in regard to the teaching position he was trying to fill at Berkeley.

Kroeber had earlier told Sapir that Radin could not be considered, which Sapir found unfair. He told Kroeber that his Berkeley colleague Tom Waterman was biased against Radin. Making clear that Radin had not solicited his support, Sapir proceeded to recommend Radin for the position.

As regards knowledge of anthropology, particularly American, Radin is head and shoulders above [William H.] Mechling and [John Alden] Mason, and, I suspect, [Wilson] Wallis. His descriptive knowledge is doubtless better and more detailed than that of Goldenweiser. For field work there is no better man to secure abundance of valuable data (whether on ethnology or linguistics) than Radin. He gets tremendous amounts of text material, hears well, and investigates problems of social organization, religion, and mythology thoroughly. On technology, I believe, he is weaker. He has had plenty of experience. His Winnebago work you probably know of. The Bureau [of American Ethnology] is getting out an annual report on his Winnebago material (general survey, which is but the merest fraction of his total Winnebago material, as I understand). For us [Geological Survey of Canada] he has done work on Ojibwa linguistics and ethnology (chiefly religion, social organization, and mythology). I have seen some of this and know it is good stuff. Then in Mexico he did a lot of work on Huave and Zapotecan. Over and above his anthropologic attainments, Radin is unusually well read on almost all conceivable topics . . . and is a man of culture. Him and Goldenweiser I frankly consider the cream of the younger anthropologists in this country. Some people, let me frankly admit, dislike him because of a certain irresponsibility (or naiveté) of demeanor. We (my wife and I) have always found him a most delightful friend. I may say that Boas was at first rather down on him, but has modified his estimate of Radin completely, as far as I know. Take my word for it—he is excellent.[72]

Intimations of irresponsibility surfaced over the years. Boas's "modified estimate of Radin" would on subsequent occasions provoke further modification, often downward, after one or another tense encounter between the two men. Still, Boas wrote on behalf of Radin, telling Kroeber that Radin was an "indefatigable and clever fieldworker and his gift of accumulating observations is very great." Boas acknowledged misjudging Radin as a student, yet informed Kroeber that Radin "is not a vigorous thinker, timid in making conclusions." Boas's qualified recommendation of Radin characterized him as a "man worth working with, notwithstanding the weaknesses I have pointed out."[73]

Radin's professional relationships were unquestionably troubled, particularly with Boas. Yet that relationship continued until the end of Boas's life amid periodic outbursts from Radin. As early as 1915, in what appeared to be Radin's determination to sever all connections with his teacher, he wrote:

My dear Prof. Boas:

In your conversation with me this afternoon, you took it upon yourself . . . to impugn my scientific honesty and accuracy. . . . I do not know the reason for this attitude on your part and can only explain it on the ground of your strong personal dislike for me which you have shown on numerous occasions during the last four years and which has led you to seriously impair my chances for advancement.

I had hoped that with increasing years you would put aside the dislike for me which you seemed to have formed quite a number of years ago but apparently it is not to be; and rather than have the present extremely unsatisfactory relation that exists between us continue, I would rather have no personal relations of any kind with you. Perhaps if you regard me as a complete stranger you will not take the liberty of attempting to humiliate me as you did to day [sic], and have done on a number of other occasions, or, at least, I will feel that I have the right to reply in any manner I deem fit.

It is far from my intention to show the slightest disrespect to you. I believe none of your pupils ever entertained as deep and sincere a respect for you as I did. I believe however that I owe it to myself to be frank and direct to you. I hardly suppose you realize that by adopting the skeptical attitude toward my work which you do, you put your activity on my behalf in securing the fellowship for me two years ago, on a charity basis.

I also feel constrained to withdraw my application for the Curtis fellowship, for I do not feel that you are recommending me sincerely. It is much against my will and my nature that I talk to you, an older man and my teacher, in this manner as you yourself must realize, but I think you have forced me to.

At the bottom of the letter Boas wrote: "This is another one of your performances that are bound to destroy your scientific usefulness. I assume that I have not received this letter."[74]

In a response to an inquiry from Kroeber two years later, Boas again conveyed his exasperation at Radin's comportment. Although Boas's professional judgment of Radin grew more critical, he was still willing to help him, at a distance so to speak, to obtain a position.

I do not think I can give very good advice in regard to the Radin matter. Personally, I have had so much trouble with him, that I do not want to have any more to do with him. I am quite willing to help him to get an opportunity for work as long as I do not need to look after it; and in this sense I am trying at the present time to see whether we can make some kind of arrangements for publication of his Winnebago material in Wisconsin.

I do not share your opinion in regard to his ability. He is a good collector, but absolutely uncritical and without any power of clear thought. His papers on religion and on literary style show that he is always swayed simply by personal sympathies or antipathies, or by personal ambition, but that he is lacking in the icy enthusiasm that is necessary for good scientific work.

In my opinion, it is a risky experiment to give him a position which gives him an income which is insufficient for his maintenance. With his complete lack of adaptation to the necessities of life, this will simply lead him to all sorts of financial makeshifts that might easily cause difficulties to you. Of course, it is possible that he may have learned something in regard to this matter, but I am not very sanguine. I wish I could write more encouragingly, but I cannot.[75]

Boas did not feel such personal antipathy toward any of his other students, although he did not hesitate to criticize them in professional terms, and rarely in the harsh terms reserved for Radin—"absolutely uncritical without any power of clear thought."

During World War I, Radin, with Sapir's help, again joined the Geological Survey of Canada, where he remained for four years, continuing his research among the Ojibwa of Ontario and writing reports ultimately published by the Geological Survey.[76] His many subsequent academic appointments provided temporary teaching or research positions in at least nine institutions. They included the University of California, Kenyon, Cambridge, Michigan, the University of Chicago, Black Mountain (the short-lived experimental college in North Carolina), Mills, Fisk, and Brandeis. He resided in Berkeley for three years, 1917–1920, offering courses at Mills College and the University of California, where Kroeber hired him in temporary positions despite Boas's misgivings. He settled in England for about five years beginning in 1920, when he lectured at Cambridge and became acquainted with W. H. R. Rivers, to whom he dedicated *Crashing Thunder.* The nature of Radin's relationship to Rivers is uncertain, but they shared interests in psychology and psychiatry, although Radin tended to be a strong critic of the latter, particularly the psychoanalytic perspectives gaining ascendancy in the 1920s. Little is known of his years in England.

Prior to his departure for England and uncertain prospects, he wrote to Boas in a disillusioned tone, dejected perhaps at the termination of his Berkeley appointment or his financial distress. Moreover, his first wife, Rose Robinson Radin, was ill with a lung condition, probably tuberculosis. Although he informed Boas of his intent to abandon ethnology, Radin never left the discipline and some of his best-known anthropological work lay ahead.

I have fairly definitely determined to give up all future anthropological work and devote my time to history and literature.

As you know, I have a large number of manuscripts on the Winnebago, the Ojibwa and the Zapotecs and I don't know what to do with them. Can you make any use of them? I do not feel that I really care to waste the time working them up, unless some monetary benefit accrued. I am not in the least bit interested in the subject of ethnography itself any longer.[77]

In the absence of evidence, one can only speculate about other sources of Radin's alienation from the academic world. While finding yet another temporary position at Cambridge, Radin was of course cognizant of the career paths of more favored students in the first cohort to study with Boas, including Kroeber and Lowie at Berkeley and Sapir, soon to join the University of Chicago and eventually a particularly prestigious post at Yale. Boas's high regard for Sapir was no secret, and indeed Boas, as noted, beginning in the early 1930s, hoped he might induce Kroeber and Sapir to come to Columbia.[78]

During his time abroad starting in 1920, Radin also lived in Switzerland, beginning his association with Carl Jung. He and Rose Radin stayed in Paris during part of their time in Europe before returning to the United States in 1925, but virtually nothing is known about the Radins' Paris sojourn, except in the recollections of his cousin, Helen Sarason. As a young woman of twenty-one, she and another cousin, Clara Schaap, met the Radins in Paris. She recalls nothing of any professional activities that might have engaged Radin's attention in Paris. Instead, her recollections confirm a picture of Radin as a magnetic, if improvident, bon vivant:

Paul was so charming, enchanting, sweet—but not the most reliable . . . Max and Herman [brothers] were. . . . In 1925 he met my cousin Clara Schaap and me at the Paris railroad stations and made us give up our hotel and go with him to live with him and Rose on the Left Bank. He took us about and brought us to parties of painters, writers, et al. Perhaps Picasso, Hemingway, [illegible]. Who knows: He borrowed money from the two of us—but he was the Golden Boy of the family. Who cared?[79]

Returning to the United States in 1925, he held a one-year fellowship at the University of Michigan and conducted fieldwork among the Ottawa. Radin arrived at Fisk in 1927, remaining there for three years as research professor of anthropology.

Resigning without explanation in 1930, he returned to the Bay Area, where he lived periodically, except for scattered appointments, for part of the next nineteen years. He continued to teach at Berkeley in temporary positions, conducted linguistic research in northern California, and worked on surveys during the 1930s of various ethnic groups in San Francisco. He also taught at the California Labor School. Traveling to Europe in 1949, he eventually settled in Lugano. A well-known publication during his stay in Switzerland was *The Trickster: A Study in American Indian Mythology,* to which Jung contributed a chapter. While in Switzerland, he oversaw publication in German of several of his books, having determined in those early postwar years that he would never permit their publication in Germany.

Radin's short-term teaching and research positions in the United States and Europe enabled him to make a bare living, as money problems continued to plague him. He was often subsidized by grants or fellowships given directly or through administering institutions. At one point when there was some question about renewal of his contract with the Canadian Geological Survey, he wrote to Sapir indicating that he had applied for a high school job in Santa Fe, where he would teach mathematics and biology.[80] Rose Radin's illness required various changes of residence, including a stay in the Southwest at a sanitarium in Santa Fe.

Radin joined Fisk University through the support of the Laura Spelman Rockefeller Memorial, creating a nearly ideal position that permitted him to pursue his primary interests in research and writing. As research professor of anthropology, he could escape much of what he deplored—the mundane administrative responsibilities and obligations attendant to a normal teaching appointment. Fisk asked little of Radin beyond the pursuit of his research project with graduate-student assistant Andrew Polk Watson.

Radin's frequent shifts in employment provide yet another indication of the professional alienation that enabled him to maintain his much cherished academic and personal freedom. He could also preserve his intellectual independence, uncompromised by the complacency, institutional loyalty, and narrowness of vision that he believed a steady, longer-term position might risk. Personal autonomy, however, created its own strains in view of Radin's continuing money woes. Thus, his resignation from Fisk in early 1930 left him with an uncertain employment future.

Once again, Sapir responded to an inquiry from Kroeber about Radin's suitability for one of the few available positions at Berkeley in linguistics. While Sapir had a high regard for Radin's linguistic skills, he nonetheless confided to Kroeber that "Paul does not seem to me to be a good enough linguist to do the kind of comparative work that you are suggesting for him." Of course, Sapir's standards were extremely high. In his view those standards exceeded even those of Boas. Sapir regretted that

> we are allowing too many poor or improperly qualified men to do linguistic work that should be entrusted to well-trained persons with a special flare for both phonetics and morphology. Boas still has very much the old pioneering attitude that the main thing is to rescue languages and put a lot of uncritical material on record. I do not subscribe to his view in the least.

While identifying a possible role for Radin after his return to Berkeley from Nashville, Sapir wrote to Kroeber, candidly acknowledging Radin's other deficiencies.

> It is true that his record is a poor one institutionally but he must be very much more sobered by events [stock market crash?] than he has been in the past and it is almost inconceivable that he should still indulge in his favorite pastime of resigning from good positions.

At the same time, Sapir said that "Paul has done a great deal of very valuable work both in ethnology and linguistics and that, in a general way, anthropology owes him an opportunity to continue." Sapir, well acquainted with the strengths and deficiencies of his friend, personally and professionally, believed that "a position in the nature of a research endowment would . . . be the ideal thing for Paul, but such things are not to be had for the asking."[81] Sapir managed to remain a loyal but not uncritical friend, interested in Radin's welfare. He recognized the high quality of Radin's research and his value to anthropology, but did not want to "oversell" Radin's achievements to anyone as informed as Kroeber.

Just prior to his resignation from Fisk, Radin sought research support and modest living expenses from the Committee on American Languages that Boas headed. Their relationship continued to be testy, exemplified by Radin's charge against Boas that "you are influenced exclusively by personal prejudice and private animosity." Sapir and Leonard Bloomfield, members of the committee, had twice supported Radin for a grant of $500.00 to continue his linguistics work in Oaxaca but were overruled each time by Boas. Radin also complained to Boas about his unnecessary "backstairs policy." Boas had approached the Rockefeller Foundation to find out how much money Radin was receiving on a grant. Responding, Radin wrote, "If you had asked me I would have been glad to let you know." Boas was likely concerned about the possibility of "double-dipping."

At the same time, Radin also accused Boas of making defamatory remarks, which "I must vigorously protest," about the circumstances of his hasty departure from Mexico sixteen years earlier. Having seen a letter from those years that Boas had written to Sapir, Radin complained to Boas: "You state that I left Mexico in 1913 because I got frightened about 'a revolution that did not amount to anything.'" Continuing, Radin corrects Boas's claim:

> First of all, that happened to be the revolution in which Madero [Mexican president] was killed; secondly, the train on which my mother, my wife, and I left was the last train that left Oaxaca for six months; and thirdly, I left because I had received a private telegram from then Secretary of State Knox telling me to leave.
>
> All of this you knew and I must ask you to correct the impression that you may have made on Sapir as soon as you can. You cannot take refuge in your age to make slanderous remarks.[82]

His extraordinary rebuke of Boas stands out against the prevailing feelings of esteem and affection that marked the attitudes of Boas's students toward their mentor. Radin's sharp reaction to Boas's letter to Sapir written sixteen years before alleging that Radin feared political turmoil and violence is hypersensitive in the extreme. Who wouldn't be alarmed at the imminent prospect of violent revolution? While the history of anthropology will hardly turn on the circumstances of Radin's departure from Mexico in 1913, the content and tone of his letter to Boas again captures the uneasy relationship between the two men.

Three years later, in the depths of the Depression, Radin reported his progress on four manuscripts earmarked for the *International Journal of American Linguistics* that Boas edited. He again approached Boas for a grant, and in a manner confessional and contrite, even groveling, he acknowledged prior failures and admitted his own irresponsibility.

I realize quite clearly that this is not a good year to ask for a grant of any size and certainly not one in which commitments can be made for a number of years. If you can obtain any money for me, would you therefore consent to my living abroad? $1000 to $1500 a year would go very far there and would be a mere pittance here. My record for living up to my contracts is, of course, very poor. I realize that fully. I think, however, that you can rely upon me this time. I would appreciate a little peace of mind and freedom from financial worries. I wish you would understand one thing. I do not believe that the world is in one huge conspiracy against me. My predicament is entirely due to the faults of my character and temperament. These can be changed only to a limited extent at my age. A university post is clearly out of the question for me. I would be perfectly content with a research position even if that, from the nature of the case, could never be guaranteed for more than two years at a time.[83]

Radin's candid admission here and elsewhere justifies the reservations about his reliability on the part of Boas, Kroeber, and sometimes his dear friend Sapir.

In spite of continuing tensions in his relationship to Boas, it does not appear that Radin's personal feelings shaped to any extent his often critical assessments of Boas's scholarship, particularly in *The Method and Theory of Ethnology.* But even that volume is not an unalloyed demolition of Boas's work, containing as it does a laudatory assessment of other aspects of Boas's scholarship, such as his role in ending the core influence of cultural evolutionary thinking in American anthropology.[84] The raw feelings between the two men, however, persisted through Boas's last years. When, for example, Boas in retirement was supervising Amelia Susman's doctoral research on the Winnebago syllabary, he suggested to her that

> through Kroeber you get in touch with Dr. Radin and see whether you cannot induce him to give you his Winnebago manuscripts. I shall advise you . . . not to say that I am connected with this work. He dislikes me and it might cause him to refuse.[85]

Still, Boas remained the most enduring influence on Radin's scholarship.

Radin's colleagues found irksome his tendency to follow personal inclinations with little restraint. Recollections by the anthropologist Robert Spencer, who completed his graduate studies at Berkeley in the early postwar years, likewise speak to Radin's eccentricities, self-indulgence, and indifference to fundamental obligations. Forty years after his student days at Berkeley, Spencer participated in an oral history project about that period. He remembered Radin's cavalier attitude about teaching as well as other responsibilities:

> [Kroeber] hired two people. He hired Paul Radin . . . and he hired Robert Lowie. Radin taught anthropology briefly at UC Berkeley in 1921. He was very, very brilliant; I knew him quite well [in the 1940s]. Yes. Radin would meet his class, and then he'd hear the Indians up on the Gila River were having a powwow or something, and he wanted to go up and see it. He'd just pack up and go, not tell anybody, and so on. And then he'd go down to Oakland to order some clothes from a Jewish tailor. I say Jewish because it fits in. And the man would make him the clothes and then Radin would fail to pay him. So the man would come to class—this happened several times—and just barge into the class and start talking to Radin in Yiddish. And, you know, Yiddish is a tremendously colorful and vituperative language, and they would scream at each other.[86]

Within the Berkeley department into the late 1960s, one could still hear the occasional anecdote about Radin's mercurial attitude and failure to meet classes.

Few students or colleagues were neutral about Radin. He aroused strong feelings, sometimes affectionate and respectful, sometimes severely critical. He might be helpful and constructive, or otherwise unconcerned and disparaging. Christer Lindberg has likened Radin to the Winnebago trickster, sometimes called the Foolish One.[87] Like the Trickster, Radin was very much the protean figure. In regard to her own work on the Winnebago language, Amelia Susman followed Boas's advice and contacted Radin, whom she described as "very gracious," offering to "help me in any way he can."[88] Three anthropologists recalled Radin during their Berkeley graduate years in the 1930s. Walter Goldschmidt said of him that his "influence on many of us was great, though often very subtle."[89] A. M. Halperin, a linguistic anthropologist and Asianist, regarded Radin as "the most important single influence on my own intellectual development." Halperin continued,

> He was, to the end of his life, childlike but not naïve, possessed of virtually unlimited curiosity and always open to new stimuli, unselfish and generous to a fault, especially with his time and the contents of his mind, and he produced fascinating, if sometimes a shade malicious table talk almost without limit. He reveled in human contacts with all sorts of people, and he treated Indian

informants with the same degree of respect and honor that biographers of Lincoln reserve for their subjects.[90]

Omer Stewart, on the other hand, remembers an indifferent, irresponsible teacher. Stewart also recalled that Radin, even when not formally associated with the university, utilized the library, signing out books in Lowie's name without his knowledge.[91]

Radin's tendency to follow his own inclinations and to take advantage of the generosity of friends often put those relationships to the test. Nancy Lurie, teaching at the University of Michigan in the 1950s, announced to her colleague, the archeologist James Griffin, that the Radins were coming to town and would stay at her house "for a few days." Recalling Griffin's response, "You mean for a few months," Lurie remarked:

> I thought he was kidding but Paul had a strong nesting instinct wherever he happened to land and they did stay about a month, completely upsetting our lives but blithely unaware of it, I think. If I'd known they would stay so long, I could have prepared but they evidently had planned to look over our situation and if they liked it they'd sort of move in. For all that, it was interesting to hear Paul reminisce [about his father, Emma Goldman, and other anarchists].[92]

Memorable and difficult, Radin was particularly rude to Mountain Wolf Woman, sister of Crashing Thunder and the eponymous Winnebago woman who was the subject of Lurie's subsequent book. She was also Lurie's guest, having come to Ann Arbor to dictate her life history.

> Paul whether in the field or elsewhere was not easy to get along with and I was appalled at the way he ignored Stella Stacy (Mountain Wolf Woman) where both he and she were at my home in Ann Arbor. If she wasn't answering questions of interest to him, he acted as if she didn't exist there at the dinner table.[93]

Research assistants also made up Radin's far-ranging network of relationships and acquaintances. Alexander Lesser demurred when asked to recount his memories of Radin, saying simply that "For the most part . . . my personal relations with Radin were unhappy."[94] Herbert Lewis recalls that, independently, Lesser and Gene Weltfish each complained to him that they had practically written the entirety of

Radin's *Social Anthropology*. Radin did not share authorship with them, instead offering a patronizing acknowledgment of

> [a] debt of gratitude which I can hardly hope to repay. By their assistance in gathering and arranging some of the data embodied in this book, they have earned the right almost to be regarded as coauthors.[95]

Radin built strong relationships with several of the Winnebago with whom he worked, but none of those relationships was with women. His viewpoint was highly gender-constricted. He had little to say about Winnebago women, as informants or otherwise. In *The Winnebago Tribe* a single index entry of two pages reads, "Women, instruction concerning treatment of." The listed pages consist of a father's advice to his son. The implications of Radin's gender bias will be taken up in chapter 5.

The Winnebago with whom Radin enjoyed close connections were Oliver Lamere, his translator, and the brothers Jasper and Sam Blowsnake, authors of the two autobiographical accounts Radin obtained. Jasper Blowsnake dictated his personal story to Radin, whereas Sam Blowsnake wrote his autobiography using the Winnebago syllabary—a writing system composed of words and syllables to transcribe the spoken language.[96] Although Radin cultivated friendships with his informants, these interlocutors were also remunerated by the anthropologist.

Other anthropologists also paid their informants. For example, Sam Blowsnake, his wife Evening Star, and daughter Whirling Eagle in the late 1930s lived in the New York area, where he served as a paid informant for Amelia Susman at the going informant rate of thirty-five cents per hour.[97] Struggling to make a living, they also sold native handicrafts, and Sam performed Indian dances in several venues, having considerable prior experience as a Ho-Chunk dancer in Wisconsin. He looked into the possibility of dancing at the 1939 World's Fair. He had previously performed in Chicago at the 1893 Columbian Exposition and again at the Chicago World's Fair of 1933.[98] Promoters of native performances since the late nineteenth century had seen potential financial gain in exploiting the public's curiosity about Indians. The more elaborate spectacles reenacted Indian-white skirmishes in which some of the Indian performers had actually participated in the last of the frontier wars against whites.[99] Indian performances for white audiences have a complex history in which one can see, as Grant Arndt has shown for the Ho-Chunk, the commercialization of tradition and, in later years, the renovation by the Ho-Chunk of their traditions within a modern context. Arndt's examination of tribal history as it reaches into the present and takes on new meanings is considerably more nuanced than the salvaging efforts of Radin and his peers. Whereas salvage ethnography focused on the vanishing past, Arndt addresses how traditional symbols and customs actively define a modern Ho-Chunk identity.[100]

Unexpectedly, Radin met Sam Blowsnake when he was performing in New York. In 1938, the Radins were invited to attend a floorshow at the Algonquin Hotel featuring Indian dancers. Doris Radin recalls that Radin's exuberance and joie de vivre were on full display as the show got underway. He recognized Sam Blowsnake, "Crashing Thunder," among the dancers. Not having seen him in almost thirty years, Radin rushed into the spotlight, uninhibited, and embraced one of his most esteemed informants. Later, inviting him to join their table, Radin with good humor scolded his friend for wearing a Crow Indian war bonnet instead of a Ho-Chunk version. Sam explained what Radin of course knew—that a Crow war bonnet was much more colorful and dramatic than the subdued Ho-Chunk headdress.[101]

The Radins visited with Sam Blowsnake a number of times. Doris Radin remarked that she had difficulty thinking of "this mild-mannered man killing a man in cold blood." Eventually serving a prison term, Crashing Thunder describes in his autobiography how he killed a Potawatomie, an act encouraged by his father. After the killing, Crashing Thunder stole his victim's horses, gun, and money. Declaring his name as he shouted a war whoop, Crashing Thunder thus counted coup, gaining warrior honors, and observing the directive of his father, who proclaimed, "Your life is no longer an effeminate one." With friends, his final act was to cut out the heart of his victim, having heard that the heart could yield medicine.[102]

Sapir and Kroeber, the latter more guarded, continued their efforts to help Radin. Kroeber's patience was surely tried when Radin accused him of having "no gift for friendship." With the same striking candor and self-assessment he displayed in his letter to Boas, Radin confessed that "I do not underestimate the unwarranted manner in which I involve people in my own private affairs and I am quite willing to admit that they should resent it [which] makes an intimate or even casual relationship with me difficult." He asks Kroeber for "a definite break in our social relationship." Radin apparently resented what he considered interference on the part of Kroeber and his own brother Max in his personal affairs, however much he may have invited it.[103] The harshness and at times ad hominem nature of Radin's disagreements appear limited to his relationship with Boas and Kroeber. His intimate friends, Sapir and Lowie, seemed to have been spared Radin's more vituperative moods.

Leaving the Bay Area for Europe in 1949, he resumed his nomadic life of teaching and research, never remaining in one place for more than a few years. Although an academic itinerant, Radin found welcome support and recognition in his relatively long-term association with the Bollingen Foundation, named for the quaint Swiss village where Jung had built a home. The foundation was funded by Paul and Mary Mellon, admirers of Jung. Without naming her, the FBI identified a "sugar mama" as Radin's patron.

> Confidential Informant [deletion] advised that he had been informed by the subject [Radin] that when he returned to San Francisco in October 1944 that he had [deletion]. The subject further advised this informant that he now has a "sugar mama" who is [deletion] and that Radin has a five year contract to finish his manuscript.[104]

The foundation provided him with a fellowship, renewed annually for fifteen years, enabling him to continue his writing and scholarship. In 1949, the Bollingen created Special Publications, reserved for Radin's monographs. He also served as an adviser to the foundation, enabling him to recommend the award of some forty fellowships supporting an extensive array of projects in anthropology and prehistory all over the world. While Radin had visited Switzerland prior to his association with the Bollingen, he and Doris Radin moved to Lugano in 1952, returning to the United States in 1956. The Bollingen was also critical in supporting the publication of some of Radin's books, including *The Road of Life and Death* (1945), dedicated to "Mary Mellon in Appreciation," *The Trickster* (1956), and *African Folktales and Sculpture* (1952).[105]

Politics and FBI Surveillance

In moving to Europe and settling in Switzerland in the early 1950s, Radin became a less visible target of the FBI. The Red Scare was near its apogee as another four years would elapse before Joseph McCarthy was censured by the Senate. With the opportunities the Bollingen presented in Switzerland, there were considerable pull as well as push factors in Radin's decision to settle abroad.

Repeatedly labeled a Communist, he was acquainted in Berkeley with other prominent faculty members under suspicion, particularly J. Robert Oppenheimer and French professor Haakan Chevalier, a Communist Party member. Oppenheimer and Max Radin were good friends, and that association at times tainted the law professor, but the cloud of Communist suspicion hung more heavily over his brother. Toward the end of the 1930s, Paul Radin belonged to a discussion group, described as "a Marxist salon," composed of various Berkeley professors and other area leftists who met regularly at Oppenheimer's home.[106] Although Radin's relationship to the Communist Party remains a moot point, his embrace of positions that garnered party sympathy was for the FBI tantamount to membership.

Because Radin apparently did not write either in letters or publications about the charges of Communism leveled against him, it would seem that he was not especially concerned about what the Communist label portended, given his sense of personal and intellectual independence. However, friends from those years indicated otherwise. The ethnomusicologist Sidney Cowell was well acquainted with the Radins during their California years and in Switzerland, where Cowell admired the work of Carl Jung. She suggested that Radin worried about detention or arrest. Recalling the period after the San Francisco general strike of 1934, Cowell reported:

> Paul was subject to sudden attacks of suspicion and dread on what seemed to me surprising and unreasonable grounds; but if your people have survived through generations of pogroms you are unable to feel safe. I have never forgotten the time, about 1938 or 39, when Paul asked me seriously whether my father and stepmother, who lived in a big house on a fig ranch . . . near Fresno—Paul asked whether if necessary they would hide him in their attic if he were pursued for his Marxist convictions.[107]

Radin was certainly a political radical, but more at home behind the lectern than on the picket line. Although very left of center in his politics and his views of race in America, he was never engaged in overtly radical action. Nonetheless, his pronouncements from the left alarmed the internal security apparatus of the United States. He taught at the California Labor School in San Francisco, Oakland, and Berkeley, a decidedly left-wing institution as its name suggests. Lectures in support of union activity, civil rights, racial justice, and equality for all people—radical positions during Radin's lifetime—provoked the attention of the FBI.[108] While Radin's investigative files have been extensively redacted, they nonetheless indicate how agents relied on innuendo and unidentified "confidential informants." Membership in liberal organizations tainted Radin along with his expressed sympathies for causes critical of the racial and political status quo. The following extracts from the Radin dossier compiled by the San Francisco field office make the point:

> On November 17, 1940 [deletion], advised that Paul Radin was a Communist and was employed by the SPA project in 1935 at the Sutro Branch Library . . . was an instructor of classes held by the American League against War and Fascism . . . with lectures on the Meaning of Fascism; that in 1939 he was a member of the Communist Party; and that in 1941 he was a member of the American Committee for Protection of Foreign Born. . . .
>
> Special Agent [deletion] obtained the following information from the Internal Security file, Berkeley Police Department. . . . That the subject at one time was a professor of Anthropology at the University of California, Berkeley . . . and a writer by profession; that in 1936 Paul Radin spoke under the auspices of the National Negro Congress at a mass meeting in North Oakland.
>
> Confidential Informant [deletion] reported on October 19, 1944 that it is believed that this book [probably *The Racial Myth*] was dedicated to [deletion]. These files also contain information that the subject is a member of the Artists and Writers Union which is Communist dominated, that in 1934 while professor of Anthropology he attempted to form his students into a Communist club.
>
> *February 24, 1945*
>
> Radin is known to be a Communist and a prominent lecturer on the Racial Question at the California Labor School in San Francisco, in which school he has professed extreme interest. He is reported to have gone to China in 1937 as a government emissary but real purpose was for the Communist Party.[109]

In summer 1935, Radin taught a Labor School class in Berkeley entitled "History of the Great Revolutions," including the English, American, French, and Russian revolutions. If not a practicum, the subject could only reinforce the FBI's interest in him. Radin's love of literature also found expression at the Labor School when he taught, immediately following the Revolution course, "a little thing called 'History of World Literature.'" Not part of the humorless Left, the Labor School noted, "Of course, it is limited in scope—from the aboriginal to the twentieth century."[110]

In the 1930s, advocates of the positions taken by those associated with the Labor School faced a near certainty that they would be tagged as radicals, subversives, and Communists. Radin's embrace of those causes and his outspoken opposition to restrictive real-estate covenants and all forms of racial segregation added to a substantial FBI dossier on his activities, travels, and associations over a number of years. A West Coast center of leftist activities, San Francisco witnessed a longshoremen's strike in 1934 that led in turn to a brief general strike, arousing fears of Communist influence throughout the area. The FBI concluded that Radin was a Communist, having noted his various associations, California Labor School activities, speaking engagements before left-leaning audiences, support of Loyalists in the Spanish Civil War, reports from informants about meetings he allegedly attended, and remarks he was said to have made. FBI sources alleging Communist Party membership are unknown. Radin's 1937 trip to China remains a mystery regarding its purpose, his activities, funding, and the like. Not even the FBI had file entries about it.

Other surveilled scholars and writers of the time either lost their jobs or found their livelihoods in jeopardy because of the Communist taint. Radin was already on the economic edge. Without a continuing academic position, his livelihood was always impermanent, his support regularly shifting as he went from one temporary job or grant to another. In Berkeley during the Depression years, he was occasionally on welfare.[111] His European sojourn beginning in the late 1940s and continuing as McCarthyism reached its height insulated him to a limited extent from an even more intense scrutiny that could have further jeopardized his dim domestic job prospects.

Radin was subpoenaed in 1946 to appear before a California state legislative committee investigating un-American activities. Those named on the subpoena included the director of the University of California Press and the physicist Frank Oppenheimer, brother of J. Robert Oppenheimer.[112] In 1950, the *Los Angeles Times* reported on testimony by a former Communist appearing before the State Senate Committee on Un-American Activities. The newspaper recounted his claims of "Communist Conspiracies in Prison, Unions, Colleges and 'High Society.'" The witness said that he recruited the anthropology professor. "Men like Radin, in the Bohemian and intellectual fringe, were encouraged to go out in society," he stated. Describing Radin as "passive," the witness reported in an unintended parody of the Left, "We put the heat on him and we asked, 'What are you doing while history is being made?'"[113]

In 1945, Radin testified in an Oakland court about the impossibility of determining race solely on the basis of appearance. His testimony represented the first time that a legal challenge to racial covenants utilized anthropological expertise. The attorney calling on Radin's testimony aimed to undermine popular, unscientific racial classifications that depended on skin color as a criterion for race designation. Radin's expertise supported a Berkeley couple threatened with eviction because of their appearance. People in the neighborhood, however, said "they knew Negroes when they saw them." Called as an expert witness on matters of race, Radin testified that Caucasian and Negro races overlap at their extremes and that even an anthropologist could not determine race simply on the basis of color. Race mixing, he said, was common in the American South beginning in the seventeenth century and, consequently, southern whites "may be not entirely of Caucasian origin."[114] While Radin's testimony exposed factual errors in conventional American thinking about race, the judge ruled against the couple and Radin earned another entry in his FBI file.

A few months after the Berkeley case, Radin again was called on as a defense witness in another losing cause when jazzman Benny Carter was found in violation of a racial covenant. Carter and his wife had purchased a home in Los Angeles from the owners who in 1928 had agreed not to sell the house to anyone not of the Caucasian race. Asked how many races of humankind anthropologists enumerate, Radin replied that "there is considerable doubt in the minds of almost all anthropologists whether it is possible to make any kind of an accurate and distinctive classification."[115] His arguments for the Carters were framed outside of the customary resort to statutory law and aimed instead to show the fallacy of racial classification. Radin testified as an expert witness in a third case that had reached the California Supreme Court. A couple denied the opportunity to marry by the state's anti-miscegenation law won that right when the California Supreme Court overturned the law by a single vote. Radin had testified that the terms Caucasian and non-Caucasian are virtually meaningless and that racial classification cannot be reduced to skin color or type of hair.[116]

Paul Radin's alleged Communist sympathies lived on after him. In 1965, a flustered and bewildered California state senate, alarmed over the emergent Berkeley Free Speech Movement of a few months before, desperately sought an explanation. With more reflex than reason, a report of the California Senate Fact-Finding Subcommittee on Un-American Activities looked for Communist influences infiltrating the Berkeley campus, particularly among its influential faculty. The state senate, six years after his death, identified Radin as an example of a faculty member who had succumbed to Communism. The committee claimed that in the 1940s he disseminated Communist ideas originating in the California Labor School. A Communist operative, according to the committee, "testified about the techniques used to indoctrinate and recruit Dr. Radin and the other members of the Berkeley faculty."[117] Unpersuasive, that claim does not comport with Radin's intellectual independence and indifference to authority. He was hardly the ideal subject for indoctrination. The report was at pains to point out that Paul Radin's brother, Max Radin, the renowned professor of law at Berkeley, was not connected to the Communist Party.[118] However, Max Radin's very liberal ideas had been sufficient to prompt accusations of Communist sympathies in the 1930s, thereby preventing confirmation of his nomination to the state supreme court.[119]

The FBI files on Radin, redundant and repetitive in the extreme, mix banality and obtuseness in equal measure. In February 1945, an agent's report asserts that "Radin is known to be a Communist and a prominent lecturer on the Racial Question at the California Labor School, San Francisco."[120] Radin's file contains numerous assertions or innuendoes of Communist Party sympathies. An agent again reports early in 1945 that Radin was the author of *The Racial Myth,* published eleven years before; yet the fact of its publication seems to have had an air of intrigue about it. A 1998 Freedom of Information request, sixty-four years after publication, elicits the following release: "Subject is author of a book entitled, "Racial Myth," which is believed to have been dedicated to [Redacted]."[121] Perhaps the redaction deletes the name of a person mistakenly identified by the FBI as the honoree. One cannot be sure. At the time of the original FBI notation, determining the identity of the person to whom the book was dedicated hardly constituted a challenge, except to an agent's indolence. The agent filing the report might easily have discovered at a public library that the book's inscription constituted nothing more ominous than a declaration of filial respect as the author remembers his much admired and inspiring father, as noted earlier. Reporting from San Francisco in August 1945, the FBI investigator indicated that he would peruse the book in order "to locate information and admissions by the subject."[122]

Months earlier Radin had spoken before the International Racial Committee and reportedly said that racial discrimination in the United States would end only with the kinds of economic and political changes that had taken place in the Soviet Union. Years before, Radin praised the Soviet Union in the concluding chapter of *The Racial Myth,* where he said the Soviets and Americans offered the best hope for creating a cooperative social order in which the myths of race and nationality, so dominant in Nazi Germany, would lose their hold. Suspiciously claiming to have read *The Racial Myth,* the agent reported that the book "failed to reveal anything of interest."[123] One can only wonder about the investigator's dedication to ferreting out radical sympathies in those Communist-obsessed times when the slightest agreement with anything emanating from the Soviet Union was alarming. Radin's career on the move in part protected him from reprisals. He was untenured throughout his working life, except his final, brief appointment at Brandeis, when the McCarthy panic of the early 1950s had subsided.

Radin derided conventional intellectual orthodoxies, including those that he believed flourished among respected scholars owing to the "well known limitations of the academic mind and the narrowness of its vision."[124] He believed, perhaps, that long-term, tenured academic employment and the pressures of institutional commitment could only compromise his independence of mind and spirit. At the same time, this attitude may have been a rationalization for his inability to secure a long-term position.

Radin's final academic appointment to an endowed professorship at Brandeis, where he also became chair of the anthropology department, provides an ironic coda to his long career. Radin died in New York in early 1959 at age seventy-five, having held his Brandeis position for less than two years. Stanley Diamond observed that the institutional burdens of the new position may well have shortened his life.[125]

Neither a theoretician of culture nor an ethnologist in the conventional sense, Radin saw his work as, at once, historical in its focus on unique individuals in their own time and place, and literary in the meanings inhering in the texts that they produced. The examination of meaning and interpretation defines Radin's humanism, setting it apart from social science models and the search for cultural generalizations. Rejecting positivist approaches to cultural phenomena, he believed that social science models destroyed the integrity of the data gathered and dissolved the differences between individuals. The idiosyncratic person, as a unique actor, thinker, and narrator, remained the central subject of Radin's humanistic anthropology, yet he was never able to transcend the limits of that perspective.

CHAPTER 2

Our Science and Its Wholesome Influence

Anthropology against Racism

ranz Boas believed that anthropology was both a profession and secular calling. Beyond his immense scholarly output that exalted his reputation among professional anthropologists, Boas's pronouncements and actions on social issues ensured his position as one of the principal public intellectuals in the United States in the first half of the twentieth century. Twelve years after his death, the literary critic Stanley Edgar Hyman observed that, along with Sigmund Freud, Boas "substantially reshaped our world."[1] No challenge was more important to him than combating the unscientific uses of biological race to limit the life chances of people, thereby corrupting human relations. His pivotal work in the opening years of the twentieth century demonstrated the instability of racial types and the fallacy of using race to explain cultural and historical differences among people. His most visible targets were physical anthropologists in the United States and Germany. Boas's ultimate success in establishing his radical views on biological race was an important part of the intellectual reordering and academic institutionalization of anthropology in the United States. Boas in effect was attacking racism both in his own profession and in the world at large.

The arguments Boas marshaled against the biopolitics of race, or the use of spurious racial theories to shape public policy, attitudes, and social arrangements, faced enormous resistance, which he continued to combat to the end of his life. Anthropology had a special liberating role to play in bringing to bear scientific arguments that might disabuse policymakers and the public of their erroneous assumptions about biology and human behavior. Boas's mission included the thorough, exacting training of young people for careers in a newly professionalized, university-centered anthropology.[2]

In this vein, Boas, writing to Robert Lowie in 1928, gratefully acknowledged receipt of a financial contribution enabling anthropology students to acquire fieldwork experience. Evident in his response to Lowie, Boas at age seventy had lost none of the youthful idealism and sense of moral purpose that continued to guide his life and career.

> It has been given to me to work for many years with the growing generations of anthropologists. If I have tried to give according to my abilities, I feel that I have continually profited by friendship with enterprising younger minds and I have to thank all of you for your stimulation that has helped me, as I feel, to remain young with you. It is my greatest desire to see our science grow and exert its wholesome influence over our civilization. Your gift shows that we are in this.[3]

Although his remarks do not specify the nature of "the wholesome influence" that Boas wanted his discipline to exert, it can be confidently assumed that exploding the myth of race through the findings of anthropology was very much in mind. This is certainly what Radin attempted in *The Racial Myth* six years later. Boas's research also had important humanitarian implications, investing it with practical potential for improving lives severely damaged by the misuse of biology in shaping law and custom. Human dignity and the realization of human potential were at stake. Yet irrational and scientifically baseless claims about racial inferiority would not yield easily, especially among the public. Boas's confrontation with racism remained constant until the very end of his long life.

In the immediate aftermath of World War II and particularly cognizant of the racial aspect of the war, J. Milton Yinger commented on the relationship between science and moral purpose in opposing racism. His observation fittingly applies to Boas: "The person who starts with a conviction of the value of science and also with a strong moral stand will be the more anxious to preserve his scientific objectivity, because he knows that in that way only can his moral interest best be served."[4] Yinger's observation remains as pertinent today as in the early postwar years when the authority of scientific findings continued to face the challenge of unfounded personal prejudice, religious belief, and political interest. To counter personal bigotry and irrational judgment, Boas promoted anthropological science in the service of a morally grounded public good. Otherwise, without scientific support, competing moral claims about race, including those he espoused, could easily devolve into political arguments resolvable only through votes, or decrees, or other instruments of state. Nazi Germany was a case in point, but so too the United States when triumphant states' rights advocacy of race-based public policy dominated the century following the Civil War. In other words, Boas believed that rigorous science, not political power or unfounded belief, should be the arbiter of questions about race. Only in that way, then, can informed understanding serve both the moral and knowledge-based interests of an inclusive humanity. Yet Boas was under no illusion about the staying power of irrational opinion. American xenophobia had reached a high-water mark during the interwar years.

Beginning in the nineteenth century, race theorists in Europe and America had provided the intellectual rationale for sterilization and other eugenics measures. Later, the perpetrators of genocide found the "scientific" warrant for mass murder in the same polluting dangers believed to be endemic among "lesser" races so identified by race scientists in Europe and the United States. Scientific racism had effectively found an influential international place for itself well before Boas's emigration to the United States in 1886. Race scientists in Europe and America were in close communication about what could be done to preserve the putative purity and health of superior populations derived from northern and western Europe.

American race theorists were particularly disturbed by the large-scale arrival of eastern and southern Europeans—Jews and Catholics, Italians and Slavs—and what that portended for the much earlier, preferred, and allegedly racially superior Anglo-Protestant arrivals. Opposition to the eastern and southern European immigration cut across the political spectrum, including not only political conservatives but also progressives, such as the sociologist E. A. Ross and the sociologically minded economist John R. Commons.[5]

The United States Immigration Commission was empaneled in 1907 to investigate widely held concerns about the impact of the "new immigration" on American society. Commission members aimed to shut it down at the outset of their work, certainly before the vast compendium of empirical data on immigrant life had been assembled. Four years later, the forty-one volume report was published. Organizing vast amounts of empirical data on welfare, fertility, urban demographics, crime, employment, and the like, the report concluded that the new immigration menaced the country and necessitated curtailment. Boas authored volume 37 of the *Reports of the Immigration Commission,* yet his findings about the plasticity of race had no bearing on the commission's final recommendations. His conclusions were thoroughly at odds with the views of commission members, who regarded the new immigrants as an unassimilable threat owing to the assumed, fixed nature of their racial background. Accordingly, Congressional legislation in 1921 established ethno-racial quotas, made even more severe by the Johnson-Reed Act of 1924. Southern and eastern Europeans, judged racially undesirable, had little chance of legally reaching American shores after 1924. Public opinion and public policy on matters of race were very much in accord, evidenced by the popular support for the quota legislation of the 1920s. Negative stereotypes of new immigrants and African Americans remained prominent features of the American social and political scene.

Immigration restrictionists merged the behavioral and physical characteristics of races, believing with eugenics proponents that these characteristics were highly stable and biologically based. If they were impervious to change, the argument proceeded, then eastern and southern European immigrants could not be absorbed into the American population. Although Boas's report focused exclusively on the physical anthropology of the new immigrants, their behavioral trajectory in the United States could only point to continuing assimilation, given the plasticity of culture and the dynamics of cultural borrowing that Boas repeatedly emphasized in other contexts. By 1938, Boas was saying explicitly that immigrant absorption was also operating at the level of acquired habit—culture, in other words—since "the mental and social behavior of the descendants of immigrants shows in all those features that have been investigated an assimilation to American standards."[6]

When he wrote these lines, American anthropology was effectively the anthropology of Franz Boas. He had begun in the early years of the twentieth century to shape the profession, both institutionally and intellectually. American race scientists who came of age in the nineteenth century had lost their influence as Boasian anthropology ascended, and prominent eugenicists such as Charles Davenport and Madison Grant no longer had standing within the profession.[7] In the Boas program, culture replaced race as the wellspring of human behavior. Moreover, external Western-bound frameworks, particularly cultural evolutionism, had given way to methodological relativism and an emphasis on specific culture histories reconstructed through fieldwork. The profession effectively represented Boas's guiding influence, augmented by several cohorts of his students then holding professional offices and academic posts in American universities. Paul Radin promoted these principles as well, but primarily through his copious writing since he lacked a stable academic position.

Boas's early successes, apparent by the time of the First World War, came at considerable personal cost, including his censure by the American Anthropological Association in 1919. George Stocking Jr. has analyzed the complex of factors leading to that rebuke. Ostensibly, Boas's famous letter to *The Nation* magazine in the closing days of 1918 provoked both the censure and a nearly successful move to expel him from the Association. He had denounced four American anthropologists who had engaged in espionage for the United States while portraying themselves as researchers in Mexico. Boas charged that their covert actions represented a breach of professional ethics and a betrayal of the principles of science.[8] Regarded as unpatriotic, Boas was a strong opponent of American participation in World War I, maintaining as he did a lifelong opposition to the nationalist, patriotic fervor that had caught up some anthropologists outside of his Columbia orbit. But at base, as Stocking has shown, it was Boas's two-decade-long effort to reshape American anthropology, as well as the accompanying personal antagonisms, that set the stage for his censure. Behind the vote were a host of professional rivalries and differing ideas of what anthropology entailed.[9]

In Europe, race science continued to flourish, reaching its florescence in Germany with the Nazi ascension to power in 1933. Eugen Fischer, the rector of Berlin University, newly "renovated and purified," in Radin's bitter words, asserted that "the destiny of peoples and states is definitely and specifically influenced by the racial traits of its carriers. Universal history is simply a segment of racial history."[10] Boas maintained an ill-fated epistolary dialogue with Fischer, even after the Nazis assumed power. Fischer, an unregenerate Nazi at war's end, was well aware of Boas's conclusions about the instability of racial types based on his anthropometric studies. But Fischer conceded nothing to Boas, saying only that "certain elements in the shape of the skull . . . are modified by environmental influences—all the rest remains part of the inalienable hereditary equipment."[11] "Hereditary equipment" for Nazi race scientists as well as for American eugenicists subsumed not only biological traits but also patterns of cultural behavior attributed to biology. After the Nazis came to power, a final letter from Fischer to Boas curtly dismissed Boas's observation of an inconsistency in Fischer's research, suggesting that Fischer had altered his views on the fixity of race. His letter closes, "Mit deutschem Gruss" (with German greeting), a conclusion tantamount to "Heil Hitler."[12]

Public Intellectual

Boas's scholarly authority and the implications of his research for a new under-standing of race and culture reached well beyond anthropology and university seminar rooms. American anthropology received perhaps its greatest public boost when *Time* magazine featured Boas in its cover story of May 11, 1936, although Boas's reputation as a public intellectual was already well established. He regularly contributed to publications of wide readership, including the *New York Times* and other metropolitan newspapers and magazines such as *The Nation, The Atlantic,* the *New Republic,* and others.[13] His regular pronouncements in popular publications were usually controversial since his subjects were typically race, immigration, marriage, war, and other contested issues of broad interest, if not agreement.

The *Time* cover story provided a synoptic view of the thesis that Boas presented in his mostly widely read book, *The Mind of Primitive Man.* Up to its publication in 1911, that book represented the best summation of his scientific views on race and culture, providing "A Magna Charta of self-respect for the 'lower' races."[14] Under the heading "Environmentalist," a term in 1936 referring to nurture or culture rather than nature, *Time* identified the two overriding themes defining Boas's career and elaborated in *The Mind of Primitive Man:* the malleability of biological types, including race, and the relativity of culture, phrased by the *Time* correspondent as "the rationale of primitive cultures."[15]

In 1939, the *New Republic* collected in a single volume, *Books That Changed Our Minds,* twelve previously published articles in a series of the same name. Radin was invited to assess *The Mind of Primitive Man.* He lauded Boas's exposure of the smug, unexamined assumptions of nineteenth-century science. Its supposed objectivity, Boas had claimed, was little more than a set of subjective, value-laden presuppositions revealing more about the culture that produced them than about the world at large. Applied to human affairs, particularly regarding race, language, and culture, that veiled subjectivity had distorted the human record. Radin thus observed that "If the data he presented were accurate, all the accepted and cherished correlations that had been established between the various aspects of our civilization, not to mention many of our accepted values, had no inherent justification." This, in effect, was an attack on the arbitrariness, complacency, and perilous irrationality of ethnocentrism, so pervasive and deep-rooted that "only surprise and a kindly bewilderment greeted what he set before the American public." In Radin's view, "the world should have been shaken to its innermost core."

However, the immediate impact of Boas's best-known book was confined to a narrow circle of his students and colleagues. Like Boas and Radin, they were convinced that widespread error corrupted purported scientific understandings of human affairs. Most people in 1911 could hardly accept Boas's fundamental challenge to their belief in an intrinsic bond between race and behavior, repeatedly shown by Boas to be a cultural invention. It was clear to Radin and to Boas that the battle they were waging against popular error would be protracted.[16]

In his added chapter, "The Race Problem in Modern Society," appearing in the 1938 edition of *The Mind of Primitive Man,* Boas courageously drew a parallel between Nazi racial policy toward Jews and American public policies of racial exclusion of black Americans, Jews, and others from hotels, colleges, schools, clubs, and the like.[17] In fact, the Nuremberg Laws of 1935, which formalized Nazi racial policies toward Jews, were in several ways less severe than strictures against black people in the United States, such as laws against black-white marriage, access to public restrooms, and membership in major professional organizations.[18] Radin praised Boas for his "magnificent stand against fascism" that also included its racial analogues in the United States and his belief that anthropologists ought to be the advance guard against it.[19] In the wake of *The Mind of Primitive Man,* scientists gradually moved away from the notion that race determines culture, but an opposite trend outside of the scientific community was occurring. Boas lamented that "among the uninformed public . . . race prejudice has been making and is making unchecked progress."[20]

Boas's faith in untrammeled humanism shaped his entire outlook and social philosophy. He observed that a fundamental human value by modern standards is the treatment of a person as a unique individual, not as a representative of a class. Writing in 1921, he despaired as American society had fallen very short of that ideal and consequently "there is no great hope that the Negro problem will find even a half-way satisfactory solution in our day."[21] The intractability of race prejudice in part motivated Boas's radical proposal in 1921 advocating miscegenation to diminish racial antagonism. Greater color uniformity through black-white intermarriage, he argued, would eventually erase color as a basis for differentiating people. Eliminating anti-Semitism would require a similar plan—the obliteration of differences between Jews and their neighbors. He asserted that "anti-Semitism will not disappear until the last vestige of the Jew as a Jew has disappeared."[22] Proposing racial amalgamation and ethno-religious effacement bespoke a bleak realism about the severity of the problem of bigotry.

Boas's support for conjugal relations between white people and African Americans flouted the most formidable barrier to social equality in the United States. From the era of slavery and long after, a proposal such as Boas's could only outrage the vast majority of white people. A sexual relationship between a black man and a white woman, or even a vague rumor or suspicion, was quite enough to spark a lynch mob and terrorist violence against black people. It would be difficult to overstate the extremity of Boas's proposal in 1921, although public opinion was hardly aroused at the endemic sexual exploitation of black women by white men, beginning in the slave era and continuing after the Civil War.

Race and Ethnicity: Shackles of Tradition

Paul Radin and Franz Boas shared a commitment to humanist principles that dignified the lives of all individuals. Human dignity was imperiled by entrenched beliefs, practices, and institutions that stifled freedom of thought or imposed destructive, age-old cultural orthodoxies that disadvantaged particular categories of people. Radin cultivated humanist values from an early age, influenced as he was by his reform-minded rabbinical father and his teachers, James Harvey Robinson, John Dewey, and of course, Franz Boas.

Boas's formula for subduing racism and anti-Semitism was linked to his family history. He came of age amid a German Jewish community in his native Westphalia, where his freethinking parents in attempting to mediate religious and national identity continued to acknowledge a familial Jewish heritage.[23] Accordingly, Boas and his siblings were brought up in the Jewish tradition that included religious teaching, although a commitment to religious practice did not follow. Efforts to reconcile the identities of religion and nation in Germany carried over to the United States, where German Jewish immigrants continued to cultivate liberalizing trends begun in their homeland. The Reform movement of German Jews set about stripping away the cultural, religious, and linguistic trappings of orthodoxy in favor of a more rational faith that eroded the symbolic and social differences between liberal Jews and their Christian neighbors. Boas's forecast of the disappearance of anti-Semitism when Jews ceased being Jews was thus a possible endpoint of an old process marked by a steady cultural convergence of Jews and Christians. Yet neither that convergence in Germany nor the outright abandonment of the beliefs and practices of the religion could protect those born Jewish from the Nazi onslaught, despite their claims that they, too, were Germans.

Boas's radical humanism not only grew out of his experience as a freethinker in a liberal German Jewish family. It also had anthropological roots as he traced the course of political development of the first human communities from small-scale groups of foragers to a larger amalgamated unit. Asserting that "our first duties are to humanity as a whole," Boas argued that human foraging communities that regarded outsiders as threatening enemies eventually gave way to increasingly larger polities that expanded the scale of internal solidarity and common interest. Nationalism arrested that process, and accordingly he condemned its role in precipitating World War I, asserting in 1917 that "patriotism must be subordinated to humanism."[24] Years later at the outset of World War II, Boas's uncompromising statement of humanistic principles appears in a letter to his esteemed Columbia colleague, the philosopher John Dewey, with whom he shared a number of progressive concerns. Written three years before his death, the letter once again reiterated his opposition to nationalism and the overweening power of states or other entities that might suppress individual freedom:

> There are two matters to which I am devoted: absolute intellectual and spiritual freedom, and the subordination of the state to the interests of the individual; expressed in other forms, the furthering of conditions in which the individual can develop to the best of his own ability—as far as this is possible with a full understanding of the fetters imposed upon us by tradition; and the fight against all forms of power policy of states or private organizations. This means devotion to principles of a true democracy. I object to the teaching of slogans intended to befog the mind of whatever kind they may be.
>
> It has always seemed to me that under present political conditions we are impotent to influence governments of foreign states and that, in order to attain our ends, we must confine ourselves to act for the ideals of intellectual freedom and of service of the state for the benefit of the individual in our own country.[25]

Boas believed that human communities embody emotional beliefs and attitudes that people justify through tradition. Many of these beliefs and attitudes, often firmly held, can produce calamitous results that Boas did not hesitate to condemn. These include the narrow loyalties of a belligerent, unthinking nationalism as well as persistent racism and anti-Semitism. The more desirable but difficult course of action against the inertia of tradition calls for reason to determine human behavior and control emotions in the first place.[26] Reason, for Boas, dictated a humanistic universalism that would submerge emotionally laden, culturally fabricated human differences that had developed in the first human communities. But in the modern world, those passionately held differences manifested themselves in the destructive nationalism and racial loyalties of the state. The process of subordinating emotion to reason thus liberates people from the orthodoxies of the past—those encompassing restrictions imposed by culture that inhibit more enlightened human possibilities. In fact, "my whole outlook upon social life is determined by the question: how can we recognize the shackles that tradition has laid upon us? For when we recognize them, we are also able to break them."[27] The liberal atmosphere of his natal home provided the model for that questioning, as his parents had broken the "shackles of dogma." Although his father maintained an emotional attachment to Jewish ceremonial, it did not inhibit his freedom of thought and inquiry.[28]

In his critical references to tradition, Boas recognized the burdens imposed by history and by their continuation in current cultural arrangements. Having done more than anyone to establish cultural relativism as a first principle of American anthropology that in turn influenced twentieth-century thought, Boas also set its limits; he condemned at once an untrammeled, self-seeking individualism unchecked by the state, and an intrusive political apparatus unrestrained by "true democracy." And while racism and anti-Semitism were decidedly products of history and culture, any effort to rationalize them in terms of cultural relativism could only be perverse. Boas was neither a moral nor an ethical relativist, unhesitating as he was in his condemnation of practices that he believed stanched human freedom and self-realization, particularly in the nations of Europe and America.

Cultural Relativism: Methodological Tool or Moral Imperative?

Boasian cultural relativism is best understood not as a moral or ethical principle, but as a methodological axiom that derives significance from within the boundaries of a system rather than from external criteria. Although methodological relativism had compelling ethical and moral implications, they followed rather than preceded Boas's emergent scientific breakthroughs in the late nineteenth century. Methodological relativism in this respect enabled the anthropologist to understand cultural practices and beliefs in their own terms—from the inside, so to speak. In that circumscribed context, cultural elements bear a relationship not only to each other but also to the larger framework that constrains them. Meaning, then, is generated from within and does not depend on the imposition of exogenous factors. By contrast, moral relativism provides a self-justifying rationale for any culturally defined behavior.

The roots of Boas's conception of relativism go back to his pivotal 1889 article "On Alternating Sounds."[29] Stocking considers Boas's paper of incalculable importance in the history of anthropology.[30] Examining the role of subjectivity in acoustic perception, Boas provided an early linguistic model of methodological relativism by showing how the misperception of speech sounds occurs when a listener "hears" unfamiliar speech sounds through the phonemic framework of his native language. Boas did not use the terms "phoneme" or "phonemic" in his paper, but he was working within a phonemic structural framework that Sapir would later elaborate.[31] That a listener to an unfamiliar language might perceive two distinct speech sounds that a native speaker would perceive as a single sound demonstrates how the human cognitive apparatus is mediated by mind and language. For example, although they differ acoustically, an English speaker hears no discernible difference between the allophonic manifestations of the phoneme /p/—such as occur in the words *pan* and *span*. However, those two manifestations of the phoneme /p/ might be heard by a non-English speaker as distinct sounds. Conversely, English speakers distinguish the two words *pan* and *ban*. The acoustic properties of the two words are identical, except for the component of voicing in the initial speech sounds, and the differentiation of those sounds that every English speaker can perceive creates the semantic difference between the two words. In English *p* and *b* are distinct phonemes. Speakers of Korean, on the other hand hear *pan* and *ban* as a single word. Phonemic analysis thus establishes the necessity of methodological relativism if we are to understand linguistic sound systems and by extension cultural differences in their own terms. In each case, differences in meaning are context and system dependent—relative, in other words.[32]

But more than this, the mediating role of language and culture has profound implications for understanding human actors—literally active, perceiving individuals—making and remaking the meanings of their social and spiritual worlds. If, as Boas demonstrated, an actor perceives experience through the filter of cultural structure or tradition—relative, that is, to local understandings—it follows, then, that new experiences are subject to reinterpretation in terms of that prior configuration. Following Boas, both Radin and especially Herskovits examined how actors within an established cultural tradition integrate and transform new elements.

In the 1930s, the growth of research on acculturation—culture contact and its consequences—sensitized anthropologists to the likelihood that cultural elements borrowed by one social group from another could take on new meanings very different from what they were originally. Herskovits, influential in establishing acculturation studies in anthropology, provides numerous examples. A case in point is his interest in syncretism, a kind of reinterpretation, illustrated by African patterns reshaping borrowed elements. African peoples in New World Catholic countries, for example, identified African gods with saints of the Church. Legba, the West African trickster, thus appears in Haiti as a mendicant in close association with Saint Anthony, benefactor of the poor.[33]

Radin, while not a theorist of acculturation, addressed the issue of reinterpretation in a different vein when he considered the impact of Christian teaching on slaves. The self-aware, creative individuals who populated Radin's ethnographic work among native peoples of the New World are equally present in depictions of men and women in bondage, who transformed the punitive, sin-obsessed divinity of Methodist and Baptist missionaries into a gentle, reassuring God. Alien to their experience and needs, white Christian conversion efforts gave way before African American religious inventiveness in the creation of a distinct African American version of Christianity that will be discussed in later chapters.

Anthropology and African Americans

As World War II was raging, Ruth Benedict and Gene Weltfish published the pamphlet *The Races of Mankind*. Their publication provoked great controversy, confirming Boas's fear about the lack of progress and even regression in racial understanding. Appended to the pamphlet and complementing its findings were "Resolutions and Manifestoes of Scientists," a series of statements voted on by professional associations of anthropologists, psychologists, geneticists, and university professors, denouncing racism and anti-Semitism. Some resolutions explicitly addressed the perversion of science in Nazi Germany. The psychologist and Boas associate Otto Klineberg joined colleagues in observing that the emphasis on racial differences in Germany and Italy was growing in the United States.

Schools, churches, and civic organizations distributed the pamphlet, acclaiming the Benedict and Weltfish plea for reason and tolerance. At the same time, committees of the House of Representatives denounced the pamphlet; it was labeled "Communist propaganda" and the distribution of thousands of copies to army personnel was halted.[34] FBI surveillance of Paul Radin had occurred in the same atmosphere of racial fear, now grown even worse. Walter White of the NAACP captured particularly well the irony of racial subordination in the military, especially after grimly observing black-white relations among American soldiers stationed in Britain, where race riots among would-be combatants in France and Germany had occurred.[35] White wrote that "Americans . . . fighting a war to defeat a master-race theory, had transplanted to other parts of the world the racial patterns and prejudices of Mississippi."[36]

At the time Benedict and Weltfish were writing *The Races of Mankind,* Ruth Landes noted the parlous state of understanding about race as a concept. She observed "the increased content of the word 'race.'" Writing to Charles S. Johnson, whom she knew when teaching at Fisk, Landes worried that

> an accurately copied Nazi viciousness has entered the meaning of this word in the last half-year. Possibly this strikes me more than it would others because I am an ethnologist. But I have in mind especially the ease with which even Zionist Jews speak of themselves as a "race." Anthropologists have never approved of using the concept with more than the thinnest of stockbreeders' connotations, finding it more instructive to speak in cultural terminology (this includes Negroes). But when I returned to "civilization" up North, I found "race" used as the Nazis use it, with fixed, ranked meanings.[37]

In those ironic circumstances, it was once again a desolate vindication of Boas's pessimism about racial progress. The same can be said of Radin's unsuccessful use of anthropological evidence to argue against the exclusion of African Americans from neighborhoods. Boas continued to be very disturbed over the standing of all minority groups that had suffered denigration and abuse by race scientists, respected historians, sociologists, and the lay public. Over the years, he found that the sheer force of malignant racism meant that the struggle for human dignity and against irrationality would be prolonged.

The social and political debilities of race remained salient features of American life during Boas's long battle against the reduction of human differences to racial variation. For two decades following the end of World War II, the American population lived quite comfortably with the idea of biosocial inferiority of African Americans, immigrants, and other nonwhite peoples and with the racist policies it justified. No one was more disappointed or less sanguine about the future than Boas himself. For politicians, racism, often in euphemism, was acknowledged as a natural feature of the American social terrain, and they shamelessly paraded that claim before a largely sympathetic citizenry. In other words, public policy before the landmark Supreme Court decision of 1954 was for the most part unruffled by Boas's influence, as residential and school segregation, economic suppression, restrictive covenants, and extralegal violence in their enforcement were mostly the unquestioned order of the day. Racial quotas written into immigration law in the 1920s, opposed by Boas on the basis of scientific research, persisted in American law until 1965. A year after the Civil Rights Act, immigration quotas were overturned by the Hart-Celler Act, recognizing that ethnic-racial quotas were manifestly out of step with the new statutes supporting black equality before the law.

Early on, Boas recognized the ubiquity of recalcitrant white racial attitudes toward black people. Giving the commencement address at Atlanta University in 1906, Boas offered inspiration and caution to the young graduates. It is telling that Boas, in now famous remarks, advised his young audience not to expect support or praise from their white fellow citizens. His specific reference was to the impending efforts of the Atlanta graduate teachers to improve the standing of African Americans in the United States. He urged the graduates to continue self-motivated achievement because "with side glances on your white neighbor, waiting for his recognition or support of your noble work, you are destined to disappointment."[38] Throughout his career, from this early engagement with African Americans until the end of his life, Boas was never optimistic about white acceptance of black people on anything approaching equal terms. Consequently, he encouraged African Americans to maintain confidence in their own efforts, bearing in mind historical examples from the African past, where they could find a gratifying and inspiring touchstone rather than the shameful, atavistic picture of popular imagination. For the young graduates, Africa embodied "the strength that was their own before they set foot on the shores of this continent."[39]

The African past was so shrouded and distorted that Boas's message in Atlanta spoke not only to the young university graduates. It proved revelatory as well for W. E. B. Du Bois himself, who came of age when prevailing views, including his own, doubted, diminished, or negated the role of Africans in history.[40] Only a few years before, Du Bois was hard pressed to find an impact that the Negro race had made on the world. It might have been through Egypt, although Du Bois indicates uncertainty about black connections to Egypt. He observed that "the Negro race . . . have not as yet given to civilization the full spiritual message which they are capable of giving."[41] He maintained those views until hearing Boas's address, which caused "a sudden awakening from the paralysis of this judgment taught me in high school and in two of the world's great universities."[42] Du Bois was particularly attentive to Boas's critique of scientific racism and its perversion of the historical record.

Some six months after his Atlanta speech, Boas envisioned a large project to increase knowledge of Africa, thereby dispelling erroneous conceptions of the continent while adding to the fund of anthropological science. In observing the "increasing antagonism between white and black races," Boas wrote to Andrew Carnegie in an unsuccessful effort to gain funding for an "African Institute." Through exhibits and publications, the proposed organization would enlighten the public about "African civilization." Boas believed that such an effort might soften white attitudes by showing what black people accomplished in Africa. Particularly urgent was the need for "thorough studies of the conditions of the American Negro on such scientific basis that the results could not be challenged." The then current state of scientific knowledge about African Americans, according to Boas, was simply too low to sustain any argument that would expose the irrelevance of race to cultural outcomes. In exploding the myth of race, scientific knowledge, not sentiment, was essential. At the same time, a new clarity about the ancestral home of Americans of African descent would nurture self-esteem among black people, demoralized from the beginning over their reviled position in American society and the many pseudoscientific fictions that rationalized it.[43] Boas and Radin understood full well the devastation wrought on the psyches of minority peoples by repeated assertions alleging inferiority and a past without historical accomplishment. The celebratory reception of Herskovits's *The Myth of the Negro Past* among black scholars and journalists more than thirty-five years after Boas's proposed African Institute was in part the realization of the scientific and psychological value that he predicted.

The "wholesome influence" of anthropology thus also included the promotion of a greater understanding of Africa and African American life on the part of the racial majority in the United States. Shortly after his speech at Atlanta, Boas wrote to Booker T. Washington, hoping to arrange a meeting when Washington would be in New York. Enclosing his Atlanta speech, Boas explained that he wanted to discuss his plan to organize certain scientific work on the Negro race which I believe will be of great practical value in modifying the views of our people in regard to the Negro problem. I am particularly anxious to bring home to the American people the fact that the African race in its own continent has achieved advancements which have been of importance in the development of civilization of the human race.[44]

There is no record of a response from Washington either in the Boas or Washington papers. Nor does there appear to be further correspondence between the two men. Boas, on the other hand, maintained a long professional relationship with Du Bois following his 1906 visit to Atlanta University.

The racial majority remained recalcitrant regarding African American aspiration, so much so that in 1938, as noted earlier, Boas compared American race policies to Nazi treatment of the German Jewish population. In 1935, Otto Klineberg appropriately dedicated *Race Differences* to Franz Boas, as the book argued that ability and human potential bear no relationship to race. Yet in conclusion, the author shared Boas's despair, recognizing the chasm separating his findings from their implementation in human affairs.

If the material collected in this volume were accepted as demonstrating the absence of any valid proof of racial differences in intelligence or character, it might conceivably lead to a more favorable attitude toward groups usually regarded as inferior. In time there might even be a change in race relations. This seems to assume that people do reason, although a little earlier it was suggested that they usually rationalize. There is hope, however, even in rationalization. The very search for reasons, even if that search is secondary, makes it possible for opinions to change, if one by one the foundations on which they rest are shown to be illusory.[45]

Arguments against unreason in racial matters resided in academic books and articles, with occasional appearances in wide-circulation periodicals and newspapers, where the anthropologists pressed for tolerance and informed understanding about biological race. The Benedict-Weltfish collaboration had broad distribution, but encountered strong, official opposition and censorship. The battle, in other words, was decidedly uneven.

As World War II raged against an enemy bent on racial domination, the United States continued to perpetuate its own variety of racial control. The tragic domestic ironies of the war were legion. Du Bois in agreement with Boas asserted that the majority of men do not usually act in accord with reason, but follow social pressures, inherited customs and long-established, often sub-conscious, patterns of action. Consequently, race prejudice in America will linger long and may even increase.[46]

Du Bois's remarks appeared in the 1944 volume *What the Negro Wants,* an exposure, without intent, of the depths of racism among those ostensibly eager to hear the concerns of black Americans.

The University of North Carolina Press, noted in the context of the times for its progressive list, commissioned the book. The press asked for contributors of diverse opinion representing "left-wing, moderate, and right-wing points of view."[47] Editor Rayford Logan, professor of history at Howard, sought contributions from fourteen notable African Americans, including Du Bois, Roy Wilkins, A. Philip Randolph, Mary McLeod Bethune, Langston Hughes, and Sterling Brown. Logan prepared the first contribution, "The Negro Wants First-Class Citizenship," which set the tone for the entire volume *What the Negro Wants,* a title recalling an article of the same name by Langston Hughes just prior to the American entry into World War II. Irony reverberated when Hughes explained that black people wanted the right to eat in any restaurant or to find accommodation in hotels, noting that "any Nazi may do so."[48]

However diverse the political views of contributors to the Logan volume might have been, they were of one mind about the book's subject. Nothing less than full civil rights guaranteed to every American citizen would do. The press responded with reactionary outrage, expressed in the "publisher's introduction" written by W. T. Couch, director of the University of North Carolina Press. Couch declared that what Logan and his colleagues wanted for African Americans was simply not acceptable. He attacked all theories explaining the debilities of black people in terms of social and historical conditions and white prejudicial actions. Included in his screed were Boasian anthropology, the concept of cultural relativism, the specific works of Herskovits and Benedict, Gunnar Myrdal's recently published *An American Dilemma,* and all assertions of racial equality.

While Couch seemed to reject innateness and fixity as the source of putative black inferiority, he believed that it could be overcome and prejudice eliminated. The burden, in his view, lay only with black people, who, if not naturally backward, were certainly culturally inferior and unworthy of equal rights. He thus argued that the African American desire for inclusion—what the Negro wants—as a citizen was illegitimate.[49] Charles Johnson concluded that Couch's retrograde dissent "heightens the challenge presented by the united front of Negro leaders."[50]

Zora Neale Hurston

Of Boas's African American students, Zora Neale Hurston holds a distinctive place. She is certainly the best known, having established her multifaceted reputation not only as a folklorist and anthropologist but also as a performer, feminist, critic, and exuberant figure in the Harlem Renaissance. African Americans in rural Florida found in Hurston an ideal recorder and interpreter of their narratives, once she stripped away the patina of a Barnard sophisticate. Like Radin working at approximately the same time in Nashville, she was a kind of documentarian seeking to memorialize the unmediated voices of a marginal community previously ignored or misrepresented. In the years since her death in obscurity in 1960 and Alice Walker's devoted efforts to revive her reputation, a large literature has developed on her life and writing, including her studies as an anthropology student in New York, where she received the unwavering but not uncritical support of Boas.[51]

Warned to avoid calling or referring to Boas as "Papa Franz," the irrepressible Hurston asked Boas about that cautionary advice before a group of anthropologists gathered at Boas's home. "Of course, Zora is my daughter. Certainly. Just one of my missteps, that's all." She continued, "The sabre cut on his cheek, which is said he got in a duel in Heidelberg, lifted in a smile."[52]

Behind that amiable recollection was a serious dedication to the studies that Boas was encouraging. Robert Hemenway describes her interest in anthropology and her devotion to her mentor.

> Boas became the most important figure in her academic life, not only because of his great personal magnetism, but also because he recognized her genius immediately and urged her to begin training as a professional anthropologist, concentrating on folklore. . . . She admittedly idolized him. Hurston could be the victim of an easily aroused, indiscriminate enthusiasm, but the commitment to anthropology was no whim.[53]

Hemenway notes that one indication of her dedication to Boas was her willingness to participate in physical anthropological studies in Harlem and to do so with a "relaxed insouciance."[54] That demeanor was well captured by Langston Hughes.

Almost nobody else could stop the average Harlemite on Lenox Avenue and measure his head with a strange-looking, anthropological device and not get bawled out for the attempt, except Zora, who used to stop anyone whose head looked interesting, and measure it.[55]

Hughes was only partly right in observing that Hurston, whether at Barnard or Columbia, "didn't let college give her a broad *a* and who had great scorn for all pretensions, academic or otherwise." In the longer term, she could not have enjoyed any success in collecting folklore had she dissembled or attempted to be anyone other than herself among rural African Americans in Florida.[56] Thus, the much greater success of her second field trip to Florida derived in part from setting aside the self-conscious artifice of a Barnard education, so distant from the people in the communities she visited.

Demanding mentor that he was, Boas nonetheless suffered some frustration in dealing with Hurston, who simply did not conform easily to the confinement and discipline of academic life, especially stringent under Boas's supervision. He pithily summarized the essence of Hurston's creativity, independence, and nonconformity in a letter to Otto Klineberg, whom Hurston, along with another Boas student, Louis King, was assisting in his studies of the relationship of race and psychology. In Boas's estimation, "temperamentally she is so much more artistic than scientific that she has to be held down."[57] But no one, including Boas, could hold her down. Nonetheless, letters between Hurston and Boas as well as Hurston's autobiographical reflections on her anthropological studies imply a relationship of mutual respect and affection. The demands Boas placed on Hurston were no more rigorous than what he expected from others.

Some support for research for African American scholars was available through Carter Woodson's organization, the Association for the Study of Negro Life and History. Woodson regularly invited Boas to attend the organization's meetings and to speak before the assembled African American scholars. They also corresponded about candidates for grants, some of whom, such as Hurston, Abram Harris, and Louis King, had worked closely with Boas.[58]

Hurston's first venture into fieldwork outside of calculating cephalic indices in Harlem took her home to Florida. That research was made possible by a grant from the Association for the Study of Negro Life and History following Boas's supportive exchanges with Woodson in November 1926.[59] Given the financial struggles of Woodson's association, he sought help from Elsie Clews Parsons, a sociologist devoted to the fields of anthropology and folklore.[60] Independently wealthy and a renowned scholar, she did research in the American Southwest as well as in the East and Southeast, where she collected African American folklore. A benefactor to colleagues and students, she provided at least half the money that would fund Hurston's Florida research.[61]

Hurston, in her own inimitable way, believed that she was engaged in salvage ethnography. In a letter accompanying her fresh transcriptions of collected narratives, Hurston tells Boas of the opportune timing of her research because much of the lore was disappearing. Many people were telling her, "I used to know some of that old stuff, but I done forgot it all." Then Hurston explains, "You see, the negro is not living his lore to the extent of the Indian. He is not on a reservation, being kept pure. His negroness is being rubbed off by close contact with white culture."[62] Comfortable in her native status among black people in several Florida towns, one might surmise that informant claims of not knowing "some of that old stuff" were probably genuine. However, Hurston confesses,

> I did not have the right approach. The glamor of Barnard College was still upon me. I dwelt in marble halls. I knew where the material was all right. But, I went about asking, in carefully accented Barnardese, 'Pardon me, but do you know folk-tales or folk-songs? The men and women who had whole treasuries of material just seeping through their pores looked at me and shook their heads.[63]

As to advice, Boas was always the engaged mentor and supervisor, not especially generous with his praise, but certainly constructively critical. Looking over folkloric materials she had sent after a few months in Florida, Boas disapproved of what she was collecting and pointed her in two new directions because "I find that what you obtained is very largely repetition of the kind of material that has been collected so much." Instead, he wanted Hurston to gather new kinds of data, including those that would reveal patterns of behavior beyond the awareness of informants, and data with ethnohistorical significance.

> You remember that when we talked about this matter, I asked you particularly to pay attention, not so much to the content, but rather to the form of diction, movements, and so on. I would also suggest that it might be a good plan to lay more stress upon current superstitions and to get as many of these as you can. We ought to compare the superstitious beliefs that occur among the English-speaking Negroes with those that occur among the Spanish and French speaking Negroes.

Also practices that refer to marriage, birth death and other important events in the life would be important. The methods of dancing, habitual movements in telling tales or in ordinary conversation; all this is material that would be essentially new.[64]

Written in 1927, Boas's advice is telling for two reasons. He advises Hurston to be aware of the dynamics of cultural reinterpretation, an issue Radin raised in his Fisk research and in *The Racial Myth*. Boas also wanted Hurston to gather data on unconscious patterns of behavior that Herskovits would later pursue in linking Africa to the New World, including the United States.

Acculturation studies were some years from reaching a central place in American anthropology through Herskovits's influence and the steady attenuation of the tribal isolate as the object of research.[65] Here, Boas is suggesting that the experience of Africans exposed to different European traditions, French, English, or Spanish, pointed to variations in "superstitious beliefs." The problem to be pursued was the nature and direction of cultural borrowing and the dynamics of reinterpretation, or the new meanings African-derived peoples were placing on the cultural elements they had borrowed. Later, Herskovits made the radical claim that Europeans borrowed and incorporated African elements.[66] Boas's advice for Hurston to look at motor habits, whether in dance or narration, likewise anticipated what Herskovits would also later examine. For Herskovits, unconscious patterns of behaviors originating in Africa—what anthropologists would call covert culture—were features fully extant in African American culture.

But for Hurston, Boas's critique was close to devastating. She undoubtedly felt that she had failed Woodson as well. Somberly, she returned to New York and met with Boas.

> I stood before Papa Franz and cried salty tears. He gave me a good going over, but later I found that he was not as disappointed as he let me think. He knew I was green and feeling my oats, and that only bitter disappointment was going to purge me. It did.[67]

Boas remained her supporter, and subsequent fieldwork proved much more successful, providing additional material later incorporated into her landmark *Mules and Men*. In his preface, Boas recognized the import of an African American researcher gathering folklore when the popularity of Uncle Remus "exerted a strong attraction upon the imagination of the American public." Part of that attraction was a reinforcement of the southern view of black people. In the Uncle Remus tales and other collections of black folklore "without end," Boas asserted that "the intimate setting in the social life of the Negro has been given very inadequately." That inadequacy, also focused on Uncle Remus, was detailed by Arthur Huff Fauset in his contribution to *The New Negro.*[68] But as a native African American woman, Hurston "was able to penetrate through that affected demeanor by which the Negro excludes the White observer effectively from participating in his true inner life."[69] Among the white scholars who wrote on black folklore, the sociologists Howard W. Odum and Guy B. Johnson were well known for their publications on folksongs. Hurston found much to criticize in their work.[70] Reviewing the Odum and Johnson collaboration, *The Negro and His Songs,* the white southern progressive Nell Battle Lewis gets directly to the issue:

> A wealth of Negro folklore and folksongs exists in the South. It is one of the misfor-
> tunes of the Negro that most of the mining of this rich material has been done by
> whites, for however well-disposed and sympathetic the white man's interpretation
> of Negro art may be, no one can speak for the Negro as well as the Negro himself.[71]

In the space of a brief introduction to *Mules and Men,* Hurston, as effectively as any other writer since that time, illuminates the complexity of insider anthropology. She examines how a local, personal identity historically bound to the community softens the seemingly impersonal professional goals of the researcher; how potential informants can embrace her personal identity while cautiously viewing her professional status; and how the native as anthropologist can see the familiar at a distance, recognizing that "it was fitting me like a tight chemise [but] I couldn't see it for wearing it."[72] Hurston's collection of tales revealed the artfulness and wisdom of people more often regarded as uncultivated and improvident. This recalls Radin's view, noted in chapter 1, that even slavery could not suppress original cultural achievements in literature and music.

Having published her first novel, *Jonah's Gourd Vine,* in 1934 and on the verge of publishing *Mules and Men* the following year, Hurston received a Rosenwald Foundation grant for further study. Chronically short of money, Hurston now seemed on a secure path to completion of her anthropology doctorate. However, the Rosenwald Foundation reneged on the promised award, claiming that Hurston's plans were too uncertain.[73]

From the outset of their relationship, Boas never relinquished his support of

Hurston, recognizing that a young woman, more artist than scientist, would not be the conventional anthropology student. That support continued, even when the Rosenwald Foundation withdrew its promise. Although she returned to Columbia, a Guggenheim grant enabled her to begin work in the Caribbean, after which she did not resume academic studies.[74]

In Boasian relativism, Hurston shared with Radin an analytic understanding of what each had always known personally—the inherent value, legitimacy, and life lessons embedded in African American traditions carried on by common folk. Hurston had gained that initial understanding as a native, someone deeply embedded within the Florida communities where she eventually returned as an anthropologist. In a very different way, Radin embraced relativism as a response to his own sense of cultural alienation that then provided a path to understanding the wisdom of others, too often diminished in the name of racial dominance or other misguided ideology.

Hurston thus rejected black elitist perspectives resonating with a part of the Harlem Renaissance. As a folklorist, she demonstrated in *Mules and Men* her regard for the narrative and vernacular distinctiveness of ordinary country people. Likewise, Radin concerned himself with stylistic and literary achievements of unschooled narrators. But for Hurston, even Boas's expansive influence, encouragement, and regard for her research were too restrictive and could not contain her drive to portray the truths of black life through fiction. As the artist recognized by Boas at the outset of their relationship, Hurston knew that novels, stories, and plays were her true métier through which she imagined rather than merely documented black cultural worlds.

Posthumous Influence

Several of Boas's students, including Margaret Mead, Ruth Benedict, and M. F. Ashley Montagu, became public intellectuals, successfully stimulating broad interest in anthropology and the scientific anti-racism that began with their mentor. At stake was the standing of all minority groups, but particularly African Americans. It is thus significant that Boas's now famous address to the 1906 graduating class of Atlanta University emphasized the cultural achievements of African peoples, thereby giving the graduates a sense of pride and self-worth. The African past was cause for celebration, not shame. Likewise, the *Pittsburgh Courier* in reporting on Radin's *The Racial Myth* similarly brought to the fore Radin's documentation of African cultural achievement. African Americans were not alone in praising Radin's observations about African inventiveness. Ben Azikiwe, who would become Nigeria's first president, wrote very favorably of Radin's observations of African cultural creativity.[75] Later, Radin would also emphasize the achievements of former slaves in creating in their narrations a literature fully worthy of that designation. Boas and Radin understood full well the devastation wrought on the psyches of minority peoples by continuing belittlement of their human capacities.

Nearly ten years after its high praise of Radin's *The Racial Myth,* the *Pittsburgh Courier* joined newspapers across the country in reporting Franz Boas's death in December 1942. With a mixture of sorrow and hope, the *Courier* editorialist stated that Boas "did more than any one man to fight the vicious fallacy of race, debunk the blonde superman and expose what he called 'this Nordic nonsense.'" Racial differences, the newspaper observed in highlighting Boas's findings, do not account for cultural differences. The *Courier* lauded Boas for exposing "grotesque racial fictions" used "to justify the enslavement and exploitation of colored nations" and for "depriving the myth of race superiority of any scientific basis." The encomium concluded with a look forward to the continuation of Boas's anti-racist mission by his students: "While his passing is greatly to be mourned, we can be thankful that his students, including Robert Lowie, Clark Wissler, Melville Herskovits, Ruth Benedict, Margaret Mead, Alexander Goldenweiser, Paul Radin, and Zora Hurston are carrying on his work."[76]

Tributes to Boas in the darkest days of World War II had a particularly searing relevance as Nazi armies were rolling across Europe. His career was in large measure defined by a lifelong moral and empirical attack against the scientific racism at the foundation of Nazism and the genocide that intensified in the wake of the Nazi juggernaut. Volumes of his scholarship were among the first to be incinerated in the infamous burning of the books in 1933, including their immolation at the University of Kiel, where he had received his PhD and then an honorary degree in 1932.[77] He had written to the German president Paul von Hindenburg pleading with him to withhold power from Hitler so that Germany might return to humanity.[78] As Lowie observed,

> The rise of Hitler stirred him to the depths of his soul. That the country whose cultural heritage he gloried in, the country on whose behalf he had suffered abuse and ostracism in the first World War, should flout the principles dear to him was

an unbearable thought. Besides, being of Jewish extraction, he had relatives in Germany whose very existence was threatened by the *Umbruch* [upheaval].[79]

He could only have been profoundly disturbed in his old age by Nazi victories and the enduring racism in his adopted country. Boas was so thoroughly committed to the scientific struggle against "the myth of race" in its many manifestations that even his last words, reported by the refugee scholar Paul Rivet and witnessed by another refugee scholar, Claude Lévi-Strauss, proclaimed that "this crusade against racism must continue, always and everywhere" [*il faudra continuer, toujours et partout, cette croisade contre le racisme*].[80]

Boas had arrived in the United States when the myth of race was shaping the anthropology of that time, owing to the grip of biopolitical and biosocial thinking on the amateurs then constituting the field from their bases in Washington, Cambridge, and Philadelphia. At great risk to his standing and reputation, he succeeded in reorienting the discipline, establishing culture rather than race as the source of human thought and action. Early on, black scholars such as Carter Woodson, W. E. B. Du Bois, Charles S. Johnson, and others recognized him as an invaluable ally against racism. Reflecting on Boas's legacy as it spoke to black scholars, St. Clair Drake credited American anthropology under the Boasian influence with changing the direction of the discipline and combating biological determinism.

> Blacks watched Boas battle against the Washington, D. C. establishment rooted in the Smithsonian Institution that tried to "destroy" him. . . . They knew where their friends were in the field as well as their enemies. And when the Boasians won and the Holocaust turned the world against racism . . . and Boas' [*sic*] students took up the anti-racist crusade, Afro-American scholars were ready to give credit to American anthropology for having purged itself of its past and for providing much of the personnel that led the fight against theories of biological determinism.[81]

William Willis also praised Boas for having "introduced a new way of looking at race." Continuing, Willis remarked that "Boas was the first distinguished white social scientist in the United States who minimized the importance of race as a determinant of human behavior."[82] In a longer note, Willis elaborated:

> Boas presented his initial remarks on racial differences in his vice-presidential address at the meeting of the American Association for the Advancement of

Science in Brooklyn, New York, in August 1894. In this eloquent tour de force, Boas employed the essential arguments that were later incorporated into *The Mind of Primitive Man.* Therefore, *The Mind of Primitive Man* did not initiate the intellectual attack on prevailing extreme racial determinism. Rather it was the culmination of an attack that had started nearly twenty years before.[83]

Boas's antagonists were numerous. None had more impact than Madison Grant, a patrician, Harvard-educated lawyer who expressed the anxious fears of many nativists in his influential book *The Passing of the Great Race.* With other prominent advocates of scientific racism, Grant argued that biology is destiny. The problems of the early twentieth century, including destitution, dependency, and associated ills, had their genesis in the allegedly heritable, unchanging defects of eastern and southern Europeans then settling in American cities. Their biological flaws endangered the vigor of the old American stock deriving from northern and western Europe. Race mixing could only result in the diminished health and vitality of offspring, for eugenicists such as Grant believed that mixed-race children would inevitably manifest the weaker traits of their parentage. Grant's theories found a ready audience not only in the United States but among European race theorists, especially among the Nazis for whom Grant's ideas provided support and vindication of their own racial doctrines.

The stark realization that American versions of scientific racism materially inspired Nazi racial policies, including genocide, emerged dramatically at the Nuremburg trials. There, Karl Brandt, SS captain and personal physician to Hitler, faced charges of euthanasia of the mentally and physically ill, and of racial minorities; executing prisoners in the death camps; and performing ghastly medical experiments on camp prisoners. Brandt defended himself by citing *The Passing of the Great Race,* published in German in 1925 and presaging the actions for which Brandt would soon be executed. Hitler had declared, "This book is my Bible."[84]

The Boasian critique of the race concept ultimately became an international concern. It exercised a genuine transnational influence, best illustrated by the UNESCO Statement on Race in 1950. The statement was motivated by exposure of the full extent of Nazi genocide, which came to worldwide attention through the witnessing of survivors and liberators and was recorded in documents, photographs, military films, and newsreels. The original UNESCO draft statement joined the views of Ashley Montagu, E. Franklin Frazier, Claude Lévi-Strauss, and others. Substantially written by Ashley Montagu, the final statement was signed by biologists and geneticists, including Theodosius Dobzhansky, Julian Huxley, and Nobel Laureate Herman Muller, cousin of Alfred Kroeber, the psychologist Otto Klineberg, and Gunnar Myrdal, author of *An American Dilemma*. In the wake of the defeat of Nazism, the statement repudiated Aryan racial delusions by asserting the unity of the human species and rejecting biological race as a concept of any scientific value. "Race mixing" was a specter that had haunted American eugenicists and their Nazi champions. The UNESCO Statement declared that miscegenation, or mixed-race unions, do not result in biological decline, contrary to the profound apprehension of generations of eugenics proponents. Moreover, the UNESCO principles affirmed that human groups do not differ in their mental qualities and that there is no demonstrable connection between physique and mental characteristics. No reputable biologist or physician, only those German scientists not charged at Nuremburg but complicit in mass murder, scorned UNESCO's rejection of the fundamental tenets of Nazi racial ideology.

Among Nazi race theorists dissenting from the UNESCO Statement was physical anthropologist Eugen Fischer, with whom Boas corresponded until 1934. Coauthor of the Nuremberg race laws, Fischer and other German anthropologists were eager National Socialists, enthusiastic proponents of an aberrant race science they eagerly pressed into the service of mass murder and torturous human medical experimentation. Fischer, director of the Kaiser Wilhelm Institute for physical anthropology, together with his colleagues trained SS doctors later posted to death camps. He advanced his research by accessing body parts from concentration camps. Fischer's close follower Otmar von Verschuer in turn trained the infamous camp doctor Josef Mengele, who at war's end escaped to South America. Fischer lived until 1967, unindicted and unpunished for promoting Nazi race policies and participating in sadistic medical experiments and genocide.[85] With his associates, Fritz Lenz and von Verschuer, he evaded justice on the gallows at Nuremberg. Instead, they eventually received university appointments in genetics.[86]

Boas's most important scientific conclusions about race carried profound moral imperatives, particularly in the wake of the defeat of Nazism and the full realization of the scale and extent of its murderous racial policies. It was his posthumous honor to have his findings rejected by unapologetic Nazis when at the same time the UNESCO Statement on Race at mid-century "represented the triumph of Boasian anthropology on a world-historical scale."[87]

CHAPTER 3

From Object to Subject

Centering African American Lives at Fisk University

T he Fisk University social science program created by Charles S. Johnson regarded African Americans as active subjects belonging at the center of social and historical research on slavery and its consequences. The program was developing when the mainstream of American historical scholarship objectified slaves and their descendants, portraying them as passive figures severely limited by an assumed innate racial disposition. Paul Radin's radical humanism, concern with self-representation, and exposure of specious race-based explanations of human experience therefore found a welcome home in the social science program. He was part of an anti-racist discipline that was waging a decisive campaign to free twentieth-century American anthropology from the moribund race science that had preceded it.

Research in the social science program took different but complementary forms, represented by Charles Johnson's work utilizing sociological survey methods and Paul Radin's probing of individual lives. Johnson, Radin, and their Fisk colleagues collectively repudiated explanations, whether emanating from sociology or history, of human experience in terms of bioracial differences. Regarding historical research on slavery and its calamitous legacy, Carter Woodson and other African American scholars found little of value in the publications of most white historians whose work was defined by an unalloyed racism. Racial explanations and biopolitics were so rife in historical scholarship that Woodson and black historians declared independence from the mainstream of their profession and created a distinctive black history. The explanatory use of biological race was more nuanced in sociology and did not provoke the creation of a distinct black sociology.

Johnson studied sociology with Robert E. Park at the University of Chicago. During his long career, he worked for the Urban League, both in Chicago and New York, and in 1928 joined the Fisk faculty. In 1946, he became Fisk's first black president, serving in that position until his death in 1956. An important figure in the fight for civil rights in the years leading up to the 1954 Supreme Court decision, Johnson was highly pragmatic in his commitment to the civil rights movement for equality and desegregation. Johnson's pragmatism included a keen awareness of both the implacable opposition of die-hard racists and the limited risks southern white liberals, such as the sociologists Howard Odum and Guy B. Johnson, were willing to take on behalf of black civil rights.[1]

Despite talent and drive, Johnson—like any other African American aspiring to a profession, academic or otherwise, in the early decades of the twentieth century—faced enormous obstacles. Park's patronage was pivotal in launching not only Johnson's career but also the subsequent careers of other renowned black social scientists, including sociologists E. Franklin Frazier and Horace Cayton Jr. and anthropologist St. Clair Drake.

Johnson assumed the chair of social sciences at Fisk, where he created a program staffed by a multiracial group of talented scholars. Radin's appointment as research professor of anthropology was made possible by a grant from the Laura Spelman Rockefeller Memorial. The Social Sciences Institute was Radin's ostensible academic home, where his status as research professor with no administrative responsibilities suspended the usual demands placed on professors. Given his chronic academic discontent as well as his indifference to mundane academic administration, Radin enjoyed a position that was nearly ideal. Johnson's biographers point out that outstanding professors enjoyed "the freedom for research in the best laboratory in the nation for race relations without many of the formal restraints of academia."[2]

As a patron, Park used his considerable influence to advance the younger man's career. Charles Johnson's entrepreneurship in seeking grants supporting social research at Fisk, and his ability to negotiate white institutional patronage and the racial politics of his time recall Booker T. Washington's diplomacy and moderation. Although his style was much closer to Washington's than to Du Bois's,

Johnson did not reproduce the strategies of compliant racial uplift of Booker T. Washington, for whom Park had served as secretary and ghostwriter prior to his turn toward sociology. Park's distaste for activist engagement against racial policies that disadvantaged black people was compatible with Washington's public philosophy of gradualism. While Park trained talented black students for advanced degrees, Washington famously promoted industrial and trade-oriented education for young black people. Johnson, however, supported academic study for African Americans.

Johnson could not have succeeded in establishing a research program at Fisk had he relied on university funds alone. External help was essential. He made ample use of philanthropic and foundation support from white-dominated organizations and in this respect differed sharply with W. E. B. Du Bois. Believing that white patronage would inevitably compromise and limit the African American push for full racial equality, Du Bois rejected the sponsorship that Johnson actively solicited. Du Bois also feared that white patrons might oppose radical tactics. Johnson, on the other hand, in highly pragmatic fashion, used his considerable diplomatic skills in the manner of Washington to secure the support of white philanthropies.[3] His quest for funds brought a renewal of the Laura Spelman Rockefeller Memorial grant that had underwritten Radin's appointment at Fisk, and he procured additional aid from the Rosenwald Fund, the Carnegie Corporation, the Rockefeller Foundation, and other agencies.[4] Unlike Du Bois, Johnson was disposed to compromise. Born and educated in the South, he pursued a career at a southern black university and therefore had developed the negotiating and personal skills essential to navigating a racial environment of uncompromising social inequality, segregation, and white domination. Southern white liberals might be allies up to a point, but unlike Radin and Boas, they backed away when black people pressed for full social equality. Still, Radin avoided forthright criticism of racial conditions while in Nashville, undoubtedly in deference to Johnson's leadership.

Johnson and the Urban League in Chicago and New York

Before completing his studies at Chicago, Johnson had served in World War I. With thousands of other black soldiers, he believed that the experience of combat would bring about a new day for the American Negro, who had demonstrated patriotism and self-sacrifice. Instead, race riots erupted in American cities during and after the war. The worst violence broke out in Chicago in 1919; over five hundred persons suffered injuries, and thirty-eight people—twenty-three African Americans and fifteen whites—were killed. Johnson had served as head of the Department of Research and Investigation of the young Chicago Urban League, founded in 1916 by an interracial group including Robert Park, the first president. Under Park's influence, the organization gave Johnson leave to become associate executive secretary of the Chicago Commission on Race Relations, created to study the devastating race riot.[5] The resulting report of more than six hundred pages, *The Negro in Chicago*, was substantially written by Johnson.[6] However, the book assigns authorship collectively to the Chicago Commission on Race Relations.[7]

As principal writer of *The Negro in Chicago* and keenly aware of ubiquitous pseudoscientific racial claims, Johnson forthrightly identified those biosocial distortions as the source of many pernicious but self-justifying white attitudes toward black people. Such views attributed black social characteristics, usually negative, to an innate lack of restraint resulting in a criminal propensity, an inferior mentality and morality, and emotionalism. Johnson instead offered sociological explanations for human behavior derived from "circumstances of position rather than . . . distinct racial traits."[8] Yet he did not have complete control over the final report, as the early statement of "The Problem" regressively points to physical differences between whites and blacks as the "natural basis for distinctions, discriminations and antipathies arising from the instinct of each race to preserve its type." Johnson could not have written these lines. Moreover, in the paternalistic tone of the times, the anonymous authors of that section state that "The Negro race . . . must base its progress upon industry, efficiency, and moral character."[9]

If not a call to radical action, *The Negro in Chicago*, in carefully chosen language, still provides an unblinking assessment of the causes of the riot, placing the onus of responsibility squarely on groups and institutions under white control that disadvantaged black people at every turn.[10] Substandard housing, job discrimination, and a labor movement hostile to black workingmen contributed to widespread black discontent. But like all urban racial conflagrations prior to the 1960s, the flash point of the Chicago eruption was white violence, provoked by imagined black offenses against white racial sensibilities. The riot erupted on a Lake Michigan beach, where angry white youth, deeply resentful of the proximity of African Americans despite their observance of the beach segregation law, caused the death of a young black swimmer.[11] Violent white gangs were a particularly raw example of racist actions against black people.[12] Although he could not name it for obvious practical and political reasons, Johnson in effect shifted attention from the diversionary "Negro problem"—a ubiquitous phrase that put the onus of responsibility on black people—to the "White problem," the actual cause of racial conflict and violence in the United States. Unlike his mentor, Johnson was not practicing the disengaged, value-free, objective sociology espoused by Park and nearly the entire sociology profession from the 1920s to the present. As summarized in a posthumous autobiographical note found among his papers, Park, a one-time journalist, wrote of his conception of the sociologist as "a kind of super-reporter," committed to accuracy and detachment.[13]

In a personal reminiscence, Ernest Burgess, a sociologist and Park collaborator at the University of Chicago, observed that both white and black students drawn to sociology tended to have a passionate commitment to the cause of black equality and were thus inclined to active engagement against racial discrimination. A residue of reformism persisted in sociology, and black students could undertake advanced research on African American social issues. But Park espoused a sociology separate from reform, claiming that the sociologist "investigates race relations with the same objectivity and detachment with which the zoologist dissects the potato bug."[14] Johnson did not adopt the clinical view of his mentor, but instead linked research to ameliorative goals. He was of course constrained by the political realities of his time and place, his sensibilities as a southern black man, and his position with the Urban League; but his research was certainly not value-free or uncommitted to ending segregation and social inequality. In that respect, Johnson's sensibilities about racial injustice were precisely those of Radin and Boas.

Following his work with the Chicago Commission on Race Relations, Johnson moved to New York where he became founding editor of *Opportunity: A Journal of Negro Life,* sponsored by the Urban League and actively promoting the Harlem Renaissance. Understated in manner, Johnson did not call undue attention to himself, but instead focused interest on the artistic talent infusing that vibrant new movement. Many of its voices were collected in Alain Locke's *The New Negro,* to which Johnson also contributed. Literary contests in *Opportunity* also helped to advance new writers, such as Zora Neale Hurston. She called him "the root of the so-called Harlem Renaissance," remarking that other people had gotten credit for its founding because of "his hush-mouth nature."[15] She was not alone in her estimation of Johnson's importance in promoting African American letters. Langston Hughes said that Johnson "did more to encourage and develop Negro writers during the 1920s than anyone else in America. He brought them together to meet and know each other. He made *Opportunity* writing contests sources of discovery and help."[16]

Opportunity joined *The Crisis* as a critical outlet for black writers, such as Hughes and Hurston, who were otherwise closed out of publications with predominantly white readerships.[17]

Sociological themes also appeared in articles challenging the claims of race scientists and popular opinion alleging black inferiority. When *Opportunity* was founded in 1923, Boas and his students were combating the pseudoscientific assertions in academic circles that human behavior, decent or degraded, reproduced itself through biological heritability. Boasian anthropology by the middle 1920s had settled the matter within its own professional ranks, undermining lingering race-based theories of behavior. However, the heritage of nineteenth-century race theory persisted, not only in the general public, but in the disciplines of sociology and history. Johnson used the pages of *Opportunity* to counter those persistent distortions and to "present, objectively, facts of Negro life."[18] Through the presentation of facts, or sociological reality, Johnson hoped to build understanding of sources of social problems and to promote interracial action to counter poor health and the defective education of a million children. The sociological and artistic dimensions of *Opportunity* were clearly related; both enhanced knowledge of black people, thus helping to neutralize ubiquitous efforts "to disparage unjustly the capacity and aspirations of this group."[19]

For example, Johnson, in an unsigned editorial in 1923, confronted the claims of eugenicist Paul Popenoe. Johnson offered a stinging methodological critique of Popenoe's racial "common sense" claim that the intelligence of black people depends on the quantum of "white" blood they possess. Johnson derided Popenoe's faulty assessment of the results of army intelligence tests showing that northern black recruits scored higher than their southern counterparts. Popenoe insisted that a higher proportion of mulattos in the population of the North accounted for the difference. Johnson showed that the alleged association did not exist and, instead, offered basic sociological data showing that states with the lowest test results also had the "fewest schools, worst paid teachers, and the greatest amount of illiteracy."[20] Publications such as the *Journal of Heredity,* where Popenoe was on the editorial board, continued in the name of a grotesque racial science to provide biological and genetic rationales for widespread institutional injustices restricting black lives.

Other race theorists claimed that mulattos, instead of elevating the level of intelligence or vitality of those classified as "Negro," are in every respect inferior to people without "mixed blood." In the second issue of *The Crisis,* Du Bois featured an article by Boas exposing the latter muddle, calling attention to the contradictory claims of those purporting to explain either frailty or vigor in people of mixed race.[21]

The Higher Prejudice: Academic Racism and the Persistence of Biological Thinking in Sociology

While no sociologist in the early decades of the twentieth century loomed as large in his field as Boas did within anthropology, Park ranked among the most influential figures in American sociology through the 1920s. Prompted by his experience in the South working for Booker T. Washington, Park was more sensitive to the "Negro problem" than most of his colleagues. His association with Washington began in 1905 and lasted nearly a decade. Compared to other white sociologists, Park had more sustained and sympathetic contact with black people. He did not make the kind of moral judgments that characterized the early work of Howard W. Odum, the influential southern sociologist. Park wanted to chart what he regarded as the progress black people were making toward incorporation into American society. As noted, he was decidedly uninterested in programmatic, ameliorative programs to address social problems. His journalistic detachment substantially shaped modern American sociology that in the early years of the twentieth century had already begun to distance itself from reformist tendencies.

While Park and his Chicago colleagues looked at race by and large as a social phenomenon, they lacked Boas's understanding of the full range of physical and cultural data driving the debate over the relationship between race and behavior. Only through the scientific understanding of biological race that Boas achieved could one finally comprehend how the ideology of race as biological limitation naturalized and therefore justified the political suppression of African Americans. Neither Park nor any other white sociologist grappled with both the physical and historical dimensions of race; they lacked the requisite expertise across the social and biological sciences even to approximate Boas's extended critique of biopolitics. Boasian anthropology alone among academic disciplines exposed both the moral travesty of racism and the scientific sham that legitimated it.

Boas's leadership in forging a new, scientific understanding of the irrelevance of biological race as a determinant of behavior had an enduring impact not only on anthropology but also on sociology. The message of *The Mind of Primitive Man* diffused slowly across academic disciplines. Sociology, burdened by the staying power of its own faulty biological assumptions, came around to Boas's thinking gradually. The grip of nineteenth-century racial thinking on that field remained so firm that even a figure as enlightened as Park was very slow to discard its remnants, often conceived as in-built temperament.[22] An exception was Park's Chicago colleague W. I. Thomas, who incorporated, without attribution, a number of Boas's ideas, particularly that "differences of mind are environmental in origin."[23] Undoubtedly pleased that his ideas were diffusing into sociology through the efforts of a scholar of Thomas's distinction, Boas was gracious in accepting Thomas's explanation for not citing his work. Thomas claimed that those ideas were already commonly accepted, although he remained troubled by anonymous reports that Boas or others were distressed that he had not acknowledged Boas's work.[24]

As to Park, he observed in 1919, skeptically it seems, that "as the anthropologists now seem disposed to do" there is little variation in average intelligence across racial groups. Nonetheless, Park still clung to a biological substrate of behavior in asserting that "we may still expect to find in different races certain special traits and tendencies which rest on biological rather than cultural differences."[25] But in his most egregious pronouncement asserting biological transmission of a presumed racial temperament, he says that among black people the latter inheres in "a genial, sunny, and social disposition, in an interest and attachment to external, physical things rather than to subjective states and objects of introspection; in a disposition for expression rather than enterprise and action." Park discussed several racial temperaments that were nothing more than stereotypes, and argued that

> the Negro is, by natural disposition, neither an intellectual nor an idealist like the Jew, nor a brooding introspective like the East Indian, nor a pioneer and frontiers-man like the Anglo-Saxon. He is primarily an artist, loving life for its own sake. His *métier* is expression rather than action. He is, so to speak, the lady among races.[26]

That the *Journal of Negro History* published Park's claims about race and nature at all or in 1919, the same year as the Chicago rampage, is particularly incongruous. Undoubtedly, Park's professional reputation, his interest in racial accommodation, and his long association with Booker T. Washington gave him considerable standing among black scholars.

At that time, Park also took issue with Du Bois's interpretation of slave songs. Whereas Du Bois called them "sorrow songs," Park said that "the dominant mood is one of jubilation." The songs pointed up the "racial temperament of the Negro," tending to be "naturally sunny, cheerful, optimistic." Despite themes of hardship, yearning, and suffering, Park instead derived racial temperament from positive emotion evident in singing style but conspicuously absent from the content of what was sung.[27]

Thirteen years later, Park still clung to the idea of innate racial dispositions. While not dogmatic, Park compared Negro and mulatto actions, attributing to the latter a greater "restlessness, aggressiveness . . . and general egocentric behavior," owing to a probable inherited temperament.[28] That someone of Park's standing and experience could sustain these regressive sentiments when Boas's assault on biopolitics was well advanced points to the depth and pervasiveness of biological thinking in the social sciences. There is some suggestion that Park later regretted his composite statements about fixed temperament. Certainly, the larger corpus of his work on race relations aimed to promote understanding between African Americans and the white majority through sociological knowledge.[29] Park won the respect, admiration, and, one must add, the gratitude of black sociologists whose careers advanced through his academic sponsorship. A year after Park's death, two of his students, St. Clair Drake and Horace Cayton Jr., never politically passive or disengaged from black activism, dedicated their 1945 landmark book on Chicago, *Black Metropolis: A Study of Negro Life in a Northern City,* to Robert E. Park, "American Scholar and Friend of the Negro People."[30] Moreover, Park maintained his ties to Johnson and Fisk University, where he held an appointment following his retirement from the University of Chicago. Park died in Nashville in 1944.

Perhaps Park's most influential contribution to the sociology of race was his formulation of the race-relations cycle, a model to account for an evolving, irreversible relationship between distinct groups. Initial contact usually results in competition over some limited resource; once competition becomes self-consciously connected to an awareness of differences—racial, cultural, social—conflict defines the next stage of struggle; when the relationship between competitors stabilizes, there is a condition of accommodation, described by Park, enabling groups to coexist in a routinized but hierarchical relationship. Although it may be prolonged, accommodation can yield a fourth stage of contact—assimilation, or the coalescence of distinct groups into a single community of shared tradition.[31] Park's model was evolutionary. The process unfolded fitfully, but its course was irreversible.[32]

In retrospect, Park's model, applied to the relationship between African Americans and white Americans, flouts reality. One only need consider the Chicago riot of 1919 to see, as Charles Johnson observed, the exploitative and repressive quality of "accommodation," a term that also subsumed the inhumanity of slavery in the Park model. No one reading Johnson's report or considering the historic record of black America could possibly envision assimilation as an end product of black-white contact. Indeed, as the 1960s arrived and Park's race-relations cycle continued to appear in the syllabi of sociology courses, the unpredicted social cataclysm and violence of those years finally rendered the model irrelevant.

As a theory of group contact, Park's race-relations cycle was much more consistent with the European immigration between 1881 and 1924 than to black-white relations during any period. The adaptation of immigrants and their descendants to American life has entailed a sweeping linguistic, social, and cultural assimilation.[33] Only the most wishful reading of American history since the turn of the twentieth century could find in the black experience a reproduction of the social and cultural processes defining European immigrant absorption into American society. Rigid segregation of schools, neighborhoods, and all other institutions of American life ensured up until the 1960s that social assimilation of African Americans could not occur. It has yet to be realized.

Among the most prominent sociologists for whom biological constants were woven into their racial viewpoints was Howard W. Odum of the University of North Carolina. A southerner and descendant of slave owners, Odum reflected deep-seated biases veiled by the putative scientific claims of sociological and psychological objectivity. Odum embarked on his career with the 1910 publication of his Columbia dissertation, *Social and Mental Traits of the Negro*.[34] At that early stage, he was bound to a worldview that centered black behavior in an unchanging nature and fixed temperament rather than in the black historical and cultural response to a particularly crushing political economy. For example, he wrote:

> The great obstacle in the way of the Negro's industrial efficiency as well as in his mental and moral character is his lack of sustained application and constructive conduct. Such a state of being is, however, but natural to a people of the Negro's temperament.[35]

A year before the publication of *The Mind of Primitive Man*, Odum's thesis reflected the failure of sociology to extricate itself from the spell of nineteenth-century biologism. His typification of black people in terms of a collective natural temperament accounted for alleged retrograde morals and emotions. Likewise, biologism further underpinned the characterizations of blacks as slothful and feckless, while also arguing that intellectual limitations were chronic. Odum was under the influence of not only his own southern background but also the racial biases of his discipline.

To his credit, Odum's racist assertions "would haunt him for many years thereafter," according to sociologist William B. Thomas, who makes the doubtful claim that at Columbia Odum found an "intellectual balance" through work with Franz Boas.[36] But not the slightest hint of that supposed influence occurs in Odum's dissertation, written when he was not far removed from direct contact with Boas. Instead, Odum's early writing finds the source of the "Negro Problem" in innate black incapacity. At that formative stage in his career and subsequently, Odum, like Park, looked away from the socioeconomic and cultural foundation of the "Negro problem," which in reality lay in intractable, state-supported structures of racial inequality. Writing a year before Odum's *Social and Mental Traits of the Negro,* Boas heralded the high craft and artistic accomplishment achieved by the Negro race in Africa, concluding that any limitations suffered by the American Negro is "due, not to native inability, but to the degrading condition under which he has been placed for generations."[37]

Odum and Charles Johnson maintained a cordial professional relationship for many years. Asking his white colleagues to waive their segregationist sentiments, Odum supported Johnson's election to the presidency of the Southern Sociological Society in 1945, a considerable victory in that highly segregated era, yet sullied when "he was denied the right of public accommodations afforded white members of the society."[38] Johnson was relegated to segregated housing, a humiliating counterpoint to his new professional office.

But beyond that election, Odum maintained the same sentiments as his colleagues, believing that voluntary changes in the segregated way of life, gradualism, and nonintervention should prevail. He was, in other words, content with the continuation of social inequality into the indefinite future.[39] In this regard, Odum and Johnson were unalterably opposed. Johnson's racial diplomacy and acute awareness of white southern sensibilities notwithstanding, he remained resolute in his opposition to racial segregation. He knew full well that the realization of black aspirations and social equality could only be achieved by transforming the repressive, white-controlled institutions that blocked black political and economic mobility.

Social science research at Fisk under Johnson's leadership was occurring when in the main a sharp methodological and interpretive divide separated black and white researchers regarding race and the nature of slavery and its legacy. This divide was apparent in sociology, where Johnson and W. E. B. Du Bois scorned biopolitics and value-free social science while locating the genesis of black poverty and misery in the institutional arrangements controlled by white people. In parts of the rural South, as Johnson demonstrated in the mid-1930s, some of those social and cultural conditions differed little from the days of slavery.[40] The fallacies of race science and the lingering biological residue within sociology attuned both Johnson and Du Bois to the work of Boas, a dependable partner in their collective opposition to social inequality and the failure of American institutions to grant black people their full rights as citizens.

Du Bois, more overtly critical of white racism than was Johnson, did not gain the equivalent attention of professional sociology. Quite the contrary. Du Bois was practically written out of the history of sociology, along with his research in Philadelphia and later studies conducted at Atlanta University during his tenure there.[41] Undoubtedly, the neglect of Du Bois's work in sociology was due to his activist political positions in the young NAACP, and his belief that the findings of sociology should advance social change.

For example, Du Bois's *The Philadelphia Negro,* intended to present empirical information "that may be a safe guide for all efforts toward the solution of the many Negro problems of a great American city."[42] In marked contrast to Park's uninvolved sociology, Du Bois thought that sociology should turn to the solution of social problems—social reform, in effect—but only after empirical research had laid bare the issues.[43] Du Bois believed that a sociologist could reject the value-free position while remaining objective in the conduct of a field study. He agreed with Woodson and Boas that politics could not provide appropriate criteria for the evaluation of research, although the political implications of empirical sociological investigations of urban black poverty were apparent. He gathered empirical data on black institutions, such as the family, churches, and businesses, identifying the problems confronting the black community without shrinking from the instrumental role of white racism in limiting black self-realization.

At the same time, Du Bois did not turn away from deficiencies within the black community, including corruption of the black vote and criminality. He outlined the "duty of Negroes," including "making themselves fit members of the community within a reasonable time." These were essential moral responsibilities, even if "the ancestors of the present white inhabitants of America went out of their way barbarously to mistreat and enslave the ancestors of the present black inhabitants."[44] Likewise, in asserting "the duty of whites," Du Bois went far beyond Park's bland descriptions to describe with controlled passion the deep-seated racial prejudice that had contributed its significant measure to the manifold human problems of black Philadelphia: "To-day . . . we must face the fact that a natural repugnance to close intermingling with unfortunate ex-slaves has descended to a discrimination that very seriously hinders them from being anything better."[45]

Like Du Bois, Boas and Radin were unconcerned about the claims of value-free social science that came to define American sociology by the beginning of World War I. The issue never arose in American anthropology at that time. The unity of early twentieth-century sociology, social work, and social reform had been shattered, and the science of value-free sociology took an independent course. Advocacy had become incompatible with the professional goals of the discipline. By contrast, the efforts by American anthropologists to disentangle race from culture had important practical implications, recognized and embraced by the young discipline. The research of Boas, Radin, and others was in no way compromised by their principled commitments and actions on behalf of human freedom and equality. The "wholesome influence of anthropology," relentlessly empirical, was anything but value-free.

The Higher Prejudice: The History Profession

The reprise of scholarship on race in the first decades of the twentieth century has thus far highlighted the signal contribution of American anthropology to the discourse on human differences and the relationship between biology and culture. The Boas group supported African American aspirations, and anthropological research provided universal humanistic and scientific warrant for those goals. At the same time, a methodological and interpretive divide separated black and most white researchers regarding the nature of slavery and the postbellum African American experience. This divide was particularly apparent in academic history, where it was much sharper than in sociology. In the history profession, Jim Crow was triumphant. Critical African American history—a narrative of active individuals confronting the race-based challenges of their time—if it was to be written in the Jim Crow era, required black historians. White historians remained captive to nineteenth-century racial interpretations of behavior that cast black people as supposed victims of an innate natural profligacy.

Radically departing from the pervasive racial caricatures woven through the work of white scholars, Radin's work at Fisk resonated with African American scholarship. An affinity in outlook joined black scholarship to American anthropology. White scholarly interpreters of black history were, in the main, describing stereotypic African Americans without individuation and forever constrained by an immutable temperament unsuited to rational, unemotional behavior. Writers in this vein remained bound to flawed nineteenth-century racialized assumptions that, in the various guises of scholarship, or reason, or science, served a postbellum ideological commitment to white southern heritage. The latter included racial stratification and supremacy, social inequality, the severest forms of economic exploitation, and extralegal violence.

Jim Crow had deep roots in American historical scholarship. Ulrich B. Phillips, a widely influential historian of the South and of slavery until his death in 1934, exemplifies this phenomenon, although it is complicated by the regard in which some of his social and economic analyses of the slave system are still held.[46] Radin and Watson both utilized his work. While offering insight into the political economy of the slave regime, Phillips's commentary on the slaves themselves betrays his Deep South origins and an especially crass racism. For example, Phillips, at the outset of his discussion of plantation labor and the new environment encountered by the native African, asserts that

> His nature was an African's profoundly modified but hardly transformed by the requirement of European civilization. The wrench from Africa and the subjection to the new discipline while uprooting his ancient language and customs had little more effect upon his temperament than upon his complexion.[47]

Elsewhere, Phillips found salutary features of the slave regime, praising its redemptive value in elevating slaves from the depths of African savagery toward civilization.[48] Other historians of the South in the main embraced the same kinds of racially driven interpretations of black-white relations within the plantation system. If the putative behavioral defects of black life were naturally endemic to black communities, it followed that the social issues surrounding race in the South were at base simply a reflection of the natural limitations of the Negro. Attributing low achievement, passivity, decadence, and other alleged deficits in black communal life to an inherent quality of character or temperament effectively mystified the oppressive social and economic order that was the true genesis of the "Negro problem."

The most fundamental repudiation of the racism of Phillips, Odum, and other white historians and sociologists of lesser renown proceeded through the forward-looking research of African American historians. While modern African American historical writing begins in the early twentieth century, it was anticipated by the groundbreaking work of George Washington Williams. African Americans in Williams's rendering are very much actors in their own history, represented, for example, in his depiction of black soldiers in the Civil War.[49] Prior to Williams's disciplined work, black writers of the eighteenth and nineteenth centuries produced a variety of books and essays on black achievement through time. The aim was, for the most part, to inculcate a confident self-regard and collective pride in black accomplishment. At the same time, writing of black achievement might serve to enlighten white readers.[50] Above all, black writers and essayists could only depend on themselves for the presentation of fully humanized portraits of black people.

Woodson followed Du Bois as the second African American to earn a history doctorate from Harvard. Through their scholarship, both men advocated an African American history that represented black people in active terms speaking for themselves. In the highly racialized climate of the time, Jim Crow flourished in the academic world and had hardened into unforgiving public policy. In that setting, black history as envisioned by Du Bois and Woodson would require black authorship. Listening attentively to black voices, they represented black people in slavery and in freedom as sentient individuals rather than the passive aggregate governed by defective, insuperable behaviors conjured by white writers. African American historians had both a personal and a professional stake in a reformulated, humanized representation of black people as historical figures responding, independently of biological race, to the social and cultural reality they encountered.

While a racial divide marked scholarship about slavery, the Civil War, and postbellum African American life, an analogous division cannot be found between white northern and southern historians of approximately the same generation. In the words of Peter Novick, a "consensual racism" linked northern and southern historians from the closing years of the nineteenth century until at least the 1930s.[51] Historians from the North were as likely to embrace racial bias as were historians from the South, such as U. B. Phillips and his mentor, William A. Dunning. Beyond the influence of southern historians on the historical writing of northern scholars, persistent scientific racism in the early 1900s also imbued the thinking of most white American historians whatever their origin. Novick has also pointed out that while few northern historians were located in the South, considerable numbers of southern historians, such as Phillips at Wisconsin and Dunning at Columbia, held academic positions in northern universities. Writing in the early years of the twentieth century, Dunning shaped the thinking of many historians of the Civil War and Reconstruction. He could not transcend the shackles of his own southern tradition that had anchored his scholarship to an intractable racism.

Although few historians defended slavery or secession with any intensity, a belief in black inferiority and disunion as racial self-protection was commonplace. A near unanimity of historical opinion condemned Reconstruction in the harshest terms, mixing criticism with stereotypic racial judgments about the incapacity of black people for probity, citizenship, and governance. Dunning asserted that in dismantling Reconstruction, "southern whites, subjugated by adversaries of their own race, thwarted the scheme which threatened permanent subjection to another race."[52] He likened "the remorseless approach of negro rule" in the decade following the Civil War to the feelings of a prisoner perceiving his cell walls closing in each day to crush him.[53] Black people, Dunning explained, had "no pride of race and no aspiration or ideals save to be like whites." Then invoking the southern obsession with black male sexual predation, he claimed that the Negro then "came gradually to understand and crave those more elusive privileges that constitute social equality." Consequently, Dunning observed, in terms and substance no different from the Ku Klux Klan, that black liberation and empowerment led to "the hideous crime against white womanhood which now assumed new meaning in the annals of outrage."[54]

"Consensual racism" among historians north and south thus was the province of major academic figures. Phillips and Dunning were among the most prominent historians of their day. But there were exceptions to the racism woven through the history profession, particularly among younger scholars with decidedly left-of-center political views.[55] One must also add that black historians, such as W. E. B. Du Bois and, later, John Hope Franklin, examined Reconstruction altogether differently from northern historians, who found common intellectual cause with their southern colleagues.[56] Included here are Allan Nevins and Henry Steele Commager, whose view of Reconstruction, while not as venomous as Dunning's, nonetheless lamented how illiterate blacks not far removed from African savagery were enfranchised with citizenship and the vote. Congressional acts to assist the freedmen "unduly invaded the authority of Southern States."[57] In the outraged language of southerners, Nevins and Commager characterized radical Republicans Thaddeus Stevens and Charles

Sumner as, respectively, "vindictive" and "fanatical."[58] White people in reaction steadily regained control, although Nevins and Commager gloss over the way in which intimidation, violence, and murder achieved that racial victory.[59] It comes as no surprise, then, that August Meier, a historian of the black experience and a Commager student, characterized his professor as "a very traditional intellectual historian, who knew virtually nothing about the history of American blacks."[60]

Novick identified "the casual, matter-of-fact racism in the writing of many interwar northern historians." In the idiom of eugenics and livestock husbandry, Arthur M. Schlesinger Sr., writing in 1933, proposed that "one test of racial capacity is the ability to breed leaders" and proceeded to name five prominent African American individuals, four of whom were of "hybrid descent." From a longer list of black figures of note, Schlesinger concluded, in reprise of the eugenicist Popenoe, that mulattos, or "mixed bloods, greatly predominated among the more gifted individuals."[61]

Yet the racial divide in the institutionalization of black history was not absolute, leavened as it was by Woodson's pragmatism in seeking renowned white scholars for the executive council of the Association of Negro Life and History. That effort gave the movement for black history considerable legitimacy when seeking philanthropic support. A member of the council, Arthur Schlesinger Sr., despite the racism defining his interpretation of "hybrid descent," admired Woodson's work, rating it as good as the higher ranks of white historians. Among supporters in anthropology, Woodson counted on Boas and Ernest Hooten of Harvard.[62]

The unity of perspective of northern and southern historians in regard to race represents an academic analog to the recurrent theme in historical writing of the reconciliation of North and South following the Civil War. As David Blight has demonstrated, the national postbellum emphasis on reunion, reconciliation, and the memory of the mutual sacrifice of warring sections of the United States proceeded only by a corresponding indifference to the memory of what befell slaves and later freedmen. Black people in effect were read out of history, as the North capitulated after Reconstruction to the doctrine of states' rights. That concession permitted the often violent suppression of Americans of African descent, negating the citizenship guarantees enacted in the immediate wake of the war. Valor and sacrifice, celebrated north and south, were dominant reconciliation refrains. But in neglecting both the genesis and consequences of the Civil War, slavery and the continuing subjugation of four million freedmen were rendered irrelevant, except in segregated African American memory.[63]

African American writers did not retreat from pressing a case about race very different from the one promoted by much of the American historical establishment. W. E. B. Du Bois observed that the white supremacist outlook of the 1930s scotched at the outset any effort to understand the past solely on the basis of evidence. Writing in 1935 in opposition to established historical scholarship about Reconstruction, he exposed the continuing legacy of biologism. In the latter view, human potential and achievement were predetermined, as nature rather than nurture shaped individual and social outcomes. Du Bois, accordingly, drew a sharp contrast between two readerships for his book on theretofore ignored activist black figures in the immediate post–Civil War period. He could only appeal to the first readership that regarded African Americans as normal people confronting the challenges of their environment. That audience would fairly evaluate the people in Du Bois's book as average individuals trying to control their lives. The other audience, Du Bois suggested, assumed an immutable black inferiority, believing that freedom and the vote for black people contradicted nature's design. Those readers would remain unconvinced by any contrary evidence Du Bois presented.[64] In regard to race, they were intellectually immobilized by nineteenth-century thinking that still had vitality seventy years after the Civil War.[65]

The pervasive influence of Jim Crow in American life thus did not stop at university gates, the editorial offices of academic publications, or in the selection of serious research topics. Historical scholarship for the most part was suffused with racial bias, springing from the rigid segregation of American institutions, social inequality, persistent biopolitics, and of course the triumph of southern historiography. Consequently, research that considered black people as central figures in their own histories and narratives—subjects rather than objects—depended on black historians. The *Journal of Negro History* in 1916 gave black scholars an intellectual community and an outlet for a different perspective on the past. Embracing a viewpoint opposed to conventional historical writing on African Americans, Woodson, like Du Bois, did not intend to substitute one bias for another, to glorify black people as a corrective to their denigration by white historians, or to evaluate scholarship by political criteria. Seeking Boas's backing for an application to the Rockefeller Foundation to assist the *Journal of Negro History,* Woodson explained "that we are not interested in any sort of propaganda. Our aim is to publish the truth to generations unborn. It should be said . . . that we shall carefully avoid the other extreme of seeking facts which seemingly support some pet theory."[66] If there was a strong ideological bent in writing the history of the African American experience, its center lay in the scholarship of white historians.

The racial bifurcation of historical scholarship is clearly manifest in Lawrence Reddick's 1937 discussion of black history. As if following the very different blueprints of Booker T. Washington and W. E. B. Du Bois for racial uplift, Reddick neatly divides black historical scholarship up to his time in two—"before and after Carter Woodson." Interpretive disagreements within the field of Negro history were contested among African American scholars espousing either an explanation of advancement in terms of self-direction, self-reliance, and personal discipline or, in the new century, a more hard-edged politico-economic orientation grounded in struggle and conflict. In either case, black historical scholarship humanized African Americans, "normal people" in Du Bois's terms, active men and women confronting life's obstacles and opportunities as they presented themselves. Reddick ignored well-known white historians of the South whose negative views of black people were prefabricated versions of nineteenth-century thinking. He focused exclusively on "Negro historiography."[67]

In the same vein, Radin rejected mainstream scholarship outside of anthropology and folklore in regard to African American narrative artistry. Only the latter two disciplines acknowledged literary creativity or literary value in the narratives of ordinary African Americans or American Indians. Radin, with no hesitation, wrote of the "literary structure" of the conversion narratives and, before that, the literary features of American Indian mythology.[68] Toward the end of his life, he made the same assessment of the African narratives he was studying.[69] Likewise, Boas did not hesitate to consider the stylistic features and literary artistry of American Indians.[70]

The historian Richard Hofstadter presenting a complementary view in 1944 criticized the biases, methodological and racial, pervading U. B. Phillips's work. Addressing paternalism and white southern preconceptions of slaves as passive figures, Hofstadter insisted on an orientation already well developed among black writers. Specifically, he argued for research by those "who have absorbed the viewpoint of modern cultural anthropology" and who would realize "that any history of slavery must be written in large part from the standpoint of the slave."[71] Hofstadter undoubtedly had Boasian anthropology in mind when he held up the discipline as a prerequisite to writing the history of slavery. The Fisk narrative collection and Radin's role in assembling it fifteen years earlier is a case in point.

Lawrence Levine, a student of Hofstadter's, more than any other white historian of the slave experience, took his mentor's advice to heart. In his preface to *Black*

Culture and Black Consciousness, Levine declared that "it is time for historians to expand their own consciousness by examining the consciousness of those they have hitherto ignored and neglected."[72] This effort required that Levine break with another legacy of historiography—the total reliance on written documents as primary source material. To realize an understanding of the experience and thought of those who suffered enforced illiteracy, Levine therefore had to focus on "the orally transmitted expressive culture of Afro-Americans in the United States during the century that stretched from the antebellum era to the end of the 1940s." African American expressive culture, or folk culture of the oral tradition, including songs and spirituals, folktales and proverbs, were the staples of Levine's research. Acknowledging the long record of research on these topics by scholars outside of the history profession—one only need consider Paul Radin, Zora Neale Hurston, Elsie Clews Parsons, and later, Roger Abrahams, Dan Crowley, and Alan Dundes—he declared, "I could not have written this book without the past and present work of scholars in folklore, ethnomusicology, and anthropology."[73] To Radin, the historiographic orientation Levine described in the mid-1970s to splendid effect would not have been novel.

Johnson's Research

Charles Johnson continued in the Park tradition but went beyond it. He aimed to support black-centered social research at Fisk, consistent with the aims of Carter Woodson and other black historians to write black actors into American history. He also saw the practical implications of sociological knowledge for improving the lives of black people; it was a programmatic goal very different from Park's view of the sociologist as disinterested reporter. Johnson built up Fisk's social science faculty with a series of distinguished research and teaching appointments that offered senior scholars considerable latitude for research with few institutional duties. In several respects, the social science research conducted by Fisk investigators was in the vanguard of studies on race, or more particularly race relations in Johnson's terms, and the black experience. The Fisk social scientists had rejected out of hand the false racial assumptions of prominent historians and sociologists.

Within this framework, Boasian anthropology as a discipline was a special case, and Paul Radin a representative of a progressive, empirical discipline unburdened by the palpably racist assumptions coursing through history and sociology.

Anthropology was well-suited to the social science climate at Fisk, where black informants and research subjects would have a dominant voice. From the late 1920s through the 1940s, Johnson recruited other prominent scholars, such as E. Franklin Frazier and a multiracial cohort of African American, white, and Asian researchers. Johnson brought sociologist Jitsuichi Masuoka to Fisk as well as Mark Hanna Watkins, the first African American to earn a PhD in anthropology in the United States.[74] Ruth Landes, like Radin a student of Franz Boas's, also joined the staff.[75]

Johnson was generous with advice to those embarking on black-centered social research in the South. Anthropologist Hortense Powdermaker, for example, then teaching in New York, remained at Fisk for several weeks before departing for Indianola, Mississippi, to conduct research among the African American population.[76] Johnson, along with his colleague E. Franklin Frazier, sensitized her to the kinds of problems she was likely to encounter as a white Jewish female in the deep South. Living on the Fisk campus and talking with welcoming teaching and research faculty and graduate students, Powdermaker recalled, "I had a sense of being in an ebony tower."[77] She continued to stay in touch with Johnson, later assisting in the Fisk study of black youth in the South.[78] He had read the manuscript of her 1939 book, *After Freedom: A Cultural Study in the Deep South.* That ironic title of a study set in apartheid Mississippi had given her pause. She wrote to Johnson, who could well appreciate her comment, "You may take the title cynically, symbolically, or as you please." But Powdermaker settled on it because her informants so frequently referred to "'before freedom' and 'after freedom' in talking about the past and present."[79]

Among Johnson's books, *Shadow of the Plantation* is a study of black farmers in Macon County, Alabama. Six hundred twelve families constituting over two thousand people were the sociological sample for Johnson and his assistants. For present purposes, this volume is particularly interesting for two reasons. Breaking through its generally distant clinical tone typical of sociological writing based on large samples are deeply human statements of rural blacks suffering the heritage of plantation slavery in exploitative tenancy or sharecropping. The book documents the entrapment of tenants and sharecroppers in debt and dependency, or what Johnson calls "the dreary cycle of life."[80] Second, the book provides a brief opening for a consideration of the substantive relationship of African Americans to Africa, which otherwise does not figure into Johnson's analyses of African American life, whether in rural or urban areas. Johnson's writings in the main were consistent with those of Park and E. Franklin Frazier in concluding that cultural linkages between black Americans and Africa had been irrevocably shattered through the experience of slavery. Park and Frazier proceeded under the assumption that black culture was in effect a partial or reduced version of the cultural patterns learned from white people.

Shadow of the Plantation documents the ways in which white domination has damaged black lives. Whites controlled all local institutions. Child labor, early pregnancy, poor schools, inadequate diet, dilapidated cabins little different from the antebellum period, personal denigration, inadequate diet—the list continues—marked that domination. Johnson's 1930s portrait of black life in southern Alabama resembled, in other words, the conditions of plantation slavery seventy years before. While the sociological survey defines the book, the personal views of Johnson's informants punctuate the overall analysis, putting a human face on the more abstracted social and economic patterns revealed by the large sample of households. In terms set forth by Clifford Geertz, Johnson combined "experience-distant" description with the highly personal "experience-near" familiarity of local peoples bearing the insufferable weight of social and economic domination through the supremacy of white people. The bloodless prose of the race-relations model gives way to personal descriptions of genuine human misery that the notion of accommodation both sanitizes and obscures. The raw suffering condensed into the pithy statements of Johnson's informants complements narrations of inhumanity documented by Radin and Watson.

A mother repeats a question about whether her house leaked. "Do it leak in here? No, it don't leak in here, it jest rains in here and leak outdoors; dis ain't no house; it jest a piece a house." (99)

The baby have to eat what we have and that ain't much. I got one old rooster. I wanted to kill him but I ain't got no grease to cook him wid. (101)

I ask Mr. _____ to 'vance me jest nuff for a pair of overalls, an' he say he need overalls hisself. (110)

Ain't make nothing,' don' speck nothin' til' I die. (120)

I don't believe the white folks are doing right by these farms. We have no water, the place is in a bad condition, and we was supposed to get a federal loan. He had all the men come up to his house and sign for it, and said he would waive the rent 'causes he couldn't get it 'less he waived the rent. He signed for all the tenants and got $1600, but he kept the money and made us pay the rent and the loans we owed him, too. (123)

I know we been beat out of money direct and indirect. You see, they got a chance to do it all right, 'cause they can overcharge us and I know it being done. (127)

Johnson's study also contains a tantalizing glimpse of African survivals in Macon County, although early on, Johnson says that black people entering the plantation did so "with a completely broken cultural heritage."[81] He observes that after arrival on the plantation from either Africa or the West Indies, the new slave, reviled by others as a "salt-water nigger," would learn from earlier bondsmen and women and the white planter what he or she needed to know. Slaves already resident on the plantation felt superior to the latest arrivals, whose recent transport provided the disdained designation.[82] These attitudes prevailed in later generations, as Johnson recorded an unrelieved scorn for those descended from salt-water men and women.[83] His observation provided "an unexpected link with Africa which might indeed yield traces of other transplanted cultural traits."[84] Johnson also interviewed an elderly man who, recalling the linguistic distinctiveness of the African arrivals, utilized West African pidgin English, unusual in the black speech of southern Alabama.[85] Only in his unpublished papers is there further interest in African survivals among black Americans. There is no additional consideration of this possibility in *Shadow of the Plantation,* although Herskovits identified, in Johnson's description of a funeral, West African Kru elements that Johnson had not recognized.[86]

Johnson remained skeptical of efforts to link black Americans to their African origins because many such historical efforts had damaged black self-esteem and, relatedly, reinforced popular notions of African peoples as primitive. As he criticized the biosocial assertion that black achievement depended on the quantum of white blood one possessed, Johnson also attacked the equally spurious biosocial claim of a "direct relationship between the distinctive traits of American Negroes and those of Africans." Those traits were most often negative, including marital and familial desertion as proposed by a long-forgotten social worker, whom Johnson thoroughly criticized. Against Johnson's commitment to advancing black civil rights, integration, and social equality—in other words, an American future in which black people would take their rightful place as fully empowered citizens—assertions about connections to Africa could only imperil those goals.

When the assimilation of eastern and southern Europeans in the 1930s was in doubt, there was even greater resistance to the institutional integration of black people. In thinking that any attention to African heritage could diminish the prospect of black assimilation, Johnson was not alone. Reviewing *The Myth of the Negro Past,* the progressive white sociologist Guy B. Johnson, agreeing with Charles Johnson on the effacement of African culture in the United States, stated: "One immensely practical problem is how to prevent this book, which has a high purpose and should do much good, from becoming the handmaiden of those who are looking for new justifications for segregation and differential treatment of Negroes!"[87]

Herskovits, too, may well have shared that caution when he reported on his research in Harlem. His contribution to *The New Negro* less than a year after the imposition of severe immigration quotas doubtless brought to mind a major restrictionist rationale—the unassimilability of aliens. That anti-immigrant credo cast doubt on Herskovits's own trajectory as the son of Jewish immigrants. A similar attitude resonated with the popular belief that Americans of African descent, even more than the new immigrants, were a people apart, consigned by in-built collective characteristics to a marginal position in American society. Suggestions in 1925 that black Americans carried with them cultural practices rooted in Africa, the "dark continent" in popular thinking, might well have reinforced the widespread belief that they would remain outsiders in the land of their nativity and citizenship. By emphasizing the "Americanness" of black people, no different culturally from whites, Herskovits established their civic belongingness uncompromised by immutable attachments to Africa.

By 1935, Herskovits turned away from his Harlem research to discover contemporaneous, observable connections between Africa and the United States. In that year, following his Caribbean and South American fieldwork and in anticipation of *The Myth of the Negro Past,* Herskovits could ask in the *New Republic,* "What Has Africa Given America?" He then wrote of the probable African origins of some features of music, speech, cooking, religious practice, and etiquette that are woven into American life.[88] Within the acculturation framework, Herskovits also pointed to the probable adoption of African cultural patterns by white southerners.

Responding to Herskovits's thesis, Johnson appeared persuaded that a case was established for African connections to South America and the Caribbean. He was unconvinced by claims about similar connections "as you move northward." But he then reports that "I noted some graves in Georgia piled up with cooking utensils and clothing, in a manner which suggested a custom among several native groups in Liberia." Like the salt-water men and women, Johnson's identification of the Georgia connection to Liberia is a passing note, little more than a curiosity that he thought the ethnohistorian Herskovits might find useful.[89] But for the most part, he remained unmoved by Herskovits's then radical thesis. Thus, Johnson's outline of a first lecture in a course entitled "The Negro in America" emphasized the nearly complete break of black Americans with Africa: "Essentially there is no reason why the study of the American Negro should begin in Africa. There is little historical connection and no continuous racial memory with this continent." Pushing his argument much further than later evidence would sustain after Herskovits published *The Myth of the Negro Past*, Johnson denied any relationship between the music of black Americans and Africa. He conceded that, despite the generalized dissolution of African links to slaves and their descendants, the Uncle Remus tales might derive from Africa. But then he speculated that they might also be Indian or Scandinavian. As to language, black patois, "which is expected to be a repository of their first and most natural culture patterns, is not African but Anglo-Saxon English of the period of Chaucer and Shakespeare." Moreover, he stressed that for black Americans there is "no more prospect of return than of the going home in mass of the early Pilgrim fathers, despite the oppression fantasies of Marcus Garvey."[90]

Johnson's position on the matter of African survivals in the United States immediately aligned him with Park and Frazier. He recognized that the American denigration of all indications of African origin effected a psychological devastation among black people. Radin, too, identified the psychological ruin of the damaged self under slavery, but additionally, how ecstatic religion might arrest the process. In an unpublished lecture for his course "The Negro in America," Johnson pointed to the cultural ideas of black Africa, ranging from standards of beauty to conceptions of God. As in any tradition, conformity was a high value. But in slavery, where black people faced standards not their own, disorganization began and its most destructive result was a "loss of self-respect and an accruing and permanent sense of social inadequacy." Under these circumstances, the immediate destruction of self-esteem begins with the physical characteristics of Africans, from skin color to hair type, which might in turn induce "a ludicrous attempt at adjustment" such as hair straighteners and bleaching powders. Psychological traits and ways of living—work, amusements, family, folklore, and religion—likewise suffered the contempt of the racial majority.[91]

Other black scholars praised Herskovits's achievement. Du Bois regarded the book as "epoch making." That historical linkages between Africa and the United States were important and discoverable was beyond question. No one writing on black achievement in America after *The Myth of the Negro Past* could, in Du Bois's view, legitimately disregard Herskovits's thesis, notwithstanding some instances where Herskovits's conclusions depended on meager evidence.[92] Likewise, Woodson identified some points of interpretive overreach in which Herskovits suggested, for example, that sometimes loose bonds in black family life in America might derive from African ideas about polygamy.[93] Beyond Herskovits's supportable substantive claims of enduring connections between Africa and the United States, Woodson particularly welcomed another critique of Park:

> So general has become the theory of the inferiority of African culture and its lack of vitality that even Negro writers, misled by the contention of Robert E. Park, fearlessly uphold the mischievous unsupported statement that the American Negro retained little which he brought from Africa except his tropical temperament.[94]

Above all, Woodson praised Herskovits for breaking with old stereotypes about the Negro past and bringing science to bear on the problem.[95] Neither Du Bois nor Woodson shared Johnson's concern that the emphasis on demonstrable linkages to Africa might damage black self-esteem or retard black progress toward "assimilation" in the United States.

Although Du Bois and Woodson each welcomed publication of *The Myth of the Negro Past,* the two pioneering scholars of black history maintained a fraught relationship with Herskovits. Personalities aside, Herskovits opposed ideologically driven research aimed at social amelioration; but he overstated this tendency in the work of Woodson and Du Bois, particularly the latter. Additionally, Jerry Gershenhorn has detailed how the tensions between Du Bois and Herskovits were part of a much larger conflict in the 1930s over the ultimately failed effort to prepare an Encyclopedia of the Negro. These conflicts do not gainsay, however, Herskovits's commitment to research that would bring to light theretofore neglected and interrelated features of African and African American life. To that end, he was also a mentor to black students throughout his career.[96]

The black press, sharing the views of Du Bois and Woodson, likewise had no anxiety about the misuse of Herskovits's findings. Quite the opposite occurred in the unqualified praise for Herskovits's exposure of lies and racist claims about

African-derived people. An editorial in the *Pittsburgh Courier,* for example, begins, "You have a past," and then proceeds to tell readers of the gratitude they owe Herskovits for exposing the self-serving, exploitative misrepresentations of Negro history. The editorial details Herskovits's refutation of claims that Africans arrived in the United States ignorant and uncivilized, possessing nothing of cultural value. Detractors misrepresenting Africa and Africans then used their propaganda and

> have justified discrimination, segregation, exploitation, expropriation and disfranchisement. It has been bad enough to have this propaganda believed and acted upon by other people. It has been tragic to find this propaganda almost as readily believed by Black people.

The *Pittsburgh Press* encomium declares that, like the European immigrant groups, black Americans have a history worthy of pride. The editorial quotes Herskovits, who said that "the extent to which the past of a people is regarded as praiseworthy, their own self-esteem will be high and the opinion of others will be favorable."[97]

If one were seeking an equally confident oppositional statement on the sundering of cultural connections between Africa and black people in the United States, except for "scraps of memory," any number of statements by E. Franklin Frazier, Herskovits's primary intellectual antagonist, could serve as a model. The following view, shared by much of the sociology profession—including, of course, Park—aptly presents Frazier's uncompromising position on the question.

> When one views in retrospect the waste of human life, the immorality, delinquency, desertions and broken homes which have been involved in the development of Negro family life in the United States, they appear to have been the inevitable consequences of the attempt of a preliterate people, stripped of their culture heritage, to adjust themselves to civilization. The very fact that the Negro has succeeded in adopting habits of living that have enabled him to survive in a civilization based upon laissez faire and competition, itself bespeaks a degree of success in taking on the folkways and mores of the master race.[98]

Published in 1939, Frazier's bitter use of the term "master race" recalls Boas's remark of the year before, likening Nazi race laws to race policies in the United States that excluded black people from schools, public accommodations, and other institutions of American life.

Fifteen years before, Frazier's contribution to *The New Negro* presented a more hopeful picture closely resembling Park's assimilationist perspective. The new Negro for Frazier was best represented by the small but emergent black middle class of Durham, North Carolina, which was the "promise of the transformed Negro."[99] The middle-class business person would imitate neither the aristocratic pretensions of the black professional nor the laborer's singular interest in consumption and leisure rather than production. Essentially, Frazier, following his mentor even more closely than did Johnson, pictured the middle-class entrepreneur in the black community as no different, except in color, from the white middle-class business person. For Frazier, the building of an African American future did not follow from the recovery of black history—a fool's errand in any case—but from adoption of the cultural and business mores of successful whites. Subsequently, Frazier scathingly depicted the black middle class in terms wholly different from his bright assessment in *The New Negro*.[100]

As black scholars were writing African Americans into history, theirs was not solely an exercise in recovering the past. Their efforts would also have equally profound psychological implications for African Americans, enabling them to nurture a sense of collective confidence and self-worth as citizens, thereby palliating generations of cultural and psychological disparagement on the part of the racial majority. Along with black scholars, Boas, Radin, and Herskovits were well aware of the salutary psychological value of that radical shift in scholarship as they also contributed to it. Identifying the critical importance of a newly configured black history and exposure of the myth of the Negro past, Arthur Schomburg, writing in *The New Negro*, stated:

> The American Negro must remake his past to make his future. Though it is orthodox to think of America as the one country where it is unnecessary to have a past, what is a luxury for the nation becomes a prime social necessity for the Negro. For him, a group tradition must supply compensation for persecution, and pride of race the antidote for prejudice. History must restore what slavery took away, for it is the social damage of slavery that the present generation must repair and offset.[101]

CHAPTER 4

The Radin-Watson Collection

Narratives of Slavery and Transcendence

P aul Radin and a narrow circle of scholars in the 1920s placed African Americans at the center of research. Addressing their personal experience, thoughts, and emotions, Radin's work represented the earliest systematic effort to document first-person accounts of enslavement, postbellum African American lives, and accompanying religious conversions. Set against the ubiquitous academic and popular racism discussed in earlier chapters, the Fisk narrative project represented a radical alternative that complemented the black history movement in attending to African American representations of their own experience.

The human centeredness of Radin's anthropology began in his earliest research among the Winnebago. Continuing at Fisk, that intense individual focus remained his signature professional contribution. He joined other scholars who had rejected the "higher prejudice" of contemporaneous academic history in rendering black people silent spectators in the world they inhabited and provisioned. In sociology, E. Franklin Frazier, much more than fellow Park student Charles Johnson, worked from a model of race relations that considered people in the aggregate. Like Park, Frazier wrote of "the Negro" in generalized terms. But in unblinking prose, his nameless subjects registered the brutalizing social forces of slavery and segregation. On the other hand, the former slaves Radin met were, like the Winnebago documented in his ethnological reports, active historical figures, whose words about their own lives took precedence over all others, including his own. Although his Winnebago informants were named, the identification of people in the Fisk project was irregular, both in *God Struck Me Dead* and in "Souls Piled Like Timber: The Religious Experience of the Pre-War Negro." In the Fisk archives, the typescripts of some but not all the unpublished interviews of elderly African Americans provide the names of narrators. Radin and Watson were attentive to the sensibilities of their very elderly informants. Where their names do not appear, it is reasonable to assume that the researchers were observing the wishes of informants. The absence of names of course does not dissolve the distinctiveness of each story, for these elderly authors produced a set of singular personal documents of crisis, conversion, and self-inscription against racialized forces of dehumanization.

Radin died in 1959 before the completion of "Souls Piled Like Timber." While many of the elderly men and women interviewed were native to Tennessee, others had settled in Nashville after leaving Virginia, South Carolina, and other southern states. Eight autobiographies and forty-five conversion narratives make up a portion of the original manuscript. The eight life-history narrators were born into slavery, whereas only about fifteen of the narrators of conversion experiences had lived through slavery. Of those who had been slaves, some underwent conversion during their servitude, others afterward. The autobiographies and the conversion narratives, although distinct, complement each other because the accounts of religious conversion yield their significance only in relationship to the experience of slavery and its postbellum aftermath as depicted in the life histories. Each conversion narrative is thus also autobiographical.

It is uncertain when Radin began the "Souls" manuscript, but various notes included with the rough draft indicate that the writing was prolonged. He worked on it in Berkeley in 1945 and Lugano, Switzerland, in 1953, when he wrote to Robert Lowie reporting on his lectures, scholarly work, forthcoming publications, and "revision of my Negro material to be published by Chicago University and some minor essays."[1] It is uncertain why the manuscript never came to fruition after so many years of work. Various institutions hold his papers, but their placement during his lifetime and posthumously was not an orderly process by any means. Radin's indifference to the routine and order of academic life extended to the organization and disposition of some of his personal papers. As noted in the preface, luck rather than design safely preserved, and then only partially, the "Souls" manuscript.

Although Radin did not complete that book, the Social Science Institute at Fisk brought out twin narrative collections published in 1945 based on research conducted by Ophelia Settle Egypt, Paul Radin, and Andrew Polk Watson.[2] Neither volume appeared with a designation of authorship or editorship. Some of the narrators provided accounts of slavery that were utilized both by Settle Egypt and by Radin and Watson, but it isn't clear if they were interviewed separately for each volume.

The first, *Unwritten History of Slavery: Autobiographical Account of Negro Ex-Slaves,* examined the institution of slavery through the subjective narrations of former slaves, mostly from Kentucky and Tennessee. Those experiences were depicted in thirty-seven narratives collected by Settle Egypt and associates and culled from interviews with over one hundred elderly informants.[3] Settle Egypt had completed a master's degree at the University of Pennsylvania before joining the Social Science Institute and the multiracial research group that Johnson had brought together.[4] *Unwritten History* contains an occasional question addressed to the narrator or a brief commentary, but for the most part simply presents the personal accounts of servitude. Looking beyond the political economy of slavery, the introductory note by Settle Egypt, Masuoka, and Johnson explains that *Unwritten History* focuses on the "moral order of personal relationship of expectations and obligations" between slaves and masters;[5] it was a "system in which the individual attitudes, sentiments, habits, and conduct are fashioned and channeled as one lives within that framework."[6] In other words, *Unwritten History* does not purport to present a conventional, objective historical narrative, but rather a slave's individual understandings of his or her bondage. That is, the subjective assessment of persons and events in the slave's own life determined how he or she assimilated those experiences, which in turn shaped the individual's human relationships and spiritual journey before and after slavery.

The second, *God Struck Me Dead,* begins with a brief introduction by Johnson. Excepting Johnson's commentary and an additional, brief introductory essay by Radin on the nature of conversion, particularly its psychological dimension, the narratives are presented without explanation or analysis. Although the narrators' religious experience is woven into the life histories, Radin's purpose in eliciting the autobiographies was primarily an examination of "the outward and inward life of the American Negro for the two generations preceding the Civil War."[7] He was particularly interested in the relationship of the slave to the master and the master's household. The spare commentaries by Settle Egypt, Johnson, and Radin indicate how important the unadorned and unredacted words of former slaves were to the Fisk scholars. They assumed that the narrators should have the widest latitude in speaking for themselves. Yet Radin also said that the narratives would permit readers to place their own gloss on the conversion accounts: "In this volume we purposely refrain from any lengthy analyses of these documents lest we defeat their very reason for publication, namely, to give each reader an opportunity to draw his own conclusions and make his own interpretations."[8] Radin's statement at first seems enigmatic in light of his earlier, vigorously expressed views criticizing the presentation of raw cultural data without comment.

But the Fisk research was unique, and Radin's earlier caveats about Boas's accumulations of raw data without commentary did not apply to the initial publication of *God Struck Me Dead.* He had severely criticized Boas for treating ethnological data as if they were natural phenomena, products of the physical world that Radin believed could, at least initially, "speak for themselves." Cultural data—the artifice and fabrication of human creators—were different. He objected to Boas's Kwakiutl and Tsimshian monographs, where "we find the bare facts presented without comment." Radin insisted that the cultural facts Boas presented differed from natural phenomena because they compelled an analyst's explanatory intervention.[9]

Although *God Struck Me Dead* avoids editorial commentary, "Souls Piled Like Timber" reproduces many of the same narratives but additionally contains Radin's analysis of the material. In the former Fisk publication, he may well have had little control over the narratives produced by his collaboration with Andrew Polk Watson. Radin after all is not listed as the author of *God Struck Me Dead.* Charles Johnson undoubtedly felt that, some seventeen years after Fisk had sponsored the Settle Egypt and Radin-Watson collections, black voices in slavery and freedom finally deserved an audience. Those voices had been so thoroughly stifled that the Fisk narrative collections might begin to correct the dominant views of the racial majority, laymen and historians alike. For over a century, the white majority had represented what they considered African American realities; they were contemptuous or at best indifferent to the voices of African Americans themselves. Devalued and dismissed in political and social terms, African Americans accordingly were ignored, but in the Fisk collections they were the narrative center. Radin, of course, understood the fact of African American silence, particularly among the elderly survivors of slavery and Reconstruction, and the importance of ending that quiescence. In a 1945 preface to "Souls," Radin thus subordinated his own views to those of his narrators, explaining that

> I felt that the primary value of the book lay in the data I was presenting and only secondarily in my interpretation of it. Since, however, it does relate to matters regarded as controversial, I hope the readers and critics of this book will not forget that what I have written is of subsidiary importance compared to what the authors of the autobiographies and the conversion experiences tell us.[10]

In this light, Radin's remarks about the social circumstances of the research and Watson's role are particularly interesting in their methodological and interpersonal implications. Considering Radin's views about the personal connection between the anthropologist and gathered data, it is very clear that he fully appreciated the importance of his informants' controlling their narrations. This was especially true in his Nashville research since the Radin-Watson and Settle Egypt projects were breaking new ground. They were the first organized, programmatic efforts enabling former slaves to tell their own stories.

Watson collected six of eight autobiographies and all the narratives of religious conversion. Radin, an urbane and cosmopolitan professor in his late forties with no prior experience in the American South, fortunately worked with Watson, an experienced younger black man, native to the area but not at all provincial. Born in Franklin, south of Nashville in 1894, Watson was well acquainted as an African American with black life in Middle Tennessee in the early decades of the twentieth century. He had prior acquaintance with some of the narrators and with other people who had lived through slavery, the years of Reconstruction, and the harsh strictures of Jim Crow, still a brutal fact of life in Nashville of the 1920s. Only a year younger than Johnson, Watson followed a similar trajectory. Before coming to Fisk and working with Radin, he had served in World War I and studied briefly at the University of Chicago. He brought a maturity of outlook and sympathetic understanding to the task of collecting the narratives while preparing his 1932 Fisk thesis, "Primitive Religion among Negroes in Tennessee," under the supervision of Radin and Johnson. Moreover, Watson was a professed Christian, although he did not come of age among the Christian practitioners of "primitive religion." Not familiar with all the religious elements within the conversion accounts, he nonetheless considered the narratives resonant human documents. While their diction and unrestrained passion were not part of Watson's personal religious background, he nonetheless comported himself as a well-trained anthropologist respectfully seeking a faithful record of practices and beliefs not his own—in this case his informants' encounters with numinous forces. Later, Watson joined the Baha'i faith, attracted by the universalism of its creed, including a belief in the unity of humankind.[11]

Visiting more than one hundred people, some on several occasions over the course of two years, Watson recorded, whenever possible, personal recollections with pencil and notebook. Sometimes informants objected, requiring Watson later to write up the session from memory. *God Struck Me Dead* contains forty-eight conversion experiences gathered by Watson. Additionally, *God Struck Me Dead* presents four autobiographies collected by Watson and two by Radin. Two additional autobiographies collected by Watson were never published.

The most immediate issue for the researchers was how to explain their presence and whether the information sought was for Radin or Watson. Both men agreed that it was best to be forthcoming and direct, indicating for whom the information was gathered. Radin explained:

> This was by [no] means an easy task to do. From my own experience I have found that the best procedure in such cases is to be honest and frank, and that is what I counselled Watson to do. Whether those being interviewed understand or belive [*sic*] the explanation is not very important. What is important is whether they accept you.[12]

Sensitive to the uniqueness of the research situation, Radin and Watson tried to take account of the advanced age of the life-history narrators—all over eighty—and their ill health and irritability. Each narrator set conditions for his or her participation, and Radin discreetly complied, saying that the investigators' only option was to accede to the wishes of their informants. As to those conditions, Radin remarked that if interference in any manner had occurred

> by asking questions or attempting to direct the narrative, the rapport with our informants would unquestionably have been seriously endangered. After all, we were asking for something highly personal, recollections some of which were not pleasant to recall and which were frequently associated with portions of one's life one did not wish to dwell upon. The only chance of obtaining such information

was to let the narrator dictate, consciously and unconsciously, the terms on which he would give it.[13]

Radin's assessment of Watson, whose work established him more as collaborator than student, indicated that the project could not have gone forward without his integral participation.

> Mr. Watson's qualifications were many. First and foremost he was a Negro who had been brought up in the immediate environment of Nashville. He knew many of the people and he understood their beliefs and attitudes. Although he did not share most of them he was in no sense antagonistic. He established contact with people with great ease. He was intelligent, kind, careful and patient and grasped what I was trying to do within a short time.[14]

Radin of course had extensive experience in the collection of texts, including life-history narratives and philosophical reflections in native North America. After all, his pioneering fieldwork among the Winnebago over the years established the value of the life history to anthropology since it was a medium of personal expression, rich in its potential for yielding important psychological and sociological insight. For nearly a century, the life history has been a fundamental feature of anthropological method.

Watson was an apt student and collaborator, carefully following Radin's instructions.

> The formal training I could give him was small. I had him accompany me when I interviewed people and I accompanied him on several occasions when he went out to interview individuals. My instructions to him were simple. He was to do what I did. There was to be no specific questioning, nothing in short, in the nature of a questionnaire. Having introduced himself . . . he was to state what he wanted in considerable detail. Where he was seeking autobiographies, he was to emphasize the fact that we were interested particularly in their personal lives during the period of slavery and the post bellum period. To this, and only to this extent, was there direction. . . . He was never to press an individual or inject himself into the scene. His function was to observe unobtrusively and to listen. The most important factor in obtaining autobiographies of the kind we were seeking, my experience has taught me, is to establish rapport with an informant that your presence constitutes

no disturbing element and that he has to all intents and purposes eliminated you. After each of his interviews we discussed what had been obtained and how it had been obtained.[15]

Written well after their fieldwork and a decade after completion of the slave narrative collection of the Works Progress Administration (WPA), Radin emphasized that he and Watson wanted to elicit life histories specifically addressing the experience of slavery and the years following the Civil War. The WPA texts by contrast contained "miscellaneous details and a merely external description of plantation life" that were woven into the narratives. Much greater psychological value inhered, Radin believed, in the more focused autobiographies he and Watson recorded.[16]

As to the conversion narratives, Radin and Watson recognized them as manifest representations of "living religious faith."[17] Radin decided again that neither he nor Watson, as they gathered these narratives, should address any questions to their informants.[18] As to the honesty and candor that Radin said would guide the research, he acknowledged a moment of subterfuge when he followed the lead of a Fisk student who had persuaded an elderly woman to permit a visit from Radin and Watson. The student informed her professor that the old woman's cooperation was contingent on his assurance that he was a Baptist. Likely arriving in customary attire of vested suit and tie, perhaps a beret, lacking any prior experience in the South, and missing a southern accent and demeanor, Radin was an unconvincing Baptist. He described the encounter, while indicating once again the critical research role played by Watson:

> I went to see her but obtained nothing. Being a wise woman she recognized that my profession of faith was untrue, that what she could tell me would be meaningless to me and being meaningless to me they [sic] would constitute a criticism, unconsciously introduce an element of doubt. Here Watson's religious faith was a tremendous asset just as was his relative youth for these experiences were something that the young should know and seek.[19]

The researcher thus could positively affect the process by his attitude,

> to stimulate the narrator to recount his experience as vividly as he can to convince him that one is a worthy receptacle for what is being revealed. Watson's extraordinary merit was that he could do just this and he was amply rewarded by what he

obtained. There is no other record of American Negro religious experiences even remotely comparable.[20]

Following his studies at Fisk and the completion of his graduate degree, Watson eventually accepted a teaching position at Wiley College, a historically black institution, in Marshall, Texas.[21]

The two autobiographies Radin collected by himself are considerably longer and more comprehensive than the other six. On the face of it, Radin's ethnographic skills, development of the life-history method in anthropology, and his two decades of prior fieldwork organized around the collection of vernacular texts would seem to account for his success with the informants, Mr. Green (first name does not appear) and Charlie Mason. Watson, too, in preparing his thesis found Mr. Green a "very reliable and resourceful informant," having interviewed him for additional life-history material just prior to his death in 1929.[22] But Radin took no personal credit for the more detailed and lengthy autobiographies he recorded, instead generously attributing his success to luck. Watson, Radin remarks, would likely have collected similarly detailed accounts had he sought extended life histories from Radin's two informants. By the same token, Radin says that had he interviewed Watson's six informants, he probably would not have produced life histories as comprehensive and detailed as those of Mr. Green and Mr. Mason.

Radin and Watson, however, recognized the obvious advantages of a sole African American investigator conducting most of the interviews among elderly former slaves, long accustomed to self-protective efforts to meet what they perceived as the expectations of white questioners. The presence of a white male investigator might especially have inhibited the candid recollections of women called on to narrate painful life events, including sexual degradation and humiliation by white masters and overseers. Indeed, of the six autobiographers Watson recorded, five were women. While relatively brief compared to Radin's texts gathered from Mr. Green and Mr. Mason, Watson's autobiographies bring their own distinctive value to the Fisk project.

For example, in one of his unpublished autobiographies, Watson elicited from his informant, Yvonne Thompson, a particularly stark portrayal of the slave experience that laid bare the cruelty, sadism, and arbitrariness experienced or witnessed by an aged former bondswoman whose memory in 1929 reached back to the Mexican-American War. Through her measured, even understated language, she reanimates an experience of utter inhumanity. A house servant who didn't suffer the same severities as field hands, she nonetheless labored ceaselessly as she endured the unrelieved fear that her children could be sold away. The contrast between house servants and field hands is particularly dramatic in her recounting of one visit to Mississippi with her mistress. There, the scale of slavery and brutality shocked even Mrs. Thompson, inured to cruelty and viciousness witnessed in Tennessee. What she saw in Mississippi further seared her memory, already deeply imprinted by beatings, mutilations, and killings at the home of her mistress.

I was born here in Nashville, but I don't know how long ago. I had two children when the Civil War started. I got my age from the people that owned me, but after I came to live with my children and grandchildren what few papers and records I had got lost. I was large enough to know a little something about the war with Mexico. Of course, we slaves didn't know no more than what was told us, or what we heard the white people talk about. But even in this way the house servants could hear a lot.

I didn't know much about the Civil War until I heard my mistress talk about it. Most of us were made to fear the Yankees. The white folks would tell us all kinds of low down things the Yankees would do to the slaves. In spite of all, though, some of the slaves ran off and joined the Union army. They couldn't have been treated no worse by the Yankees than many of them were treated by their masters, for I have seen any number of both men and women with fingers and even arms cut off, and I have seen them die from whippings. Many of them lost limbs and fingers for serving or nursing their babies while working in the fields without permission from the overseer.

My mistress was a teacher, and I was the nurse and house-servant, so I went with her on trips to Chattanooga and Mississippi. I didn't go to Mississippi but once, and God knows I don't want to go there anymore. I never saw so much cotton and so many slaves in my life. As far as the eye could see there was cotton, cotton, cotton and the fields were just lined with slaves, men, women and children.

Nearly every morning, away before day, I could hear some of them getting a whipping and they would be just hollering and pleading, "Oh, pray master! Oh, pray master!" After the lashing, they got their backs greased, and then went on to work. Some of them were too sore and stiff to bend over, but they went on. I guess that is one thing that made them pray so hard for God to deliver them from their sorrows.

It was also the custom among some of the big slave-owners to have the Negroes come up in the yard and dance and amuse the white folks after supper. One night, after everybody except old man Jones had left, the white folks got on him to dance. He had the reputation of being the preacher for the slaves, and when they called on him he wouldn't dance. They kept after him but he just wouldn't. His master got sore at him and began to whip him and just whipped the old man until he died. The last words he said were these, "You can punish this old earthly body but you can't kill my soul." I will never forget that night and that poor man as long as I live. I was certainly glad to get away from Mississippi. I never have wanted to see that place again.[23]

Mrs. Thompson's tone conveys resignation to the past without overt, vengeful feelings, although the latter were certainly represented in other Fisk narratives.

May Anson also tells of the same brutalities, not only the repeated blows to the head and verbal abuse inflicted on her but also the acts of rape and child murder perpetrated by "the devil here on earth," the slave-owner on an adjoining farm. Mrs. Anson felt relieved that the vicious treatment she suffered was not more severe and remained convinced that a hell must exist for those who committed such atrocities. Although she had a profound Christian faith, she was in no sense resigned to the past, and her narration expresses a hatred of the sadists and abusers she recalled. Mrs. Thompson and Mrs. Anson experienced many personal outrages, yet amidst the broadest range of human misery each woman could point to atrocities that had exceeded her own humiliations. Appropriately, Radin and Watson entitled Mrs. Anson's autobiography "Slavery Was Hell without Fires."

When I was little I used to work around the big house, cleaning floors, polishing silver, wiping floors, waiting on the table and everything. My mother was the cook. My mistress was awful mean and exacting. I had better not do anything wrong. She used to beat me like I was a dog; hit across the head with tongs and poker or anything. There were some wooden steps in the hall leading upstairs. One day I was going up them. She got mad because the steps creaked. She hollered at me and called me to her and said, "You black bitch, you go up those steps like a horse. I'll kill you." Hardly a day passed that she didn't beat me for something.

On the farm adjoining ours was another plantation and from what I saw old Man F. do to the slaves I think I was blessed to be treated no worse than I was. He had a lot of slaves and he was a devil here on earth. I never saw as many dead babies in my life as I did on his farm. He used to walk or ride down through the field and take his foot and kick poor women that were with child and cause them to have miscarriage right there in the field. Then he would call the Negro foreman to bring a cart and "haul away this damn . . ."

Women with small babies were allowed to take their babies to the field and put them under trees until nursing time. A woman had better not stop to suckle her baby until she was told to do it, else she would be beat almost to death. I actually saw old man F. walk through the field and seeing a baby crying, take his stick and knock its brains out and call for the foreman to come and haul off the nasty black rat.

Yes, in them days it was hell without fires. This is one reason why I believe in a hell. I don't believe a just God is going to take no such man as that into his Kingdom.

Them were some awful times. Many of the slaves were taught to steal from neighboring plantations. They would slip out at night and steal a cow or hog or corn, and bring it home and lock it up in the smokehouse. They would steal to make their provisions hold out. If a neighbor came to inquire about anything missing the master would deny any knowledge of it. "No, I don't think any of my Negroes did it." They would say this, knowing all the time that the meat or corn was locked up in the smokehouse.

Now these white folks are always talking about the Negro stealing. If they do steal, it is mostly because they were taught to do it in slavery times. Not only stealing but a lot of other devilment. Look at old Nason that lived on the other side of us. He forced nearly every decent-looking slave woman he had. Williamson County is full of half-white children he got by his slaves. I used to hear my mistress talk about him a lot, but I had better not be caught listening. I heard just the same, though, but I didn't have to hear. I had eyes I could see with and I knowed there wasn't no white slaves over there. I saw and heard, too a lot more than they thought I did. [24]

While brutality—whipping, mutilation, and killing—were meted out both to male and female slaves, women were also subject to rape as Mrs. Anson's autobiography makes clear. The men, too, spoke of witnessing sexual outrages against female slaves, indicated in the following excerpt from Mr. Green's autobiography.

Ever since I got freed I have been trying to figure what made that man so mean. After thinking about him I have come to believe that he was so mean because he felt that the war was coming and that we would be freed. You see, some foresaw the war and the freedom of the slaves while others didn't. He was one who thought that in case of war the South would win. So he bought slaves while everybody else was selling theirs. When he saw that the war was coming he got harder and harder.

He was as hard on the women as on the men. Some of the things I saw him do to women is too low to tell. He used them and abused them in public and in private. But all of these things I have put behind me. At times I look back over the road I have traveled and wonder how I am still here.[25]

He described one of his owners as sometimes physically abusive, but usually restrained by his wife. He was not restrained, however, whenever he wanted to rape one of the slave women. Of the owner, Mr. Green said that

he was bad among the women. Married or not married made no difference to him. Whoever he wanted among the slaves, he went and got her or had her meet him somewhere out in the bushes. I have known him to go to the shack and make the woman's husband sit outside while he went in to his wife.[26]

Little of substance distinguishes the conversion narratives of men and women, given the thoroughgoing degradation of both sexes. While a woman was raped, her husband could only suffer helpless degradation and emasculation at his inability to protect her, unless he was willing to die. That was the case when the slave owner, Sam Watkins,

who would ship their husbands (slaves) out of bed and get in with their wives. One man said he stood it as long as he could and one morning he just stood outside, and when he got with his wife he just choked him to death. He said he knew it was death, but it was death anyhow; so he just killed him. They hanged him.[27]

Unwritten History thus documented occasional, violent resistance to slavery as well as more covert acts of defiance such as theft, lying, abetting escape, and other "weapons of the weak."[28] Equally oppositional, the narrators in *God Struck Me Dead*, playing on black reinterpretations of white Christianity, unequivocally asserted the humanity of slaves.

The bitter feelings expressed by Mrs. Anson were unexceptional within the context of both Fisk publications—*Unwritten History* and *God Struck Me Dead*. Settle Egypt's collection of thirty-six autobiographical reflections of former slaves living in Tennessee and Kentucky record rancorous feelings and hatred that could come from the memory of particularly brutal treatment or from the fact of slavery itself, even if one suffered less than others. Every slave surely believed human bondage was contrary to the divine will, despite what white preachers told them. White people visited every kind of cruelty on their slaves. A Nashville centenarian described child murder, also referenced by Mrs. Anson, and beheadings that occurred during the rumored slave insurrection of 1856 in Stewart County, Tennessee, and Trigg and Christian Counties in Kentucky.[29] Rare among former slaves, he was an atheist, according to his son, as he was unable to understand how God could punish the wicked as well as the innocent—"plenty folks went crazy trying to get that thing straightened out."[30] Unmitigated by Christian belief, his most intense hatred centered on his white father:

> I was riding on a street car long after freedom and I passed the cemetery where my father was buried. I started cussing—"let me get off this damn car and go see where my God damn father is buried, so I can spit on his grave, a God damn son-of a bitch." I got no mercy on nobody who bring up their children like dogs. How could any father treat their child like that? Bring them up to be ignorant like they did us. If I had my way with them all I would like to have is a chopping block and chop every one of their heads off. Of course I don't hate them that is good. There are some good white folks. Mighty few, though.[31]

Likewise, an *Unwritten History* narrator saw a continuous line joining the era of slavery to the world of 1930:

> Times are bad enough now, but you ain't seen nothing. White folks will always be hard on niggers and niggers will have not a chance. I hope God will help the niggers and they will help theirselves. But I ain't never seen how God can forgive those mean white folks for what they done to niggers way back yonder, nor for what they are doing to them now.[32]

At about the same time as the Radin, Watson, and Settle Egypt collections were underway in Nashville, John Cade of Southern University was collecting first-person accounts of former slaves in Louisiana.[33] Joining other black writers interested in documenting the primary experience of slavery, Cade directly addressed the value of black scholars interviewing black informants. He granted to white writers an ability, unavailable to black investigators, to portray white attitudes and behavior, however disagreeable toward blacks. There was certainly no shortage of such examples. But more significantly in terms of filling an enormous historical void, black writers, as Cade argues, can portray black people more dependably than white observers and will thus represent the "real black man as he was, is, and hopes to be."[34] Restrained but unmistakable in intent, Cade dismisses the failed scholarship of Jim Crow apologists.

Prior to the Fisk and Southern University collection projects, there were of course other pieces of revealing testimony in a number of slave autobiographies published before the Civil War, including those of Henry Bibb, William Wells Brown, and Solomon Northup.[35] Additionally, scattered sources from the eighteenth century through the 1930s recorded the voices of escaped or manumitted slaves as they spoke in letters, speeches, brief autobiographies, and in interviews with newspaper and magazine writers, folklorists, and others.[36] Prominent historians such as U. B. Phillips were of course well aware of the published accounts of life in the slave regime, but dismissed those narratives as abolitionist propaganda. The historiographic bias against recollection, oral testimony, or any non-documentary source produced well after the fact was also at play. Phillips summarized inadmissible sources in his study of slavery:

> Polemic writings also have been little used, for their fuel went so much to heat that their light upon the living conditions is faint. Reminiscences are likewise disregarded, for the reason that the lapse of decades has impaired inevitably the memories of men. The contemporary records of slaves, masters and witnesses may leave gaps and have their shortcomings, but the asseverations [declarations] of the politicians, pamphleteers, and aged survivors are generally unsafe even in supplement.[37]

Radin was familiar with Phillips's methodological skepticism and even shared some of it.

> Now where one deals with articulate individuals, particularly when they are quite old, a question naturally arises. To what extent are their narratives really authentic? Such persons are bound to be imaginative and often creative. Will they not reorganize and elaborate their material? There is . . . no way of controlling their statements. But there is absolutely no reason for believing that any of the incidents they narrate are untrue or have been deliberately invented. At worst, it can be said that, like the authors of all autobiographies, they distort and dramatize certain events and place incidents in a false perspective. Since there was no way of

checking the accuracy of the specific incidents, particularly those highly repugnant to our feelings, the best we could do was first, to find out whether such incidents could have taken place, and secondly, to try to learn as much about the narrators as possible in order to determine the kind of dramatization and distortion they were likely to indulge in. Unfortunately in only two instances, the autobiographies which I myself obtained, was this reasonably successful.[38]

Radin's insight into historical source material was particularly shrewd in its modern recognition that all autobiographers "distort and dramatize," whether their medium is the written or spoken word, whenever it was produced. Zora Neale Hurston's *Dust Tracks on a Road* is an excellent case in point, dramatizing, for example, her coming to grips with a complex personal identity, encompassing both the down-home Eatonville girl and the New York writer, scholar, and Harlem Renaissance figure. For Hemenway, "Zora seems to be both an advocate for the universal, demonstrating that this black woman does not look at the world in racial terms, and the celebrant of a unique ethnic upbringing in an all-black village."[39]

While oral testimony challenges the critical skills of the scholar, Radin believed that none should be dismissed ipso facto. That view is closely related to the fundamental difference between his attitude and that of Phillips toward slaves as persons. In reducing slaves to an aggregated, regressive mass, Phillips and contemporaneous historians for the most part either did not accept the full humanity of captive African people and their descendants or denied a slave's capacity for independent thought and belief. Radin, however, accepted only one approach, that of the culture historian whose prime function is to proceed with a sense of humility and "to listen, and to understand sympathetically what he is being told and to eliminate himself as much as possible from the picture."[40] Early on, Radin had produced a considerable body of person-centered writing on native North America. At Fisk the same radical humanism repudiated the prevailing racial clichés and stereotypes that dominated popular and academic opinion through the first half of the twentieth century.

While the Tennessee and Louisiana collections of Radin, Watson, Settle Egypt, and Cade present their own distinctive tests of the historian's skill, those narratives provide a context often missing in the series produced by the WPA.[41] For example, the latter texts provide little information about the collectors, their backgrounds, or qualifications. Likewise, the physical and social circumstances under which the WPA narratives were collected remain for the most part opaque. The interviewers and editors, moreover, say nothing about the use of Standard English in some narrations and vernacular black speech in others or, in that vein, the relationship between the narratives submitted to the WPA and the actual texts collected. While a number of deficiencies mark the two Fisk collections, including almost no data about the informants and their contemporary social circumstances, some of the more troublesome aspects of the WPA collection were avoided in the Radin-Watson and Settle Egypt collections.[42] Significantly, Watson, Settle Egypt, and Cade were black researchers investigating black lives, while Watson's mentor, Paul Radin, brought to bear a lifelong sensitivity to black civil rights issues and a radical understanding of race in America. Above all, the Fisk researchers approached their aged informants respectfully, reflected in what was certainly an intentional editing strategy that preserved black vernacular expressions and idioms without attempting to reproduce the exact diction of the narrators. The effort to transcribe black speech in many of the WPA documents, on the other hand, perpetuated the stereotypes and minstrelsy pervasive in American media of the time.

On several levels the Fisk inquiries about the lives of people in slavery and the postbellum years broke new ground in understanding the African American past. The researchers assumed that they were interviewing people whose intellectual maturity and capacity for reflection was, as a human given, no different from their own. Their view of slavery had to begin with the slave as a person. The investigation, moreover, was undertaken by anthropologists and sociologists well acquainted with interview techniques and sensitive to the fraught nature of their subject. With much empathy, they were, in other words, asking people to recall defamation, misery, and the recurrent personal tragedies that slavery guaranteed, which, taken together, constituted an unrelieved denial of their humanity.

From Crisis to Conversion

Despite the grim memories of bondage and the early postbellum years, Radin raised the question of why "so few individuals escaped complete demoralization and so few developed neuroses." The answer, he suggested, lay in the texts detailing conversion. However, the basis of Radin's psychological assessment of the vast population of former slaves and his assertion that few freedmen suffered mental problems is unclear. That conversion brought solace, peace, and a new self-definition to each individual is beyond doubt. But to assert that such experiences therefore accounted for the putative mental health of millions is not so much wrong as unsupported by the data that Radin and Watson gathered.

This is one of several instances in which Radin's interpretations moved well ahead of the historical and ethnographic evidence necessary to support them. It is more argument by assertion than by substantive demonstration. At several points in "Souls," Radin acknowledges as much, citing the insufficiency of personal data on informants that would permit deeper insights into the psyche of individuals. Given Radin's commitment to an ethnology that encompassed both psychological and historical perspectives—a point he wrote about while at Fisk—he regretfully had to forego an intense analysis of each text, lacking as he did the deep knowledge of each narrator required for such an exercise.[43] Moreover, as noted earlier, he advised Watson not to question informants beyond what they had volunteered in their narratives. That lack of knowledge was due to the difficulties attendant to working with people of extreme old age, including some who could not accommodate revisits from the researchers for reasons of illness or fatigue.

Nonetheless, the personal experience of conversion resulting in deliverance from uncertainty and chaos effected a profound, life-altering change as narrated by each individual. Narratives describe what the convert knew to be actual encounters with divinity and the devil, heaven and hell, death and rebirth. Neither Radin nor Watson gainsaid these accounts, for they eschewed judgments about the spiritual journeys recounted. Instead, they recognized that for their elderly narrators belief *is* experience. Radin found in the texts convincing testimony explaining how individuals managed to avoid personal demoralization and reach a "new individuation, an inward re-integration."[44] The psychologically damaging conditions of servitude and postbellum brutality that certainly impaired self-realization motivated the religious awakening and personal transformations that Radin and Watson tried to understand. In other words, dehumanized as mere property and later reviled as free men and women, converts found a new status, ordained by themselves, and not acknowledged or even recognized by white people. Nonetheless, the religious ecstasy of experiencing heaven and being found by God or his angelic surrogates brought recognition and a redemptive, positive self-definition to each convert.

Similarities across narratives in the Watson collection indicate that each testimony was not solely a spontaneous inspiration and was in no sense a random or unique text. Although conversion tended to be a solitary experience, patterns emerge across the entire corpus of narratives. In other words, the individual religious journey later recounted in worship service amid great emotion exercised some influence on others, thus accounting in part for the recurring style and content of the narratives. Conversion during a church service or the recounting of prior conversions by congregants were public events during which symbols of coming to God were abundantly in evidence and doubtless internalized by witnesses. Subsequent public recitations by the converted thus reiterated a general structure of the narratives. The authority of African American elders, particularly powerful ministers, perhaps beginning in the early nineteenth century, also played a role in shaping the pattern of the recounted conversion experiences.

What mattered for Radin, characteristically, during his Fisk appointment were the thoughts and emotions of real individuals, aged African Americans living out their final years in Nashville. They were among the last who could speak personally and authoritatively about lives in chattel slavery. Later, they struggled through a brutal post-Reconstructionist period that suppressed all efforts to exercise their rights not only as citizens but often as human beings. That oppression is palpable in many of the Fisk narratives, autobiographies and conversion testimonies.

As slaves, they had found nothing of comfort, existential meaning, or respect in the barren versions of Christianity promoted by white churchmen or missionaries sent among them by slave owners. Urged in the name of Christian obedience to accept their lot as property, and powerless to mitigate materially the daily humiliations of enslavement, including physical brutality, men and women created beliefs and rites of great psychological value. None could possibly believe that slavery was a just condition of life or that God demanded its acceptance. Instead, personal experience, sermons about biblical figures, particularly Moses and Jesus, and, perhaps, African survivals combined to form a new spiritual world of value and personal standing within a community of shared, unrelieved suffering. Obedience to the master's power mystified by white churchmen and missionaries as a divine order was transformed into an obedience to a reconceptualized God. This was only possible through a reinterpretation of Christianity motivated by a driving need to repair the spiritual and psychological damage that slavery and its aftermath had inflicted. The conversion narratives were thus not a black imitation of white theology but a unique bricolage, a new configuration of meanings fabricated out of familiar elements, including those of the predominant faiths, Methodist and especially Baptist, that surrounded the slaves.

Whereas Methodist church organization was hierarchical, investing bishops with considerable authority over local congregations, the Baptist church was highly localized, each church tending toward autonomy. Baptist congregations were not accountable to higher church authorities in the manner of Methodism. That local independence invested the Baptist pastor with near absolute authority, particularly in those leaders of what Watson identifies as "The Negro Primitive Baptist Church."[45] The latter church, like its white counterpart, organized itself on what it considered "original" principles of Christianity, rejecting all accretions to Baptist faith and practice not ordained in the Christian Bible, whether Sunday school, musical instruments in worship, or even pastoral training in theological institutions. Adults or younger people who could articulate their beliefs, not the newborn of conventional Christianity, underwent the ritual of baptism occurring through total immersion in a river.

That practice recalls African religious rites among the Yoruba, Ashanti, and Fon focused on possession by river deities, among the most powerful in the pantheon. Memories of Africa, not part of the consciousness of Watson's informants, could, in the Herskovits scheme, nonetheless have passed unconsciously across generations that associated rivers, divinity, and rebirth, thus providing a partial structure through which Christian teaching was reinterpreted.[46] However, it must be remembered that, although the importation of slaves to the United States after 1808 was constitutionally banned, those born in Africa might well have been living when the Civil War ended. Illegal importation of slaves was also a possibility, the last and best-known case reported by Zora Neale Hurston.[47]

The possibility of African survivals in the United States was acknowledged by Radin in *The Racial Myth,* as noted in the Introduction. It was not, however, a question that he pursued. Nor did Watson, in examining the roots of the Primitive Baptist Church, raise the possibility of Africanisms among his informants, instead doubting, with other black scholars of the time, their persistence among slaves.[48]

Nonetheless, Herskovits, although lacking strong evidence, raised the possibility not only of African cultural resonances in the United States but also of white cultural borrowing from black people. Anthropologists inspired by Herskovits and others have of course analyzed the dynamics of culture contact. The processes attendant to the interactions of people of diverse traditions—acculturation, in other words—point to the near inevitability of a two-way flow of ideas and practices, even amid enormous power disparities among those in contact. The embedded racism of the era, however, could hardly admit of any black influence on white people. But pressing on, Herskovits observed that phenomena such as river baptism and "shouting," a joyful element in the conversion narratives, may well have derived from the deep emotionalism woven through the religions of West Africa. Against the grain of conventional thinking in 1941, Herskovits remarked that "there is a strong probability that these patterns were themselves of importance in giving to the whites just that tradition which among Negroes is customarily ascribed to white influence!"[49]

Additional Texts

The Primitive Baptist Church became the spiritual home for people following their conversion. Having passed along the edge of hell, they were guided by God or an intermediary through an ordeal testing their faith on their way to salvation and eventual rebirth into heaven. The God-centered narrative that follows aptly illustrates Watson's observation that "It would be hard to find a people whose mind is more fixed on God and His attributes than that of the Negro Primitive Baptists."[50] In "Born in a World of Heaven," abbreviated below, river baptism is the culmination of the conversion experience when divine grace is forthcoming only when doubt has disappeared. But the narrator continues to doubt, even after she was struck dead and envisioned heaven, hell, and the Trinity. Lacking a perfect faith in God—perhaps the greatest of all sins—her doubts bring on punishment in the form of sickness and an inability to walk. As in other narratives, sinfulness or disobedience induces physical maladies or bodily torment—such as pain, paralysis, sickness, and finally, in the journey to grace across the border of heaven and hell, death. Struck dead and later afflicted because she questioned God's word, the narrator describes her bodily sensations. As in other narratives of conversion, the coming of absolute faith and turning away from sin and doubt are powerfully expressed as re-embodiment through rebirth into heaven. Some narrators describe seeing their old bodies as their spirits are liberated in heaven.

BORN IN THE WORLD OF HEAVEN

I have always been a sheep. I was never a goat. I was created and cut out, and born in the world for heaven. Even before God freed my soul and told me to go, I never was hell-scared. I just never did feel that my soul was made to burn in hell.

God started on me when I wasn't but ten years old. I was sick with the fever and He called me and said, "You are ten years old." I didn't know how old I was, but later I asked my older sister and she told me that I was ten years old when I had the fever.

As I grew up I used to frolic a lot, and was considered a good dancer, but I never took much interest in such things. I just went many times to please my friends and later my husband. What I loved more than all else was to go to church.

I used to pray then. I pray now and just tell God to take me and do His will, for he knows every secret of my heart. He knows what we stand most in need of before we ask for it and if we trust Him He will give us what we ought to have in due season. Some people pray and call on God as if they think He is ignorant of their needs or else asleep. But God is a time-God. I know this, for He told me so.

I remember one morning I was on my way home with a bundle of clothes to wash—it was after my husband had died—I felt awfully burdened down so I commenced to talk to God. It looked like I was having such a hard time. Everybody seemed to be getting along well but poor me. I told Him so. I said, "Lord, it looks like You come to everybody's house but mine. I never bother my neighbors or cause any disturbance. I have lived as it is becoming a poor widow woman to live, and yet, Lord, it looks like I have a harder time than anybody else." When I said this something told me to turn around and look. I put my bundle down and looked towards the east part of the world. A voice spoke to me as plain as day, but it was inward and said, "I am a time-God, working after the counsel of My own will. In due time I will bring all things to you. Remember and cause your heart to sing."

When God struck me dead with His power I was living on 14th Avenue. It was the year of the Centennial. I was in my house alone, and I declare unto you when His power struck me, I died. I fell out on the floor flat on my back. I could neither speak nor move for my tongue stuck to the roof of my mouth. My jaws were locked and my limbs were stiff.

In my vision I saw hell and the devil. I was crawling along a high brick wall, it seems, and it looked like I would fall into a dark roaring pit. I looked away to the east and saw Jesus. He called to me and said, "Arise and follow me." He was standing in snow, the prettiest, whitest snow I have ever seen. He commanded me the third time before I could go. I stepped out in it but it didn't seem a bit cold nor did my feet sink into it. We travelled on east in a little narrow path and came to something that looked like a grape-arbor, and the snow was hanging down like icicles. But it was so pretty and white that it didn't look like snow. He told me to take some of it and eat but I said, "Lord, it is too cold." He commanded me three times before I would eat any of it. I took some and tested it, and it was the best-tasting snow I had ever put in my mouth.

The Father, the Son and the Holy Ghost led me on to Glory. I saw God sitting in a big arm chair. Everything seemed to be made of white stones and pearls. God didn't seem to pay any attention. He just sat looking into space. I saw the Lamb's Book of Life, and my name written in it. A voice spoke to me and said, "Whosoever My Son sets free is free indeed. I give you a through-ticket from hell to heaven. Go into yonder world and be not afraid, neither be dismayed. You are an elect child and ready for the fold." But when He commanded me to go I was stubborn and didn't want to leave. He said, "My little one, I have commanded you and you shall obey."

I saw, while I was still in the spirit, myself going to my neighbors and to the church, telling them what God had done for me. When I came back to this world I rose shouting and went carrying the good news.

I didn't go like the Lord told me though, for I was still in doubt and I wanted to make sure. Because of my disobedience He threw a great affliction on me. I got awfully sick and my limbs were all swollen so that that I could hardly walk. I began to have more faith then, and put more trust in God.

He put this affliction on me because it was so hard for me to believe. But I just didn't want to be a hypocrite and go around hollering, and not knowing what I was talking and shouting about. I told God this in my prayer and He answered me saying, "My little one, My grace is sufficient. Behold I have commanded you to go and you shall go."

When I was ready to be baptized, I asked God to do two things. It had been raining for days and on the morning of my baptism it was still raining. I said, "Lord, if you are satisfied with me and pleased with what I have told the people, cause the sun to shine this evening when I go to the river." Bless your soul! when we went to the river it looked like I had never seen the sun shine as bright.[51]

"God Struck Me Dead," the eponymous title of this conversion narrative originally appearing in the 1945 Fisk publication, was retitled without explanation by Radin, "Born in a World of Heaven." Published under the new title, it appeared with two other conversion texts in *Circle Magazine,* a short-lived avant-garde periodical of literature, criticism, and the arts published by a Berkeley bookstore in the mid-1940s. Radin did not explain why he selected "Born in the World for Heaven" for republication, nor did he offer any commentary on either the text or Watson's informant. What can be said is that Radin found artistry and literary merit in this drama of a heavenly visit, the sight of Jesus and God, and the experience of death and rebirth.

The literary deftness of the narrators derived from their skill in selecting pertinent events in their own personal experience that they then knit together with fixed forms. The latter included biblical passages and references, such as the invocation of Christ as the "Lamb of God," learned orally, and in a few cases by reading, hymns, sermons, and even passages from such books as *Pilgrim's Progress* learned from unknown sources. Sometimes there is a rephrasing of biblical verses or passages, then integrated into the conversion narrative.

> The penitent is not transported to hell but the "greedy jaws of hell." Angels do not simply gather around an individual but a "host of angels, even a great number, [gather around] with their backs to me and their faces to the outer world." People do not dwell on this earth. They are placed on the "rock of eternity." They are "shod to run the race with patience"; they work "in a newness of life"; they are "chosen vessels before the wind ever blew or before the sun ever shined." They describe the vicissitudes of their religious life thus: "Falling down and getting up, I keep my eye on the bright and morning star."

Together, these elements and techniques combine to create "a special form of American oral literature."[52] It was thus especially important to remain faithful to his informants' words, not only in the interest of African American self-representation about slavery and postbellum adjustment but also to discern the intrinsic literary value of the narratives.

Radin noted in *Circle Magazine* that the narratives "were obtained by me in 1928 from individuals who had been born in slavery. They are presented exactly as they were obtained."[53] The ambiguous implication here is that Radin either gathered the narratives directly from informants or from Watson, the actual collector. Moreover, Radin's statement seems to lay to rest any question one might have about editorial intrusion, redactions, and the like, especially when researchers did not utilize recording equipment.[54] Although Radin suggested that the texts were reproduced with no editing at all, any reader might be forgiven some doubt, given the degree to which many of the texts approximate Standard English. Watson resolved this matter in his thesis when he discussed the collection of the narratives, stating that "The dialect in nearly every case, direct quotations included, was changed to more ordinary English."[55] Watson, rather than Radin, probably was responsible for the "ordinary English" renderings, but beyond Watson's efforts there is no evidence suggesting that substantive altering of the texts occurred.

The narratives frequently define a period of uncertainty, a kind of hovering between heaven and hell, life and death, or even a condition regarded as death itself from which the supplicant might believe himself or herself literally to have been reborn. In "Born in the World of Heaven," the narrator faced the ordeal of avoiding the devil and the dark pit of hell, separated from heaven by a brick wall along which she crawls. This period of uncertainty—marginality or liminality—induces visions among believers, putting them into a direct communication with God, or Jesus, or another heavenly source bringing a message from Divinity, or even an inner voice directed by God. Finally, there occurs a reintegration into an interior psychological world of clarity, of balance in the relationship of the newly self-defined individual and his or her environment, or, as Radin put it, an achievement of "a status that he himself had ordained, not a fictitious one imposed from without."[56]

"I Am Blessed but You Are Damned!" illustrates the motif of newness that occurs in a number of conversion texts. Here, it focuses particularly on embodiment, wherein the narrator describes sickness and paralysis after hearing the voice of divinity offering reassurance. The narrator then gazes not only on his new hands and feet but also on his old body suspended over the pit of hell. God lovingly addresses the person as "my little one," as if talking to a child, thus reiterating the theme of newness, purity, regeneration, and certain benevolence. Fearing a beating from his master for destroying part of the corn crop, the narrator instead persuades the master through the exuberance of his words that he is in fact a preacher to whom the master must listen. Probably for the first time, he speaks to his master boldly and without fear. His is a new sense of self, a significant, emboldened individual. In other narratives, dread of the master is expressed by representations of the devil with his "hell hounds," which allude to vicious dogs some slaveholders maintained to keep their slaves in check.

I AM BLESSED BUT YOU ARE DAMNED!

One day in the field ploughing, I heard a voice. I jumped because I thought it was my master coming to scold and whip me for ploughing up some more corn. I looked but saw no one. Again the voice called, "Morte! Morte!" With this I dropped the plough and started to run, but the voice spoke to me saying, "Fear not, my little one, for behold I come to bring you a message of peace. Be upright before Me and I will give you a message of truth."

Everything got dark, and I was unable to stand any longer. I began to feel sick and there was a great roaring. I tried to cry and move but was unable to do either. I looked up and saw that I was in a new world. There were plants and animals and all, there. Even the water, where I stooped down to drink, began to cry out, "I am blessed but you are damned; I am blessed but you are damned!" With this I began to pray, and a voice on the inside began to cry, "Mercy! Mercy! Mercy!"

As I prayed an angel came and touched me, and I looked at myself and I saw I was a new man. I looked at my hands and they looked new; I looked at my feet and they looked new. I looked and saw my old body suspended over a burning pit by a small thread like a spider web. I again prayed and there came a soft voice saying, "My little one, I have loved you with an everlasting love. You are this day made alive and freed from hell. You are a chosen vessel unto the Lord. Be upright before me and I will guide you unto all truth. My grace is sufficient for you. Go and I am with you. Preach the Gospel and I will preach with you. You are henceforth the salt of the earth."

I then began to shout and clap my hands. All the time a voice on the inside was crying, "I am so glad! I am so glad!" About this time an angel appeared before me and said with a loud voice, "Praise God! Praise God!" I looked to the east and there was a large throne lifted high up, and thereon sat one, even God. He looked neither to the right nor to the left. I was afraid, and fell on my face. When I was still a long way off I heard a voice from God saying, "My little one, be not afraid, for lo: I am with you always." All this He said but opened not his mouth while speaking. Then all those about the throne shouted and said, "Amen."

I then came to myself again and began to shout and rejoice. After so long a time I recovered my real senses, and realized that I had been ploughing and that horse had run off with the plough and dragged down much of the corn. I was afraid and began to pray, for I knew the master would whip me most unmercifully when he found that I had ploughed up the corn.

About this time my master came down in the field. I became very bold, and answered him when he called me. He asked me very roughly how I came to plough up the corn and where the horse and plough were, and why I had got along so slowly. I told him that I had been talking with God Almighty and that it was God who had ploughed up the corn. He looked at me very strange, and suddenly I fell for shouting and I shouted and began to preach. The words seemed to glow from my lips. When I had finished I had a deep feeling of satisfaction, and no longer dreaded the whipping I knew I would get. My master looked at me and seemed to tremble. He told me to catch the horse and come to the barn. I went to get the horse, stumbling down the corn rows. Here again I became weak, and began to be afraid of the whipping. After I had gone some distance I became dazed, and again fell to the ground. In a vision I saw a great mound and beside it, or at the base of it, stood the angel Gabriel, and a voice said to me, "Behold your sins are a great mountain, but they shall be rolled away. Go in peace, fearing no man, for lo: I have cut your stammering tongue and unstopped your deaf ears. A witness shalt thou be, and thou shalt speak to multitudes and they shall hear. My word has gone out and it is power. Be strong, and lo! I am with you even until the world shall end. Amen."

I looked and the angel Gabriel lifted his hand and my sins that had stood as a mountain began to roll away. I saw them as they rolled over in a great pit. They fell to the bottom, and there was a great noise. I saw old Satan with a host of his angels hop from the pit, and there they began to stick out their tongues at me and make motions as if to lay hand on me and drag me back into the pit. I cried out, "Save me! Save me, Lord!" And like a flash there gathered around me a host of angels, even a great number, with their backs to me and their faces to the outer world. Then stepped one in the direction of the pit. Old Satan and his angels, growling with anger trembling with fear, hopped back into the pit. Finally again there came a voice unto me saying, "Go in peace and fear not, for lo! I will throw around you a strong arm of protection. Neither shall your oppressors be able to confound you. I will make your enemies feed you and those who despise you, take you in. Rejoice and be exceeding glad, for I have saved you through grace by faith, not of yourself but as a gift of God. Be strong and fear not. Amen."

I rose from the ground shouting and praising God. Within me there was a crying, "Holy! Holy! Holy is the Lord!" I went on to the barn and found my master there waiting for me. Again I began to tell him my experience. I do not recall what he did to me afterwards. I felt burdened down, and that preaching was my only relief. When I had finished I left a great love in my heart, that made me feel like stopping and kissing the ground. My master sat watching and listening to me now he, too, began to cry. He turned to me and said in a broken voice, "Morte, I believe you are a preacher. From now on you can preach to the people here on my place, in the old shed by the creek. But tomorrow morning, Sunday, I want you to preach to my family and neighbors. So put on your best clothes and be in front of the big house early in the morning, about 9 o'clock."

I was so happy that I did not know what to do. I thanked my master and then God, for I felt that He was with me. Throughout the night I went from cabin to cabin, rejoicing and spreading the news.

The next morning at the time appointed I stood up on two planks elevated in front of the porch of the big house and, without a Bible or anything, began to preach to my master and the people. My thoughts came so fast that I could hardly speak fast enough. My soul caught on fire, and soon I had them all in tears. I told them that God has a chosen people, and that He raised me up as an example of His matchless love. I told them that they must be born again and that their souls must be freed from the shackles of hell.

Ever since that day I have been preaching the Gospel, and am not a bit tired. I can tell anyone about God in the darkest hour of midnight, for it is written on my heart. Amen.[57]

As in other conversion texts, the protagonist is freed from the fear of both hell and his master. He gains a new earthly role, elected as a preacher carrying the divine word.

Originally titled "I Came from Heaven and Now Return" in its Fisk publication, Radin renamed the text that follows, "The Water Cried, 'Unworthy, Unworthy'" in his "Souls" manuscript. Taken together, the titles capture the dominant conversion feature of movement toward redemption. After an initial vision of a kindly, wordless man, the narrator describes her burden as "it seemed that everything had turned against me" and even her drinking water cursed her. Muteness and immobility accompany the initial vision. Then, she "was killed to sin" and reborn through Jesus. In what Radin called "the crucial vision," the narrator walks through hell, seeing the devil and a mass of suffering people, but does not dwell on that encounter, instead following her deliverer into heaven, where she finds a welcoming home with God. A sense of regeneration, "I was new all over," accompanies her return to normal life, forever changed and anticipating her ultimate return to heaven.

The Water Cried, "Unworthy, Unworthy"

I was born a slave and have lived through some very hard times. If it had not been for my God I don't know what I would have done. Through His Mercy I was lifted. My soul began singing and I was told that I was one of the elected children and that I would live as long as God lived. I rejoice every day of my life for I know that I have another home, a house not made with human hands. A building is waiting for me way back in eternal glory, and I have no need to fear. He stood me on my feet and told me that I was a sojourner in a weary land. I came from heaven and now I am returning.

I have prayed ever since I was big enough to call on God. I was sold into slavery and sent to Mississippi to work on a cotton plantation. Even there I prayed; and after the war, I continued to pray.

In my first vision I saw, one evening, a man, tall and calm, come from the southwest and stand before me. He did not speak but he smiled and vanished.

A few days later, while I was living at Squire X, my husband took my daughters to a dance and I was left alone. I felt burdened down and it seemed as if everything had turned against me. I reached for a drink of water and the water cried out, "Unworthy, unworthy!" I ran into the other room and fell across the bed. There, I declare unto you, I was killed dead to sin and made alive again in Jesus Christ. I heard my husband when he drove up, heard him when he came into the house and heard him as he said, "Martha, what is the matter?" But I could neither speak nor move. My jaws were locked and my tongue stuck to the roof of my mouth.

In my vision I saw hell and started to walk through. I went a little way and came to a door. Then I saw a man, his head as white as cotton and clubfoot as red as fire. I looked beyond him and saw a great host of people with heads as white as cotton they were all groaning and wandering around as if in pain and sorrow. My heart became heavy and I prayed. I looked up and saw a man, unlike anyone I have ever seen before. He showed me a little path and said, "Follow me!" I cried out, "I thank God! I thank God!" This was all I could say. We walked on and climbed Zion's hill and there I saw the city. A voice spoke to me, "Come into Father's welcome house!" I entered and saw a host of children, all the same size, sitting around a table. The number was so great that I could not count them. They all have bowed to me three times and in unison cried, "Glory be the Lamb that was slain for the sins of the world!" A voice said, "Amen!"

When I left heaven I didn't walk. I seemed to have been rocking along.

When I came to, I looked at myself and I was new all over. I looked at my hands and my hands looked new; I looked at my feet and my feet looked new. I began shouting and praising God. I loved everybody and every creeping thing and I felt like getting down and kissing the very ground.

One night after this, while I was in bed with my husband, I saw a woman come out from the east. She was snow-white, and her hair hung down over her shoulders and her wings reached from her head to her feet. I wakened my husband and tried to make him see her but he said he didn't see anyone.

When God got through with me I spoke out of a full heart and said things that I didn't know I had in me. God has His own time and way of taking hold of His people and His words more than we read and think about. He is a true God and He won't make haste.[58]

In the dehumanizing world of slavery, the experience of conversion protected people from total derangement when they could not find the slightest human accommodation for themselves in unremitting servitude and brutalization. They suffered an unbroken assault on selfhood. Their humanity was in effect denied, even by the most benign slave masters, who could only see slaves as governed by coarse natural inclinations. The slave regime had portrayed the movement of Africans to the American South as acclimatization to a new environment, not to slavery itself. That is, slave owners believed that the institution of slavery was well known to Africans. As slaves in the New World, they left heathen darkness behind and entered civilization, where Christianity promised uplift and spiritual reward while providing slave owners a self-righteous myth of justification.

Of the collection, approximately one third of the narratives derive from people who were slaves but underwent conversion after 1865. A few depicted conversion during the slave era. The remaining narratives recall conversion in the years after the Civil War by those whose parents had been slaves. Although each account is highly personal, taken together they represent variations within an overall structure that reiterates the general pattern Arnold Van Gennep identified in his cross-cultural examination of rites of passage.[59] Each person underwent conversion through an individual experience, neither guided nor scripted by elders or others who had undergone conversion. There was no collective ritual socially embedded or located at a sacred site in the manner of many cross-cultural ethnographic cases. Those undergoing conversion, the large majority of whom did so individually outside the formal setting of a church service, sought to sever their relationship to an old life defined by slave masters or their successors; they were eager to separate themselves from a condition over which they had little control and particularly to transmute an identity that masters and overseers had imposed upon them. The radical change in self-conception, in one's orientation to the social and natural world, was in effect a rebirth, possible only through death of the old self.

People through Christian faith were seeking a lodestar, an immutable reference point, and a means of personal and communal validation and control in a world that for them was wholly unstable and uncertain, except for its callousness. In religion, the slave or survivor of slavery entered a supernatural world where his or her desired status was assured through conversion.

But theirs was a Christianity very different from what slave owners had promoted in their naive belief that Christian missionaries preaching acceptance of one's condition would stifle the slave's desire for freedom. Ever the rationalist, but respectful of the diverse worldviews he encountered in his own fieldwork or in other source materials, Radin could not avoid the obvious question he posed to an elderly man, a former slave who had endured much more than the usual cruelty. How was it possible for the old man to reconcile the abuse he suffered at the hands of Christians with his unquestioning belief in the benevolence of the Christian God? To Radin, he thundered, "Son, I put that doubt behind me long ago!"[60] This made perfect sense, for the rejection of Christianity, the only available system of transcendent meaning and certainty available, would have meant further psychological fragmentation and descent into emotional chaos.

A substantial part of the answer to Radin's question also lay in the slaves' reinvention of the Christian God. Alien to their experience and their needs, white Christian proselytizing gave way before African American religious inventiveness. That self-fashioning nurtured a new world of human dignity and promised immortality, ordained by a forgiving, compassionate divinity. The religious transformation effected by a distinctly black Christianity made people whole. That new state of being occurred through a rite of passage narrated as an experience of individual ordeal and death followed by spiritual rebirth and liberation of the soul unencumbered by the sin of doubt. The soul, on its odyssey toward deliverance, experienced physical obstacles and Satan and his minions. The journey, or travel of the soul, is sometimes rendered, without any loss of meaning, as "travail of the soul."

Thus in the eponymous "Souls Piled Like Timber," the narrator told Watson that God "began to talk and reveal Himself to me." Still, overcome by loneliness and worry, she sought solace in her Bible, when she spoke to God and He replied. Spurning hell and seeing "souls piled like timber," she took the road to heaven, delivered by God, who reassures her that He has protected her. As in other conversion texts, the narrator here is overcome with loneliness and despair. Her young daughter has died but comes to her with the reassurance that she is happy in heaven. Likewise, her deceased mother appears, telling her, "Don't forget the old folks."

It gives me pleasure to talk about God for He has done so many wonderful things. I could not, if I would, refrain from talking about Him. How He has dealt with others I do not know, but I do know what He has done for me.... One night, while I was cooking supper, I suddenly got very lonely and felt burdened down. I stopped cooking, got my Bible and sat down to read. Shortly after I started I lost sight of the world and saw myself (in the spirit) being led down a dark and lonely road, and as I went down the road it seemed to close behind me. I was praying inwardly to God saying, "Lord, have mercy!" For some reason I was caused to look up and I saw a light on my right. I said, "Lord, where am I?" He answered, "The road you are on leads to hell but the road on your right leads to heaven."

I looked down that dark pathway and saw what He called "the gulf of despair." I looked again and saw ... human souls piled like timber and everything was gloom and sadness. I cried to the Lord to deliver my soul and He lifted me from that gulf of darkness and started me to travelling in the upward road. . . .

I can never tell all that I have seen and heard for He has been so good to me. Once I prayed and said, "Lord, you have been so good to me." A voice answered, "Yes, I have been good to you. I stayed the hand of your enemies like as I stayed the hand of Abraham when he would slay his son, Isaac."[61]

While hell and the devil figure in many conversion narratives, they are more backdrop than developed features, and eternal torment and punishment receive equally scant narrative attention. Although the supplicant sees "souls piled like timber," the narrator is unconcerned with why they line the pathway to perdition, looking instead toward the upward road to heaven and the promise of grace. The secondary place of hell and the devil in the conversion narratives represents a defining transformation of the preachments of white ministers, as black people made Christianity their own, turning away from the white Christian view that sinfulness alone disqualifies one from heaven.

Radin argued that for black people, fitness for heaven was for the most part unrelated to sinfulness. The sinner, in the black perspective, is not condemned to eternal damnation and the fires of hell; he or she only suffers a delay in the ultimate redemption and rebirth. In the earlier text, "Born in a World of Heaven," the narrator has no fear of hell: "Even before God freed my soul and told me to go, I never was hell-scared. I just never did feel that my soul was made to burn in hell.[62] Black people could not easily accept the idea of hell presented by white preachers and, consequently, altered it to the point of reversal. That is, black people do not choose heaven, or prepare for it, but rather give themselves up completely to the will of God. The pattern of the conversion texts indicates that

God chooses His people and God comes at His own time. Again and again the narrators assure us that God does not come before time or after time, but just on time. It is God who does the choosing and the calling, not man. In other words, the moment a man feels heavy at heart, the moment he hears the voice, he really knows that he is to be saved from the jaws of hell; he will see himself in two parts and come back to life and human consciousness again, happy and shouting.[63]

Radin concluded that for the converted, "the two alternatives are not so much heaven or hell as heaven or nothing."[64] A white person, however, seeking heaven yet never knowing what his fate will be "debases himself more and more [and] emphasizes and exaggerates his sinfulness and complete unworthiness."[65] In this way, white people prepared themselves without certainty for what they hoped would be God's deliverance, although hellfire remained a real possibility.

Mr. Green was one of the two elderly former slaves from whom Radin collected life histories and whom Watson interviewed for his thesis. Regarding Mr. Green and Mr. Mason as authors, although nearly illiterate, Radin was reiterating a theme running through the entire body of his work. He consistently argued that intellectual unity characterized humankind and that analytical thinkers, or native philosophers, inhabit every society. Although a minority in each community, they are all equally capable, in Radin's view, of reflective metaphysical and existential thought, independent of the kind of society in which they live or their medium of expression. Writing and speaking are simply different channels for communicating ideas. Radin was not hesitant in referring to folklore and other spoken genres as "oral literature," a particularly clear effacement of the distinction between written and spoken forms. Thus, as an author, Mr. Green crafted an autobiography and a conversion narrative that eloquently conveyed the depravity of slavery and its perpetrators, the crushing debasement of human lives, and the unbending religious faith through which people humanized themselves and each other.

A thoughtful, reflective individual, Mr. Green was born in South Carolina. He believed that the lot of slaves among whom he lived was much better than on most plantations. But a fundamental cruelty of the slave system was particularly evident when his master decided to sell Mr. Green, then a young boy, who suffered throughout his life from that early separation from his mother. In conversion accounts, the journey to heaven is usually preceded by physical symptoms of heaviness, lethargy, pain, and the like. At other times, an overwhelming sadness, often recalling the death of a close kinsman, precedes the transcendent experience. For Mr. Green, a particularly admired informant both for Radin and Watson, a traumatic despondency following separation from his mother was the defining experience of his life.

On the morning I was sold and went to tell my mother good-bye she fainted. She was in the bed and I went to the door and said, "Good-bye, Mama, good-bye. It nearly broke her heart. She was in bed sick from the thoughts of me going away. She turned her face from me when I spoke and gave one groan and said, "Farewell, son, farewell." I left her with those words ringing in my soul and I have never ceased to remember that farewell until today.

On the day I left home everything was sad among the slaves. I took my little bundle of clothes, a pair of slips, a shirt and a pair of jeans and went to give Mama my last farewell. As I went, she came to the door and threw up her hand at me and said, "Farewell, son, farewell." When she said that she fainted and fell. Aunt Patsy picked her up and carried her back to her bed. I never expected to see her again in this life. But I did. It was after the war, though, and I had got free and found God and was preaching the gospel.

I went to Charleston. My master had a house there. He hired me out and I drove a cart until fall. The prices usually went up on slaves in the fall of the year. Along in September what was known as "nigger-traders" started to coming around Charleston which was a great trading post. When selling-time came we had to wash up and comb our hair so as to look as good as we could so as to demand a high price. Oh, yes, we had to dress up and parade before the white folks until they picked the ones they wanted. I was sold along with a gang of others to a trader and he took us up to Louisiana. There, I believe, I was sold to the meanest man that God ever put breath in. I got scars on me now that I will take to my grave. He knocked and kicked from sun to sun. Out of seventeen of us sold to him only four of us got back home. Some died, others he killed. He whipped from about three o'clock in the morning until eight and nine o'clock at night. It was awful to hear the poor slaves crying, "Oh, pray, master." Both men and women were whipped alike. I held one old man to be whipped and saw him beat to death. I don't know how many he beat to death but I came near being killed myself. I have a scar on my chest now as large as my fist that came from a blow he gave me with a knotted stick. He not only beat his slaves nearly to death, but he took many of the women off and cohabitated with them almost in our sight. I lived through it all praying to God every day for deliverance.

Up until the time I was sold down in Louisiana, I didn't know what hard times were but from the first day I got on that plantation my troubles began and they lasted until I got free. I was a young boy and had never done much work. About the time I was sold I had just started to driving a cart about the place, hauling wood, trash and doing odd jobs. Aside from this I used to take care of the slave babies while the parents in the field at work. So I hadn't done any work like I had to do in Louisiana.

As I look back over it now I don't wonder that I felt as I did. I just gave up all earthly hopes and thought all the time about the next life. I had promised to meet my mother in glory and I never missed a day going out in the bushes to pray. I didn't pray much. The biggest thing I would say was "Lord, have mercy on me" or "Lord, save my soul." I was whipped and knocked every day for what I had done as well as for what I failed to do. I will go to my grave with that knot on my chest as big as a man's fist. It is the result of a blow my owner gave me with a stick. Though I suffered then from hardships and though I still have pains from this scar I hold no hatred toward anybody. I have always said that man was a devil on earth, but I have forgiven him. The same God that made the good made the evil and I guess He knows what is best.

After the war I got a partner and we started out sharecropping. I took fresh courage and began to see life a little different but there was one thing that never left me and that was the last promise I had made to meet my mother in Glory. I had never ceased to pray, but it looked like my burden got heavier. I went around some with other boys and danced and had a good time a little, but every now and then the thought would come to me, "Remember the promise you made to your mother to meet her in Glory." This thought always restrained me whenever I would attempt to go too far. I kept praying and seeking because I thought my mother was dead or even if she wasn't dead, I didn't know that I would ever see her again for every way I turned I found somebody looking for mother, father, sister, son or brother. In many cases separation had been so long that many times brothers and sisters would meet and would not know each other. They were sold here and there and changed their names so much that it was hard for even mothers to make themselves known to their children, if lucky enough to find them.[66]

Mr. Green told Radin of his crucial vision, immediately prompted by the great despair he felt in trying to reunite with his mother. He was so burdened that he could only think of death and his promise to his mother to meet her in heaven, although she survived and was living in South Carolina. He was uncertain about how he could travel there from Louisiana, where he had been sold. While working, he was overwhelmed by hunger, faintness, and illness, and collapsed, believing he was about to die. He also struggled with unidentified sins. Envisioning the brink of hell described by many other narrators, his soul took flight from his body as he heard a reassuring voice saying, "Trust and believe." As in other narratives, the voice might be that of God, or Christ, or a divine messenger. Significantly, Mr. Green likened hell and heaven to enslavement and emancipation, each pair thematically reiterated by the difference between darkness and light, the old body and the new.

CONVERSION OF MR. GREEN: AN ABBREVIATED VERSION
AS TOLD TO ANDREW POLK WATSON

From the time I was sold away from my people in South Carolina and carried and sold to that mean man in Louisiana, I prayed every day. I wasn't nothing but a young boy, but I didn't see no hope for the future. The last word my mother said to me when we parted was "Son, remember to pray and try to meet me in heaven." These words stayed with me. I never missed a day praying. There wasn't nothing to live for. I just gave up to die. I would have welcomed death. But the Lord had a work for me to do. The war came and the slaves got freed. This gave me hope. But my thoughts stayed on God and the last words of my mother: "Pray son! Pray and try to meet me in heaven." Along about the close of the war, after I got freed and started to working for myself, I began to feel burdened with sin. My food seemed to swell in my mouth. Finally I gave up everything, stopped trying to eat and told my partner that I would not try to eat and drink until I had found God. He said, "I'll be damned if you won't die." About two days later while I was chopping in the field, my burden got heavier than I could bear. I fell to the ground on my face. I said, "Good-bye everybody. I'm going to die." I immediately lost sight on the world. When I found myself, I was stretched out on the brink of a dark pit. I heard voices crying, "Cool water! Cool water!" I saw my helpless condition and surrendered myself to God. A voice on the inside of me began to cry "Lord have mercy, save my soul." No sooner had I surrendered myself and the voice on the inside cried that the work was done. It was like lightning. A great light shone from above. A calm but powerful voice spoke from mid-air saying, Free, Free! Lo, I am the way; trust and believe." When I heard these words, a burden seemed to fall from me and my soul took a leap. A man came out of a man. It was my soul all dressed up and having wings to fly like a dove. I flew into a world of light with thousands of other beings like myself. I left my old body stretched out on the brink of hell. I have never experienced such joy and happiness as I came into that morning. I will never forget it, for it was the day that me and God met. All the time we were flying along, a voice was crying, "Peace, peace!" I don't know where it was coming from nor the light either. Neither do I know when my soul came back to the old earthly body or whether it ever came back. I only know that when the heavenly vision faded, I found myself there in the field where I first fell on the ground. From that day, I felt called to preach. For sixty years I carried the message of God. I didn't know how to read, but God opened my understanding.[67]

The self-aware, creative narrators in Radin's ethnographic work among native peoples of the New World are equally present in "Souls Piled Like Timber," where they experience the gentle, reassuring voice of a loving God. Accordingly, the religious reformulation documented by Radin and Watson spurned the punitive, sin-obsessed divinity of white preaching and doctrinal Christianity. The religion of the slave master and his successor had spoken little to the needs of human beings oppressed at every turn. Threats of hell, eternal damnation, or a lurking Satan had little place in an evolving black theology attuned to people experiencing an earthly hell each day. The hell that threatened white Baptists and Methodists who violated canonical Christianity had little place among the narrators. For the latter, less than perfect faith was the greatest sin, while the worldly transgressions of white Christianity, such as drinking and sexual indulgence, were of little note in the black conversions.

In Watson's view, emergent African American religion was fulfilling the spiritual longings of enslaved field hands in a way that the early nineteenth-century white-led camp meetings in the woods of Kentucky and Tennessee could not. Unlettered and degraded, these same field hands, as Watson remarks, had turned their "originality and ingenuity," their "imaginative genius" to a profoundly meaningful reformulation of the beliefs presented to them by white missionaries and others.[68] In Radin's summation of the reinterpretive process, it appeared that people were not so much seekers after God but rather those whom God was seeking. They had to be worthy. And in the process of conversion, God became, unalterably, the immovable point of reference that enabled people to gain a wholly new personhood, deserving of love and respect if they would only embrace an unshakable faith. The slaves thereby repudiated what every slave owner depended on—an encompassing denial of their humanity. At the same time, they also gained the certain expectation of heaven, which they had already seen, having died and been reborn into paradise before returning to their mortal lives, spiritually emancipated from the fearful and denigrating circumstances that enveloped them. Religion embodied a human resourcefulness—psychological, intellectual, and emotional—enabling slaves to separate themselves from the dehumanizing circumstances of daily life. Through the efforts of Radin and Watson, their purposeful voices of travail and transcendence endure as a unique historical record.

CHAPTER 5

The Winnebago Narrations

Tradition and Transformation

Beginning in 1908 and for the next five years, Paul Radin visited Winnebago settlements in Nebraska and Wisconsin. Publishing his doctoral dissertation in 1911, Radin focused on the Medicine Dance, the single most important ritual among the Siouan-speaking Winnebago. He compared it to the Mide'wiwin, or medicine societies of the Ojibwa and Menominee, Algonquin-speaking peoples with whom the Winnebago shared a considerable array of cultural features. The Winnebago had guarded the cosmological secrets of the Medicine Dance, believing that its betrayal to uninitiated outsiders would bring death. Radin's recording of the Medicine Dance occurred as the new, schismatic peyote religion was emerging. The converts to peyotism, Radin's most important informants, cooperated in his research. They told him of the new religion and disclosed the esoterica of the Medicine Dance. The latter no longer defined their religious lives, and, newly liberated from the fearful consequences of narrating the ritual, they conveyed its mysteries, including the all-important ceremonial sequences ensuring reincarnation. Radin pursued details of the Medicine Dance, knowing that his research was exacerbating the religious and social breach between the peyotists and followers of the old ways. The ethical sensibilities of Radin and his peers were quite obviously very different from those of post-1960s anthropology.

Equally divisive were very different visions of the role of Earthmaker, or God, in the lives of people. The traditional relationship between human beings and Earthmaker was indirect. Various spirits served as intermediates between humanity and divinity. While Earthmaker gives life to humans, he does not grant blessings, nor do humans worship him. While Earthmaker created humanity, spirits, and lesser deities, "neither the spirits and deities nor man regard this fact as entitling him to gratitude or worship."[1] He is rather a supreme god far removed from humanity, entering into a relationship with people only through the intercession of mediating transcendent powers, to whom people make sacrifices, particularly tobacco.[2] Of profound import, tobacco is the single object of creation that Earthmaker placed under human control, thus establishing a continuing interdependence between spirits and people. Coveted by the spirits, burnt tobacco as an offering to them represented a channel of communication to the numinous world and guaranteed that they, rather than Earthmaker, would turn their powers toward the needs of their human supplicants.[3] This is an ethnographic fact of considerable importance, since the traditional role of Earthmaker was inverted by the peyotists, who spurned tobacco sacrifice, the spirit world, and their personal use of tobacco. That is, the new peyote religion defined a direct connection, unmediated by spirits, between peyote worshippers and divinity. That immediacy appealed to adherents of the new faith, or at least to Radin's principal informants, as their easy access to Earthmaker was enabling them to remake troubled lives.

The disruption of familiar life patterns and beliefs in the wake of white intrusion across the broad range of American Indian societies provoked a variety of religious and cultural responses, including peyotism. These changes were unfolding even as native peoples continued to maintain some hope of turning back white settlement. Religious changes ranged from revivalism and nativism in A. F. C. Wallace's terms, to the adoption of Christianity and accompanying European cultural practices.[4] Among the Winnebago prior to white contact, clans and religious societies, each part of a complex division of ritual and ceremonial labor and organized in relationship to particular spiritual powers, had controlled human access to unseen forces. The success of ritual and ceremonial action and its continuity through time depended, then, on stability and order in the structure of social life, particularly in those groups charged with religious responsibilities. Peyotism entailed almost immediate accessibility to Earthmaker, once the drug was ingested. The new religion flourished amid changes in the social units that had once looked to spirits and other mystical forces rather than to Earthmaker for blessings and religious direction.

Converts to peyotism on whom Radin relied included John Rave, Oliver Lamere, Jasper and Sam Blowsnake, and Albert Hensley. They spurned drinking, gambling, and flouting of kinship obligations, explaining that the new religion arrested all destructive behaviors associated with white conquest. Their accounts of adopting peyotism contain some striking convergences with African American conversion narratives, including particularly direct communication with Earthmaker, the perception of one's death and rebirth, and a near-ecstatic, sublime joy in the feeling of connectedness to all people and all things. Similarly, neither African American converts nor Winnebago peyotists blending peyotism and Christianity expressed undue fear or concern about hellfire, the devil (sometimes expressed by the Winnebago as evil spirits), or eternal damnation. The immortality of the soul was a promise both in African American conversions and in peyotism. The lack of fear among the Winnebago peyotists is associated with a general rejection of traditional religious elements in favor of the acceptance of a new, personal relationship with Earthmaker, spontaneously realized after peyote consumption.

Dismissive of composite representations of people that filled the pages of anthropological monographs, Radin was determined to bring to light distinct personalities, their social relationships, and their rejection of the Medicine Rite. Yet that interest in unique individuals is belied by his attribution of particular statements to more than one person. For example, one of Jasper Blowsnake's accounts of the peyote religion and his experience with the drug that originally appeared in 1923 reappears in nearly verbatim form three years later in *Crashing Thunder,* narrated by Sam Blowsnake.[5] It is more than ironic and not a little confusing that Radin would attribute the same words to Sam and to Jasper Blowsnake. This is not a singular case since Radin in a number of other instances assigns authorship of the same narrative passage to different people. With the same indifference, Radin sometimes lifted passages from his previous publications and inserted them into new articles without informing the reader. Since there were two Crashing Thunders—the real named individual (Jasper) and the published narrator, his brother (Sam), who assumed the name, Radin either conflated those identities, wittingly or not, or else felt that the issue didn't matter. But of course it does matter, especially in light of Radin's robust, oft-stated views about the narrations of named, historical individuals.

Radin wanted his readers to believe that the Blowsnakes and others were best understood by closely attending to their words and to their representations of personal experience as they knew it and lived it. Their words might appear in their life histories, or in their narrations of the myths and rites of the Medicine Dance, or in their experiences with peyote. Radin had no a priori expectation that because two people were Winnebago their experiences in any domain of social life would be the same or nearly so, shaped and directed by cultural tradition. For that reason, the Two Crows phenomenon of inconsistent testimony from multiple informants, a problem for Edward Sapir, was in Radin's view more pattern than exception in anthropological fieldwork and required no explanation. Ostensibly keeping the unique person in view, Radin did not accept the tendency of his colleagues to posit the representative individual, embodying his or her culture as abstracted by the anthropologist from field notes. John Rave, who introduced peyotism to the Winnebago; Lamere; the Blowsnake brothers; and Hensley were his principal informants and are thus well known in his writings and in a large secondary literature. The lives of these informants and others reflected the changes, including religious conflict, that inevitably altered Winnebago society. Consistent with Radin's vision of anthropology, their identities were never subordinated to, inferred from, or utilized to create a cultural template.

Radin's extensive Winnebago publications reach into the thousands of pages, requiring for present purposes a careful selection that establishes, on the one hand, the context and purpose of his Winnebago fieldwork and, on the other, the relationship between his Winnebago and African American research. After examining Radin's findings on Winnebago expressive culture—the meanings inhering in ritual, folklore, and visionary experience—it will then be possible to ask what bearing that work had on his subsequent collection of African American narratives. That is, can it be ascertained if—in working on the Nebraska plains beginning in 1908, then in Wisconsin, and some twenty years later in Nashville—Radin discovered a shared understanding of revelation and self-inscription, a unitary psychic substrate below the variability of culture and experience? The question certainly interested him throughout his career, and the possibility of a universal cross-cultural psychology inevitably touched the interests of Carl Jung and others associated with the Bollingen. But characteristically, Radin followed his own path, remaining skeptical of Jung's quest for universals in the absence of field experience. For Radin, fieldwork was the sine qua non for writing authoritatively about religion, philosophy, or any other dimension of non-Western experience. Still, the question of the psychic unity of humankind is apparent in much of Radin's work, ranging from the universal character of the trickster, as creator and destroyer, to the sagacious meditations of philosophers in every kind of society, to the psychological requirements of the normal self. Radin's ruminations about selfhood within a distinct cultural context provide the most promising point of comparison between his Winnebago and African American findings.

Winnebago, Nebraska, 1908: Radin Begins Fieldwork

The arrival of an anthropologist at a new locale sometimes prompts local speculation about the sudden appearance of the stranger.[6] In Nashville, Radin's presence among elderly African Americans was substantially mediated and explained by his student and collaborator Andrew Polk Watson. Despite Radin's empathic understanding of the devastation of slavery and the myth of race, the barriers of history and color were so formidable that it is very unlikely he could have proceeded without Watson or another equally talented African American investigator, particularly one associated with Fisk University. A number of the former slaves lived nearby. There is no record, however, of any Nashville informants pondering the reason for Radin's presence beyond what he and Watson said when presenting themselves.

A very different response occurred twenty years earlier when Radin, at Boas's suggestion, embarked on doctoral research among the Winnebago of Nebraska.[7] Radin's arrival, coinciding with John Rave's initial success in gaining converts to peyotism, evoked a remarkable local response. Described by the anthropologist, "I was the preordained one who had sensed what was the proper time to come to the Winnebago, and this legend he [Crashing Thunder] diligently disseminated among all his relatives and subsequently embodied in certain autobiographical snatches I obtained from him."[8] In Mark Van Doren's more dramatic version, Radin's would-be informants concluded that "he must have been sent by God, since he came at precisely the moment in their history when success was possible."[9] Yet Radin, the young fieldworker not yet thirty, embarked on his initial ethnographic investigation unaware of these circumstances:

> Why 1908 proved to be so propitious for Rave's propaganda it is difficult to say. But it did prove so, and the Nebraska division of the Winnebago soon found itself split into two contending camps, the peyote-eaters and the so-called pagans.
>
> It was into this atmosphere of conflicts and dissensions, where all men's minds were unusually disturbed and perturbed and where feelings and emotions ran high, that I unwittingly stepped on my ethnological field-trip. Nor was I in the least aware that my coming at that particular time meant more than it would have

meant five years before. As it was my first anthropological field-trip, I was both bewildered and ill at ease.[10]

But Radin soon realized that he had before him the extraordinary but unanticipated opportunity of documenting the birth of a new religion.

It was as if an anthropologist had witnessed the earliest successes of the Seneca prophet Handsome Lake, or the Paiute visionary and Ghost Dance founder, Wovoka. In the latter case, James Mooney worked with Wovoka and was a participant-observer in Ghost Dance performances among several Plains tribes when the movement held its greatest appeal in late 1890 and the early months of 1891. This fieldwork was of course the basis for Mooney's great landmark work on the Ghost Dance.[11] His ethnographic coverage also included a visit to the Winnebago, who had remained indifferent to Wovoka's movement.[12] Although the Ghost Dance enlisted many believers among the Lakota (Sioux) and other Plains groups, Radin was unconcerned with understanding why the Winnebago turned away from the Ghost Dance. The reasons for their indifference might well have shed considerable light on the dynamics of social change, but Radin was much more committed to the recovery of Winnebago tradition.

Siouan speakers originating in Wisconsin, the Ho-Chunk had absorbed multiple influences of the linguistically related Iowa and Oto as well as proximate Algonquin speakers, the Fox and Ojibwa. Along with other anthropologists of the Boas group, Radin wanted to document a way of life prior to the accumulating acculturative transformations refiguring American Indian societies. There was inevitably a sense of urgency in view of the ubiquitous evidence that the social order of personal relationships, economic and political arrangements, and religion—integrally formed generations before—had waned, and that memories would also fade in time. Much of the motive force driving those changes was the injustice of government Indian policy. Omer Stewart succinctly described the conquest and reservation resettlement that instigated the changes radically altering the way of life of the Winnebago. It was a continuing process that modeled the nineteenth-century experience of Indian peoples across the Plains:

> They had suffered as others had in the thrust of civilization, their numbers being greatly reduced in the middle of the nineteenth century as a result of disease, warfare, and continual displacement by the U.S. government. After giving up their lands in Wisconsin, they were forced for a time to live in various places in Iowa,

Minnesota, and South Dakota, where they were usually so unhappy that they were only kept on their reservations by the use of troops. Finally, in 1863, most Winnebago accepted a reservation in northeastern Nebraska next to that of the Omaha, who sold part of their reservation to accommodate the Winnebago.[13]

Radin observed that the fundamental reordering of the political economy in the wake of conquest effectively marginalized Winnebago culture, while daily living became "a hopeless blend of Indian and white."[14]

Marginalization occurred in relationship both to American society and to Winnebago aboriginality, set in motion at the point of European contact, when the French appeared in the mid-seventeenth century.[15] Economic destruction, the breakdown of village organization, and the development of labor patterns virtually indistinguishable from whites did not at the same time signal integration on equal terms of the Winnebago and white settlers into the widening American political order. Other ruinous changes in Winnebago expressive culture, including religion, ritual, and mythology, were also occurring much more slowly.

The Winnebago religious complex that remained intact was losing relevance to new ways of reservation living. In short, ideology and social life were no longer synchronous. The still existent system of meaning, woven through ritual and myth, had been cut adrift from its social moorings; it then underwent what Radin called "petrification." He observed that the disjunction between the old Winnebago ideological superstructure and social, political, and economic life in 1908 spurred "a complete retreat from reality." By this phrase, he did not imply mental disso-ciation or disturbance but rather the unreality of an ideological system with no ostensible relationship to contemporaneous social and political circumstances. The breakdown of unilineal descent embedded in the clan system and exogamy, for example, diminished the ceremonial cycle organized through kinship. Likewise, time-honored ceremonies that centered on war bundles and the accumulation of prestige in battle, or counting coup, lost their immediate raison d'être with the enforced termination of warfare.

Radin wanted to obtain a true insider's account of Winnebago life rendered directly and in the vernacular. When he began, he was not cognizant of John Rave's growing success in challenging the old rituals and ideological order. The steady adoption of the new religion freed people from the fearful customary constraints against revealing the secrets of Winnebago ritual, particularly those that had surrounded the sacrosanct Medicine Dance. In seeking an inside view of Winnebago traditional practice, Radin at an earlier time would probably have failed to procure texts describing the Medicine Dance. However, his arrival in 1908 was perfectly, if unintentionally timed, for at that moment conversion to peyotism was accelerating, memories of the Medicine Dance were immediate, and fear of divulging its secrets by former Medicine Dance participants was abating. Obeisance to traditional religion, once imperative, was losing its hold among an increasing number of people.

The new religion mixing Christian elements with the visions induced by consumption of the hallucinogenic peyote mushroom brought the converts into an immediate relationship with God, whom the new adherents identified with peyote itself. The rapid growth of peyotism near the moment of Radin's arrival culminated in the formation by the Nebraska Winnebago in 1921 of the Peyote Church of Christ—the first Plains group to incorporate a peyote church outside of Oklahoma. The following year it was renamed the Native American Church of Winnebago, Nebraska.[16] At the same time, Radin gained access to the complex of rites constituting the Medicine Dance since his peyotist informants were intimately familiar with its cryptic inner features but no longer in its thrall. He proceeded to gather the texts that would not only portray the perspectives of his key informants, but would also sketch the community of which they were a part.

Text and Language

Radin, in a preface to his wide-ranging ethnography *The Winnebago Tribe,* acknowledges his mentor to whom "he is under especial obligations for directing him to the Winnebago, for the methods of research inculcated in him at Columbia University, and particularly for impressing upon him the necessity of obtaining as much information as possible in text."[17] Radin sought native verbatim accounts of religious ritual and belief in the spirit of Boasian salvage ethnography and the native point of view. He wanted to document Winnebago religion while it was still possible, but by 1908 when he began fieldwork, the acculturative process had rendered a number of ritual and religious practices inaccessible except through memory. He was thus unable to witness many of the ceremonial behaviors that his informants described. It is important to note, however, that Radin had little interest in participant-observation, and across the wide range of topics he wrote about, very little derives from close scrutiny of events as they unfolded, or from a personal response to local activities he witnessed.

Although interested primarily in religion, ritual, and worldview, Radin did not restrict himself to those topics. He also documented traditional Winnebago social structure, which provided the organizational framework, particularly through clanship, of the religious practices that consumed his attention. But here too, particularly, any observation of the functioning of clans and their religious duties was also unattainable, according to Radin, who provided the following warrant for salvage ethnography:

> The Winnebago social organization has long since broken down, but its details are still so well preserved in the minds of the older men, and particularly in the literature of the tribe, that no difficulty was experienced in reconstructing it.[18]

Radin's claim was overstated. Important but often unanswerable questions arose, such as the relationship of the Winnebago moiety system, or the "twofold division of the tribe," to their respective social and ceremonial functions.[19] Other questions also failed to provide fully satisfactory answers in the process of historical reconstruction.

Radin's interest in texts and self-inscription converged in three landmark autobiographies. Beginning with his doctoral dissertation, "Personal Reminiscences of a Winnebago Indian,"[20] Radin focused on Jasper Blowsnake, born "Crashing Thunder." Subsequently, Radin published *The Autobiography of a Winnebago Indian* in 1920 and a revised and expanded version, *Crashing Thunder: The Autobiography of an American Indian,* in 1926, based on the first-person narrations of Sam Blowsnake, Jasper's younger brother. Sam at birth had received the name "Big Winnebago," chosen by his maternal grandmother to mark her unmixed Ho-Chunk ancestry. According to Nancy Lurie, Radin believed the name "Big Winnebago" might convey a kind of mockery, or, as Lurie put it, the "'heap big Indian school' of fiction writing."[21] Consequently, he decided on the much more stirring and evocative "Crashing Thunder," the actual name of his favorite informant, Jasper Blowsnake, and his first life-history subject.

Radin's rationale for collecting autobiographies occurs for the first time in his introduction to *The Autobiography of a Winnebago Indian.* He remarks that a particular shortcoming in ethnology is the difficulty, "one might almost say the impossibility," of securing a view from the cultural inside. Usually, informants are content simply to meet the expectations of the ethnologist, often resulting in a failure to secure the true subjectivity that an inside view affords. Most informants, further, are too busy living their culture rather than reflecting about it and cannot provide the kind of intimate, immersive perspective Radin sought. An extended period of residence, even to the point of becoming a member of the community, could obviate some of the obstacles the ethnologist faces, but investigators can hardly devote so large a segment of their lives to a field project. Autobiography provided one way out of the dilemma since many informants are willing and interested in providing personal reflections, sometimes at considerable length.[22] This was certainly the case with Jasper Blowsnake and Sam Blowsnake. The anthropologist's subsequent account would then derive neither from his own suppositions nor from an informant's fragmented answers to direct questioning, but rather from "an interpretation of his life and emotions from within."[23]

Devoted to history and believing it integral to anthropology, Radin nonetheless had a very jaundiced view of professional historical scholarship. He objected to historical generalizations about matters that, "from the very nature of the case, he [the historian] could only remotely understand." Frequently occurring scholarly mistakes, "ludicrous and appalling," occur in dealing with human complexity, "man himself in all his vagaries, his inconsistencies, and his lack of direction." As a result, Radin cynically concludes that a common attitude regards "history as a pleasant, amiable, but wholly imaginative record of man as he never existed." His remarks appear in *Crashing Thunder,* a book he believed would point the way toward proper historical and ethnological scholarship.[24]

Radin's singular commitment to understanding how people thought about their world in their own terms through their own language tested his formidable linguistic proficiency. Still, Radin made ample use of the services of a translator, Oliver Lamere, although J. David Sapir, in his posthumous tribute to Radin, remarked that he "spoke their language as well as any white man could hope."[25] Radin, more than many anthropologists, was commendably forthright about his language skills in the field. They were considerable, but he never achieved near-native competence in the language, and despite his abilities, he made no attempt to translate texts without the participation of Lamere.[26]

Like Radin, Boas had posited ideal but unattainable conditions for fieldwork, including very long-term residence and near native fluency in the local language. Every anthropologist, then, could only achieve a very imperfect outcome. Boas and Radin also were of one mind in focusing on the insider's point of view through the collection of native texts. But as to autobiographical narratives, Radin's mentor had little regard for them. Boas believed that life histories deal with memory, conditioned by various factors at the moment of collection, not with facts. Personal experience, particularly, is subject to the vagaries of time, resulting in variations in the same narrative line collected at different periods.[27] By current standards and what anthropologists have learned in the interim, Boas's reservation is a point well taken. Nevertheless, oral history remains a valued tool for unlocking the past if the historian or anthropologist applies the same critical scrutiny to the oral "document" as he would to any conventional written source. Boas's critique focused too sharply on the "historicity" of oral narrative, for he left aside the utility of the life history in revealing the contours of social relationships and cultural values. Radin said as much when he introduced *The Autobiography,* saying his aim was "not to obtain autobiographical details about some definite personage, but to have some representative middle-aged individual of moderate ability describe his life in relation to the social group in which he had grown up."[28]

For collecting texts, Radin utilized three methods. One, phonographic recordings played a very minor role in his research and were employed primarily for Winnebago songs. Far more important was Radin's transcription of spoken texts using modified phonetic symbols, eventually streamlined by his own notations, "a kind of shorthand" enabling him to produce written texts at a rate only slightly slower than the informant's narration. Radin's success in transcription derived not simply from his very substantial linguistic abilities but also from the social situation. He was trusted by his informants, almost all of whom were peyotists interested in the research. At times, he also paid informants. Lamere's presence also conveyed the feeling among informants that Radin was an appropriate audience. A narration also went well when the narrator simply forgot Radin's presence, an indicator of success that Radin later achieved in Nashville, where he claimed a self-imposed rule of never interrupting a narrator. Watson, like Lamere, also reassured informants in Nashville that Radin could be trusted.

Radin's third and most frequent method of text collection depended on the Winnebago syllabary, a set of symbolic notations each representing a syllable. Adapted from the Fox syllabary in the 1880s, the Winnebago version was utilized by key informants such as Sam Blowsnake in writing his story for the anthropologist. Radin was well aware of the advantages and disadvantages of his methods of recording narratives, recognizing that each instance is artificial, whether an informant speaks into a mechanical device, dictates to an ethnologist, or writes without an audience. Well in advance of other anthropologists and folklorists, Radin raised the question of how writing influences oral literature, noting how the medium produced new opportunities for creativity and self-expression, particularly for the Blowsnakes. For example, using the syllabary, Sam Blowsnake included his personal ruminations about the narrative he was setting down on paper. Radin felt that such digressions, uncharacteristic of oral performance before an audience, represented innovations made possible by writing, owing to "elimination of an immediate, visible and controlling audience and the leisure provided for reflection, selection and correction."[29]

Peyotism against Tradition

Radin's original plan depended on a willingness of key informants to reveal heretofore secret lore at the heart of traditional religion without fearing that betrayal of abstruse rituals and beliefs would bring catastrophe and death. His principal collaborators and informants were adherents of peyotism. They rejected key elements of traditional belief and practices, including conceptions of God (Earthmaker), reincarnation, tobacco offerings, puberty visions, war bundle ceremonies, and the all-important Medicine Dance with its accompanying ceremonies and mythology.[30]

In cooperating with Radin, the peyotists helped to defuse the power that the Medicine Dance held over individual lives. Spurning the promised oblivion fated for those revealing Winnebago mysteries to the uninitiated, they believed that the continued observance of traditional religion was detrimental to proper living. Prepared and even eager to disclose and discredit once venerable beliefs, Radin's informants faced the strong opposition of conservatives equally committed to the preservation of the religion they had always known. Believing that it was doomed but determined to document precontact religion, Radin could do so through the cooperation of the peyotists. The latter doubted the value of the remaining customary rituals, rooted in an earlier time when they had defined the Winnebago as a people and were integrally linked to social and political organization.

Among the Nebraska Winnebago, there was no middle ground between Rave, Lamere, the Blowsnake brothers, and other converts to peyotism, on the one hand, and religious conservatives, on the other. Tensions over traditional religion and practice sharply defined the contours of the old and new faiths. While the peyotists had no objection when Radin sought information from the conservatives, the opposite was not usually the case. The conservatives were unwilling to reveal secret knowledge to anyone who had not been initiated into the Medicine Dance, including Radin, whose access to ritual secrets was considered illegitimate.[31] Consequently, virtually all of Radin's understanding of local religion, particularly, derives from people who had adopted the new peyote practices, although somehow he managed to attend two meetings where a Medicine Dance ceremony was performed.[32] Intriguing as this is, Radin, who preferred talk to observation, did not describe what he witnessed. Likewise, other features of "tradition" in its various mutable forms and fragments had a discernible staying power, recognized by Radin but far afield from his interests.

Some traditionalists, however, cooperated with Radin but only in regard to the narration of a narrow range of tales. In one instance, the incongruity of traditional ideology and contemporary life is manifest in Radin's introduction to the myth "How an Orphan Restored the Chief's Daughter to Life." It is a notable example of Radin's textual recording, using his modified phonetic system. The myth, one of a corpus of four myths concerning the human connection to the spirit world, death, and reincarnation, presents an anomaly, analyzed in Lévi-Strauss's structural tour de force, "Four Winnebago Myths."[33] Radin collected the aberrant myth in 1909 from Charles Houghton, "without question the best raconteur I encountered among the Winnebago." An important figure in the Medicine Dance and an implacable opponent of the peyote religion and any other influence that questioned or undermined religious custom, Houghton of course knew of Radin's association with the peyotists. Yet he remained an amiable informant, restricting his cooperation, however, to the narration of myths and folktales that did not reveal the arcana of rituals and ceremonies connected to the Medicine Dance. Although part of the conservative faction that protected cosmological tradition, he was decidedly not conservative regarding Winnebago material changes. That is, Houghton was convinced that the traditional economy could not be recovered and that Winnebago adoption of the new economic order should proceed quickly. Houghton's attitude is indicative of the generally uneven pace of social change.[34]

Houghton's ready acceptance of the new economy amid his deep religious conservatism suggests that the Boasian preoccupation with salvage ethnography was likely less nuanced than it might have been. Tradition, including institutions, practices, and beliefs, is not unitarily swept away; components of a particular way of life do not change in tandem. Believing that reliable historical reconstruction depended on the survival of those who had participated in the old ways, the Boas group proceeded with a distinct urgency. However, some traditional practices and beliefs actually persisted amid change, sometimes in modified form and integrated into new patterns of behavior. A case in point is the diffusion of the peyote cult across the Plains.

Radin observed that a unique feature of peyotism—the abandonment of traditional ceremonies and the older ways of living—derived immediately from Rave's teaching. But the relinquishment of existent cultural features in favor of new elements was in principle thoroughly out of keeping with Plains history, where various tribes were accustomed to borrowing cultural elements from other groups without jettisoning their own practices. Those that adopted peyote did so without a wholesale condemnation of former religious traditions. Instead, they accepted in pragmatic fashion new ritual forms that could incorporate customary practices, or accommodate traditional observances, or rework borrowed elements as syncretic reinterpretations.

Lurie studied the Winnebago nearly forty years after Radin's initial work, focusing particularly on the life of Mountain Wolf Woman, youngest sister of the Blowsnakes. The anthropologist noted the bitterness of the schism between traditionalists and peyotists, and the unique religious profile this created for the Winnebago. That acrimony was atypical of other Plains groups, where imported religious innovations could be adapted to existing cultural practice. In many places, one could thus find activists combining Christianity and traditional religion, peyote and Christianity as in the Native American Church, and even traditional religion and peyote. But among the Winnebago, the latter possibility did not occur. Agreeing with Radin, Lurie observed that "peyote and traditional activists just don't exist."[35]

That peyotism was new or that it incorporated Christian elements was of little concern to the conservatives.[36] They opposed the practitioners of the new religion, for the latter had turned their backs on the rites of the ancestors and in various ways were emulating white people. Particularly troubling to conservatives was the rejection of the belief in reincarnation and the adoption of Christian ideas concerning the immortality of the soul. Finally, traditional believers disdained peyotists because the latter were literally iconoclasts, destroying sacred objects, including war bundles and medicine bags.[37] Stewart, however, took strong exception to the Lurie-Radin view, claiming that Rave and Albert Hensley, who expanded the Christian elements within peyotism, continued practicing traditional religion.[38]

Radin thus began his first fieldwork in an anxious, overwrought Nebraska community divided between adherents of the new faith who would cooperate with him and those holding onto long-established, closely guarded religious practices. Ironically, his access to the secrets of the Medicine Dance depended on those for whom ostensibly it held the least significance, if he and Lurie were correct. The peyotists, they believed, actively repudiated the sacrosanct core of traditional cosmology, thus precipitating a deep factional rift. Despite the schism, Radin was able to ease his way into Winnebago society as he carried a letter of introduction from Angel De Cora, an activist, artist-illustrator, and cousin of Oliver Lamere. De Cora had studied art at Smith College, graduating in 1896. Well acquainted with Boas, she taught at the Carlisle Indian School, where she introduced Boas to Indian students who could serve as linguistic informants.[39] She had also worked with Boas on the Winnebago language shortly before Radin went to Nebraska.[40]

The Moment in Their History: Emergent Peyotism and the Visions of John Rave

Peyotism began in Mexico, eventually moving northward, where Oklahoma became the epicenter of its rapid diffusion across the Plains. Many features of the peyote rite recur, shown by Stewart in his peyote element distribution survey covering some thirty societies.[41]

Ritual use of the hallucinogen presented the Winnebago with an alternative to traditional religion following acculturative changes that had swept over native North America. Widespread claims that peyote possessed near-miraculous healing properties induced many people to ingest it for the first time. A large number of first-time users were seeking relief from conditions resistant to other remedies. After a few peyote services, many looking to peyote only for relief of illness saw images of God. At a time when some people believed that the old ritual strategies had failed them, those visions quickly established the religious aura of peyote.

Rave first ingested the drug in Oklahoma in the early 1890s. In the manner of other Indian religious prophets, Rave also experienced personal crises prior to the onset of his visions. He had been a heavy drinker and irresponsible husband to a succession of wives. He was, moreover, severely distressed by the recent death of family members. Beginning in 1901, Rave tried to introduce peyote to the Nebraska Winnebago following his stay in Oklahoma. Initially, he found few converts. By 1905, however, a notable increase in peyote believers occurred as people found compatibility between peyotism and Christianity. Described by Radin, "many people now noticed that those connected with the Peyote cult were the only people in the tribe leading a Christian life."[42]

As a young person, Rave suffered great discontent, even torment when he failed to receive a puberty vision and the spiritual blessings that would accompany it. That his parents likely informed him of what the puberty vision would entail undoubtedly compounded Rave's distress at not achieving that spiritual coming of age and a relationship with the unseen world. The Winnebago puberty vision was akin to the vision quest of so many other American Indian groups on the Plains and eastward. Undoubtedly related to his inability to enter into spiritual contact in a puberty vision, he was ineligible for induction into the Medicine Dance. Although Rave was able to participate in other ceremonies, Radin inferred that his failure to realize beneficent spiritual contact in puberty and his consequent exclusion from the Medicine Dance ensured that he would have no public impact on the community. Rave's sense of alienation and status deprivation was so keen that his rejection of traditional religion was more than a matter of indifference. He had developed a deep animosity and contempt toward the Medicine Dance, finding his own religious salvation in the oppositional beliefs and practices embedded in peyotism.[43]

Rave's initial experience with the drug was terrifying, for he felt an alien presence within himself that would not leave, followed by images of a snake and the Winnebago water spirit. The latter two were harbingers of death in traditional thought, once again showing the persistence of customary belief amid social change. A third image conjured the devil, probably a composite of the Christian devil and an evil Winnebago spirit. Rave finally comprehended that peyote brought about the visions, including the final vision of God. However frightening, Rave's initial consumption of peyote brought on his first but very belated spiritual experience. Although he failed to achieve the expected revelations as a young person, peyote-induced visions followed the structure of the traditional puberty rite and lent some legitimacy to what he was experiencing under the influence of the drug. That is, the old puberty visions induced by fasting tended to elicit images of three spirits, all deceptive, followed by a fourth, or true spirit. For Rave, that true spirit was peyote, or God. He saw the beginnings of a new religion.

The next evening Rave, in company but fearful, once again ate peyote.

In the middle of the night I saw God. To God living up above, our Father, I prayed. Have mercy upon me! Give me knowledge that I may not say and do evil things. To you, O God, I am trying to pray. Do thou, O Son of God, help me, too. This religion let me know. Help me, O medicine, grandfather, help me! Let me know this religion!"

Thus I spoke and sat very quiet. And then I beheld the morning star and it was good to look upon. The light was good to look upon. I had been frightened during the night but now I was happy. Now as the light appeared, it seemed to me that nothing would be invisible to me. I seemed to see everything clearly.

Rave went on to celebrate the healing qualities of the drug, which remarkably cured him and his wife of a long-standing disease. The incipient religion was also a force for good, as it steered people away from destructive habits and, in the rapturous glow of a new, transformative faith, represented "a cure for everything bad."[44]

In common with other revitalization phenomena, peyotism among the Winnebago began with the visions of an individual in crisis.[45] As founder of the peyote cult among the Winnebago, Rave enjoyed growing success and personal recognition because he had become a proselytizer and prophet of a new gospel. (The term "cult," long embedded in the literature, like "primitive," has many negative connotations, yet flourished among anthropologists writing sympathetically about peyotism.)

Prophets were not a new phenomenon for the Winnebago, appearing periodically among native peoples of North America throughout the nineteenth century. The Shawnee prophet Tenskwatawa, brother of Tecumseh, influenced the Winnebago through his fateful predictions, advising people to abandon European practices and their own "bad customs." A revivalist, he urged a partial restoration of old values and ways that had fallen into disuse. Only in that manner could the people thrive in the radically altered circumstances created by white conquest.[46] Given the Shawnee prophet's disparagement of some Winnebago practices, peyotists felt a line of continuity from the prophet to the new peyote religion nearly a century later.[47] But whereas Tenskwatawa exhorted a selective revival of traditional practice, Rave disparaged both the recent and distant past through the embrace of a completely new religion that nonetheless contained unacknowledged elements of the old faith. For example, the sequence of three deceptive visions followed by a fourth, or true vision characterized what had long defined the fasting experience, and it carried over into Rave's revelatory understanding that his fourth vision under the influence of peyote was God.

The broad perception that the social order was no longer meeting the psychological needs of the people set the stage for Rave's success. According to Radin, Rave had to confront the source of anguish to succeed in his preaching. Local distress was due either to the many personal and social dislocations associated with white conquest and perfidy or to defects in the traditional way of life. "He accepted the second alternative," Radin writes. Then, he adds, "Why, I do not know. It was clearly one of the possible interpretations and had been taken by Winnebago prophets before him."[48]

Rave's attack on tradition derived, as noted, from his own inability to experience a puberty vision or to find efficacy in the Winnebago custom of ritual fasting. Sacrificial presentations to Earthmaker in the form of tobacco, eagle feathers, or other ritual objects held no meaning in light of his failure to experience the spiritual blessing at puberty when it was most important. But peyote gave him a direct, unmediated experience of God, liberated from all of the ritual and symbolic accoutrements of tradition that were at the same time emblematic of his spiritual inadequacy. He no longer needed or lamented them, once he prayerfully gave himself up to Peyote/God/Earthmaker:

> O medicine, grandfather, most assuredly you are holy! All that is connected with you, that I would like to know and that I would like to understand. Help me! I give myself up to you entirely!

Rave's salvation lay in turning away from the source of his torment—his failed internalization of the Winnebago sacramental complex—and his achievement of a new self-acceptance and status made possible by peyote. Exclusion from the Medicine Dance no longer mattered. In this respect, his conversion to peyotism recalls African American conversion as a redefinition of a person's relationship to God, bringing both certainty in one's worldview and a new, valued status and recognition. Ultimately enlisting other, like-minded people, Rave in his personal crises stimulated, in Wallace's revitalization formulation, "a deliberate, organized conscious effort by members of a society to construct a more satisfying culture."[49]

Radin's statement that Rave's preaching emphasized the defects in traditional life rather than acculturative changes begs an important question that Radin had no interest in addressing in a systematic way. Whether recognized or not by the actors, personal and social discontent rooted in conquest, reservation confinement, economic change, and the like certainly played a role in establishing their susceptibility to radical religious change, including the repudiation of the most sacred features of tradition. It could not have been otherwise, unless we mistakenly assume that psychological states occur outside of social and historical frameworks. Certainly, the individual psychological dimension looms large in peyotism, as it does in numerous revitalization movements, and Radin illuminates it in considering the subjective world of his principal informants. Any personal charisma Rave exhibited could have attracted some early followers, but it alone could not sustain peyotism as a revitalization movement. Similarly, peyote, owing to its medicinal qualities, might well have remained another efficacious botanical within the Winnebago pharmacopeia without stimulating a transformative movement. Notwithstanding Radin's pioneering work on how Rave and others represented the peyote experience in their own words, it leaves unanswered questions about how social and historical ferment led people to embrace a new religion. In other words, Radin did not address the social and historical genesis of psychological stress and dislocation except through the detailed experience of particular individuals.

Christian elements within Winnebago peyotism proved compatible with the burgeoning religion from the very beginning. The second night that Rave consumed the drug he saw God, invoked Jesus, and personified peyote with the honorific "medicine grandfather." The growing impact of Christianity on Winnebago peyotism, however, derived principally from Albert Hensley, a one-time student at the Carlisle Indian School. Having led a dissolute life like Rave—gambling, drinking, and doing the devil's work—Hensley found his salvation in peyote, which he easily incorporated into an abiding Christian faith. Through Hensley's influence, the Christian Bible found an important place in the new religion. Hensley likened the antagonism to peyote by established churches to hostility to Jesus's message at the outset of his preaching. Of peyote, Hensley said,

> It is a true religion. The peyote is fulfilling the work of God and the Son of God. When the Son of God came to the earth he was poor, yet people spoke against him; he was abused. It is the same now with the peyote. . . . They say that this is merely a plant, that it is the work of the devil. They are trying to stop its use and they are calling it an intoxicant. But this is a lie. If they will but come and see this ceremony they will realize this.[50]

Unlike Rave, who directed his anger against old Winnebago practice, Hensley saw his target as the traditional church, opposed to peyotism and constituted of people who had not achieved the "inner purification" that peyote made possible.[51]

The division between traditionalists and converts to the new religion was very much a division between old and young. The latter were able to press folklore into the service of the new religion by using the protean figure of Trickster, whose foolish behavior represents the unthinking actions of the Winnebago.

The old people often spoke of the Trickster, but we never knew what they meant. They told us how he wrapped a coon-skin blanket around himself and went to a place where all the people were dancing. There he danced until evening and then he stopped and turned around. No one was to be seen anywhere, and then he realized that he had mistaken for people dancing the noise made by the wind blowing through the reeds. So do we Winnebagos act. We dance and make a lot of noise, but in the end we accomplish nothing.[52]

Another brief tale tells of Trickster's chicanery when inviting birds to dance to his songs but with their eyes closed. In turn, he kills each bird that passes, interpreted as follows by dissenters from tradition.

So are we Winnebagos. We like all that is forbidden. We say that we like the medicine dance; we say that it is good and yet we kept it secret and forbid people to witness it. We tell members of the dance not to speak about it until the world shall come to an end. They are afraid to speak of it. We, the Winnebago, are the birds, and the Trickster is satan.[53]

Although well aware of divisions between old and young, traditionalists and peyotists, Radin had little to say about gender differences generally or in regard to peyotism in particular. His ethnographic portrayals of the Winnebago society are decidedly male in their focus, neglecting the important question of the differential impact on men and women of radical change, including peyotism. For Radin, the new peyote religion promised the fulfillment of spiritual and psychological needs that customary religion could no longer provide to men. Traditional male behaviors suitable to a nearly vanished world lacked vitality and relevance to daily living, yet they persisted. Young men continued to be trained as warriors when traditional fighters no longer had a viable place in the society. Crashing Thunder (Sam Blowsnake), for example, supported by his father, sought warrior recognition and the opportunity to count coup well after the cessation of intertribal fighting; he then killed a Potawatomi and seized his property, as noted in chapter 2. For counting coup through killing and theft and therefore no longer following the female path, Crashing Thunder established his manhood and won the approval of his father. But instead of finding wider, unchallenged approbation and the status recognition of an earlier period, he was arrested and imprisoned. At the same time that young males continued to be socialized into an irrelevant warrior role, they also received training as hunters and shamans. The viability of those once esteemed and vital pursuits, however, had also diminished.[54] White intrusion had interrupted and undermined the male pursuits of hunting and trapping that once lay at the center of economic life. People increasingly depended on wage labor on white-owned land, where they were employed in harvesting farm produce.

To a limited extent, Lurie's work with Mountain Wolf Woman widens the gender-constricted angle of vision in Radin's work. Forty years after publication of *The Autobiography of a Winnebago Indian,* Lurie recorded the life history of Mountain Wolf Woman, including her experience with peyote and traditional practice. Winnebago women did not seem to suffer the psychological devastation experienced by men in the wake of the many changes that brought about reservation life. Socialized into the role of wife, mother, and caretaker of the home and family, women had to continue to fulfill those domestic and familial duties in the wake of radical change. In other words, women occupied a role marked by much greater continuity and stability than the male role. They did not have to contend with radically altered expectations of their duties, despite the refigured social and economic environment of reservation life. The absence of men who were periodically engaged in war had also nurtured a level of female self-sufficiency that undoubtedly eased the burden of acculturation. When the cash economy dominated local life, people turned to wage labor on white farms where their role in harvesting closely approximated a traditional female activity. Even the coming of tourists seeking native crafts such as beadwork and baskets benefited the producers, who were women. Social change brought a less severe disruption of women's activities compared to those of men, in effect enabling women more than men to find familiar sources of self-esteem and status under altered conditions.[55]

After taking into account the age differences between brother and sister, Crashing Thunder and Mountain Wolf Woman, and the four decades between the collection of each narrative, Lurie concluded that gender more than any other factor accounted for the striking differences between the two life histories. Thus Crashing Thunder and Mountain Wolf Woman responded to peyotism very differently. His life was one of dramatic conflict, crisis, and struggle involving womanizing, frequent drunkenness to the point of delirium, murder, and prison. Compounding his sense of personal failure, he had believed that a destiny of more than ordinary accomplishment awaited him. His uncle, White Cloud, had told Crashing Thunder's mother: "You are about to give birth to a child who will not be an ordinary individual."[56] But instead he led a life of dissipation and frightening visions until he was baptized into peyotism and swore to serve Earthmaker and never again take part in the Medicine Dance.[57]

Mountain Wolf Woman, on the other hand, suffered through none of the traumas that punctuated Crashing Thunder's years. Her early experience with peyote was to relieve the pain of childbirth, thus following an established pattern of initially treating the peyote as a medical curative. Continuing to use peyote, Mountain Wolf Woman under its influence no longer felt shy or retiring, but joyful and happy, as described by other users. Her use of peyote seems to have been continuous with her generally serene outlook on life. Early on, she had a vision at a peyote meeting of storms and thunder, high winds and impending disaster. People were running in panic seeking safety. Mountain Wolf Woman wondered what kind of shelter they were seeking when none was to be found. She thought to herself, "Jesus is the only place to flee to." Continuing, Mountain Wolf Woman said, "Then I saw Jesus standing there." She felt a new sense of contentment, pleasure, and joy. "Now I was an angel. That is how I saw myself. Because I had wings I was supposed to fly but could not quite get my feet off of the ground. I wanted to fly right away, but I could not because my time is not yet completed."[58] Her experience of bliss, happiness, and delight is consistent with the equally exultant emotional states described by other peyote users. Those ecstatic feelings also recall the supersensory encounters of African American narrators in their journeys to heaven.

The Subjective Experience of Peyote Consumption: Expanding the Self

Radin's understanding of peyotism among the Winnebago derived from narrated accounts, not from observations of peyote ceremonies or personal experience with the drug. He was not a participant-observer in peyote ceremonies, preferring instead to document this and other cultural practices through the verbal accounts of religious adherents. There is no indication that he ever tried the drug, even out of curiosity. He thus relied on statements about behavior, for his interest ultimately lay in the articulation of human thought and meaning through words. Moreover, participation in the new religion would likely have eliminated what little access he had to traditional religious practitioners.

Prior to Radin's work, James Mooney of the Bureau of American Ethnology, a consummate fieldworker and advocate for the rights of American Indians, was perhaps the first anthropologist to investigate the religious uses of peyote among several American Indian groups. At great professional cost and with characteristic moral courage, Mooney concluded from his ethnographic work, including his participation in peyote consumption, that the sacramental role of peyote was a legitimate and integral part of the new religion developing among Indian people.[59] Alfred Kroeber early in his career also ingested peyote and commented briefly about the experience.[60] Peyotism engaged the more sustained attention of a subsequent generation of anthropologists, including David Aberle, Omer Stewart, Weston La Barre, and James Slotkin, all of whom acknowledged their use of peyote.[61] Stewart considered participant-observation an essential part of anthropological fieldwork, including peyote consumption if that was a central feature of research, and he criticized anthropologists, such as Radin, who demurred.[62]

Lowie, who began research among the Crow at about the time Radin first encountered the Winnebago, documented Crow Indian culture prior to white intrusion. Whereas Radin could not avoid the role of peyote among the Winnebago if he hoped to document traditional religion, Lowie did not face a similar imperative among the Crow and turned exclusively to salvage ethnography: "In 1907 it was borne in upon me that, if the old Plains culture had in large part disappeared as a tangible phenomenon, it survived very much alive in the Crow and Blackfoot consciousness."[63] His esteemed interpreter, Jim Carpenter, presented Lowie with the opportunity to study the peyote religion, given his own interest and a kinsman's devotion to the new faith. But Lowie was indifferent to peyotism and other post-contact changes on the Northern Plains. His Crow ethnography contained no discussion of the Ghost Dance religion or the new peyote faith.[64] His brief account of peyote in *Primitive Religion* draws its examples not from the Crow, but from Radin's work among the Winnebago.[65] There is little question that Lowie, like Radin, did not participate in peyote meetings, preferring instead, unlike Radin, to remain bound exclusively to the reconstruction of Crow society prior to white contact.

Following Mooney's lead, Slotkin, La Barre, Aberle, and Stewart defended the sacramental significance of peyote. The anthropologists likewise regarded the Native American Church as a legitimate religious institution. They joined Sol Tax and David McAllester, an ethnomusicologist, in signing a "Statement on Peyote" during a particularly vociferous national campaign against narcotics.[66] Although Radin's most important informants were peyotists, he did not participate with colleagues in public defense of the religious use of peyote. In no sense an activist, Radin's political sympathies were more likely to be expressed in his teaching, lecturing, and writing. He was probably indifferent to the political issue that peyote had become, drawn instead to his ultimate, unsentimental interest in salvage ethnography, particularly precontact Winnebago religion. For Radin, peyotism was in effect an object of study through texts as well as the way forward in understanding the Medicine Dance and the precontact social order.

The people who joined the peyote movement did not linger over their decision. It seemed that they were for the most part predisposed to the new religion after participating in a very small number of peyote events. Beyond Radin's descriptions of the experience on the part of Winnebago participants, Aberle among the Navaho and Slotkin among the Menominee as participant-observers offered particularly telling personal insights into the peyote experience. They emphasized its compelling psychological appeal that undoubtedly motivated, at least in part, its use among native peoples, including the Winnebago.

In his Navaho research, Aberle participated in eleven peyote meetings, consuming the drug on each occasion. From that experience and his discussions with informant participants, Aberle said that the drug induces a feeling of *"personal significance* of external and internal stimuli."[67] In Aberle's view, the self through peyote engages every dimension of life, finding personal meaning in the connections he or she discovers when encountering other people, the environment, personal visions, meditative reflection, and virtually all else impinging on the self. The enhancement and intensity of one's personal significance in the world is the foundation of the religion, a remarkable parallel to the new feelings of self-worth and connectedness born of the conversion experiences of former slaves. Beyond the expansion of the self, peyote could also create conditions in which an individual experienced a force beyond himself or herself that exercised a power to control unpredictably thought and emotion.[68] Slotkin, whose intense engagement with peyotists included his membership in the Native American Church, in which he also held an office, describes the peyote experience in terms similar to those presented by Aberle. That is, peyote induces a "heightened sensibility" to oneself or to others. That sensibility promotes introspection, self-assessment, personal prayers to God, and a confession of sin. As an emetic, peyote may enable an individual to purge himself of sin by vomiting. Slotkin also notes a revelatory quality to peyote, enabling the user to encounter spiritual forces, whether God or Jesus.[69] With little detail, but seemingly consistent with the reports of Aberle and Slotkin, Kroeber briefly described his peyote experience during his fieldwork among the Arapaho. He noted the drug's effect "of stimulating . . . the intellectual faculties" and the feeling of "intense exaltation."[70]

The analytic representations of the peyote experience offered by Aberle and Slotkin following their own drug encounters resonate with the native descriptions that Radin collected. The accounts of the anthropologists provide a level of understanding unavailable to Radin, who could only accept at face value his informants' descriptions of the drug's effect. He offered several narratives of peyote use beyond Rave's account of his early conversion to the new religion. Sam Blowsnake (Crashing Thunder in his autobiography), for example, provided particularly telling detail as he recalled the events that brought him to peyote and his decision to forsake all traditional rites. He acknowledged his evil deeds in the past, such as his false claim that he secured blessings from the spirits, his pretense therefore as a healer, and his deceit and philandering. His thoughts often remained unspoken within the assembly of peyote eaters; he was convinced, however, that they shared thoughts in a telepathic manner, consistent with analytic descriptions of the expansion of the self and wordless communication with other selves.

The sense of spiritual belonging among peyote eaters was also revealed in Sam Blowsnake's visions at the point of his conversion:

> It was now late at night. I had eaten a lot of peyote and felt rather tired. I suffered considerably. After a while I looked at the peyote, and there I saw an eagle standing with outspread wings. It was as beautiful a sight as could well be observed. Each of the feathers seemed to have a mark. The eagle stood there looking at me. I turned my gaze, thinking that perhaps there was something the matter with my sight, but then when I looked again the eagle was still present. Again I turned around and when I looked at the spot where the eagle had stood, it was gone and only the small peyote remained. . . .
>
> Suddenly I saw a lion lying in the same place where before I had seen the eagle. I watched it very closely and when I turned my eyes for the least little bit, it disappeared. "I suppose all those present are aware of this and I am just beginning to find out," I thought.[71]

There is a very slight variation in the above passage, taken from *Crashing Thunder*, and its original publication in *The Autobiography*, an unexceptionable exercise of the anthropologist's editorial discretion. But once again this is another example either of authorial confusion or legerdemain. Without explanation Sam Blowsnake's narrated vision of the eagle and the lion also appears nearly verbatim under the heading "J. B.'s [Jasper Blowsnake's] Peyote Experiences" in *The Winnebago Tribe*.[72]

Indicative of the "personal significance of external and internal stimuli" that Aberle described, Sam Blowsnake referred to this mystical expansion of the self when praying to God in a peyote meeting.

> As I prayed I was aware of something above me and there He was, He to whom I was speaking, God. That which we call the soul, that it is which is God. This is what I felt and saw. The one called Earthmaker, God, is a spirit and He it was I felt and saw.... I instantly became their spirit; I was their spirit or soul. Whatever they thought of I immediately knew. I did not have to speak to them and get an answer to know what their thoughts were. Then I thought of a certain place far away, and immediately I was there. I was my thought.[73]

At another time, Blowsnake reported that "I died and my body was moved to another life," where he encountered Christian-inspired messages of biblical authority and fidelity to God. In this vision, Blowsnake is no longer "my thought," but rather it is his body that saw the Bible: "My body spoke of many things and it spoke of what was true. It spoke of all the things that were being done by the Winnebago and that were evil. It spoke a long time and then stopped. Not I, but my body standing there had done the talking." It is an index of the depth and completeness of Blowsnake's conversion that his visions can encompass, on the one hand, pure mentation in which the "I" is tantamount to thought itself and, on the other, pure embodiment in which the "I" is absent until "I returned to my normal condition."[74] As part of conversion to peyotism, Winnebago seekers envisioned an experience of death and rebirth familiar in the Radin-Watson collection and indicative of the dramatic social and personal transformations often accompanying rites of passage worldwide.

Sam Blowsnake concludes his autobiography with a renunciation of traditional Winnebago religion:

> On one occasion while at a meeting, I suffered great pain. My eyes were sore and I was thinking of many things. "Now I do nothing but pay attention to this ceremony, for it is good." Then I called the leader over to me and said to him, "My elder brother, hereafter I shall only regard Earthmaker as holy. I will make no more offerings of tobacco. I will not use any more tobacco I will not smoke, nor will I chew tobacco. I have no further interest in these things. Earthmaker, God, alone do I desire to serve. Never again shall I take part in the Medicine Dance . . . I intend to give myself up to God's cause."[75]

Disclosing the Medicine Dance

In salvaging the intricate ritual and mythic complex of the Medicine Dance, Radin depended on informants not only willing but also eager to flout the admonitions that once ensured its secrecy. Jasper Blowsnake, an acolyte of peyotism, was particularly important. Radin was in the field only a brief time when the elderly father of Oliver Lamere, a convert to peyotism, wanted to assist Radin in learning about the Medicine Dance, although the elder Lamere had never belonged. Radin took advantage of his curiosity about the Medicine Dance as well as his desire to undermine passionate traditional opponents of peyotism.

Still, a certain fear, even among the committed adherents of peyotism, attended the betrayal of secrets. Three elderly former members of the Medicine Dance agreed "to recount to me the most sacred of all the myths in the tribe and one that only members of the Rite knew, namely the Origin Myth of the World, of the Indians and of the Medicine Rite." But they would do so only away from the reservation and seemingly beyond the scrutiny of the traditionalists. With Radin, they traveled the short distance to Sioux City, Iowa, where they booked rooms in a hotel. With doors and windows covered, the narration began at midnight, continuing until completion five hours later. Radin worked without his interpreter Lamere present, and recorded the myth in phonetic script. Despite their precautions, people throughout the Nebraska reservation very quickly learned of the excursion to Sioux City and its purpose. Young and old among the peyotists who had not belonged to the Medicine Dance pressed Radin to read the myth publicly. Some forty people assembled, with

> no question of awe and respect that this assemblage of unbelievers and renegades to the old beliefs paid to this first public narration of what they had always been taught to regard as the great secret which members of the Medicine Rite alone possessed. Part of this awe and respect, mixed with amazement at my supposed courage, was passed on to me.[76]

Some peyotists, although critical of traditional religion, questioned the value of disclosure and the inevitable offense to the sensibilities of the traditionalists. Others believed that in public view the former secrets would appear foolish, thus advancing the alternative peyote religion.[77] Radin gave little thought to the resentment toward him that the traditionalists certainly felt.

An opposing opinion allegedly held that recording essential features of traditional religion would express respect for the ways of the ancestors, now fading, by sustaining a record of those practices for future generations. Hence, as Crashing Thunder explained, "I thought I would write down and tell you all these things so that those who came after me would not be deceived." While the American anthropologists of the early twentieth century were driven by strongly preservationist motives that Crashing Thunder appeared to share, it seems that more mundane reasons for native cooperation might well have been at play. Crashing Thunder thus assisted Radin in exchange for money. Radin of course remained fully in control of the texts he collected, as Walter Krupat has observed. Moreover, with many fewer footnotes than *The Autobiography,* the much longer *Crashing Thunder* also contains numerous editorial changes that Krupat suggests may have reflected an intent by Radin to mask his active role in the production of the texts. Perhaps, but Radin reminded the reader both in *The Autobiography* and in *Crashing Thunder* that the protagonist's stated motive of preserving Winnebago culture for posterity was actually supplied by Radin.[78] The final footnote in *Crashing Thunder* reads, "This is the reason I gave when trying to induce the Winnebago to give me information."[79] Several levels of irony are thus evoked in the Radin-inspired title of Krupat's admirable book on American Indian autobiography, *For Those Who Come After.*[80]

After a hiatus of nearly a year following his initial fieldwork, Radin returned to Winnebago where he met Jasper Blowsnake, a peyotist and recent dissenter from traditional practice who agreed to narrate the entire Medicine Rite. He sought no remuneration, stipulating only that Oliver Lamere serve as interpreter and that Lamere inform Radin of all the dangers surrounding the exposure of Medicine Rite secrets, including the fact that someone could die. Having abandoned such beliefs, including the certainty that someone's death would follow, Blowsnake nonetheless wanted to disclose the latter danger to Radin. With increasingly sharp linguistic skills, Radin transcribed in his modified phonetic script Blowsnake's narration nearly at the pace it was spoken. Based on six-hour workdays each week, the entire narrative unfolded over the course of two months and formed the bedrock of *The Road of Life and Death.* Whatever lingering fears that Blowsnake harbored about his betrayal of Winnebago secrets were realized the day after completion of the narration when he learned that Radin had to return to New York. He had received a telegram announcing the serious illness and imminent death of his father, the venerable rabbi, Adolph Radin. He remained in the East for eight months, carrying with him the valuable text but without a translation. Jasper Blowsnake decided to withdraw from any further work on the Medicine Dance project and undoubtedly believed that in any case Radin would no longer require his services as informant.

Radin took the ill-fated position with the Bureau of American Ethnology, noted in chapter 1, and, while living in Washington, secured the translation services of an American Indian having some familiarity with the Winnebago language. He provided Radin with a literal translation of the text transcribed from Jasper Blowsnake's long narration. It was incomprehensible, however, lacking as it did the figurative and connotative referents of words and the embedded cryptic meanings all but inaccessible in the literal translation. Radin's translator maintained he understood each word yet had no idea what the narrative was about.

The anthropologist once again needed the assistance of Blowsnake so that he and Lamere could create a meaningful translation. Blowsnake, informed of Radin's impending arrival, fled the area, having told Lamere that he wanted nothing more to do with the project in light of the portentous death of Rabbi Radin. Renting a buggy and two horses, Radin set out in search of Blowsnake. Eventually he found him, and Blowsnake again agreed to work on the translation. In another marathon of six-hour workdays over the course of two and a half months, the translation was completed.[81] Blowsnake's sudden change of heart after fleeing just before Radin's arrival puzzled the anthropologist. The hold of tradition remained strong, as Blowsnake, for all his disavowals of the old ways, still felt considerable anxiety about any role he might have played in the death of Radin's father. Radin later learned that before they were reunited, Blowsnake had consumed a large amount of peyote and heard an emboldening voice, saying, "You are the one who is to tell of the Medicine Rite." The next morning he was baptized in a syncretic ritual combining peyotism and Christianity. At the same time, Jasper Blowsnake disavowed sacrifices to the spirits, ceremonial feasting, and all traditional religious beliefs, including, presumably, the power of the spirit world to protect Winnebago ritual secrets from outsiders.[82]

Radin's effort to preserve Winnebago history took maximum advantage of the divisions segmenting reservation life. His determination to secure texts proceeded through payment, manipulating community factions, indifference to local taboos, and cueing informants. No one can be certain to what extent such practices continue among anthropologists despite the professional code of anthropological ethics adopted long after Radin's death. At the least, contemporary feelings about ethical issues since the late 1960s ensure that no anthropologist would readily acknowledge engaging in similar field practices. Radin at the same time gave wide latitude to human agency and self-determination, and in this respect his vision of anthropology is starkly modern. While he exploited community factionalism, segments of the community likewise took advantage of Radin's research goal of "finding the native" to advance their own plan for a spiritual future very different from the numinous visions of the recent past.

Conclusion

Although Radin offered no explicit linkages between his Winnebago and African American research, common themes conjoin those separate projects and invite the comparisons made here and in previous chapters. In each locale, religion, conversion, and autobiography were Radin's entry points into individual lives, reflecting the unity of method, purpose, and anthropological perspective that informed all his work. For different reasons, Radin's Winnebago and African American informants had faced inner emotional and psychological turmoil until each found a self-reported stability and equilibrium following their respective transcendent experiences. This is clear in the texts Radin recorded both on the Plains and in Nashville. His Winnebago informants, after ingesting peyote, achieved in their inner transformation intense feelings of personal significance, an unbounded feeling of connectedness to persons and things, a commitment to purposeful living, and above all, an immediate and personal connection to God. Similarly, the elderly African American narrators, induced by their individual but unsought encounters in heaven, experienced a concomitant liberation from anxiety and fear as they gained a new sense of self.

Beginning his career in the first decade of the twentieth century, Paul Radin was an exemplar of the new professional course Franz Boas was charting. With others, Radin focused on fresh memories of American Indian lifeways before white conquest and the loss of political autonomy. Inscribed in the notebooks of admiring and sympathetic anthropologists, those historical reconstructions became invaluable and durable records of ways of life that otherwise would have receded beyond recovery. Contemporary American Indians excavating their tribal pasts and anthropologists and historians with complementary interests are the beneficiaries of those early preservation efforts. None could rival for sheer volume, detail, and linguistic acuity Radin's documentation of Winnebago practice and belief before the reservation confinement that motivated his remarkable efforts at ethnographic reclamation.

Entering the twentieth century, the once implacable and reviled Indian, the savage foe of American civilization and expansion, ceased to be a threat and instead entered the popular and literary imagination as the ennobled symbol of independence and freedom. Later regarded as the wise steward of venerated tribal land, the envisioned American Indian became a model of ecological responsibility and reverence for the earth. In the case of African Americans, a corresponding renovation of their national image did not occur. The popular and literary imagination gave very little quarter to Americans of African descent. Instead, a consensual racism and denigration of black people across the broadest spectrum of American society has persisted from before the Civil War into our own time. The legacy of slavery defined African Americans as a people deservedly apart, separate and justifiably unequal.

African American historians, Radin and his Fisk colleagues, and other white confreres recognized that African Americans had to speak for themselves if slavery as an institution was to be understood and historical error exposed. This was an especially acute necessity for the elderly last witnesses and casualties of the slave system and its desolate postbellum vestiges. They were a fragile resource. The Radin-Watson collaboration, like a substantial part of Radin's Winnebago work, was thus a variety of salvage ethnography, the raison d'être of American anthropology. Radin and Watson seized one of the last opportunities to record the life histories, including the religious and conversion experiences, of former slaves. There they found religious beliefs pulsating with human meaning and new self-definitions that demanded attention.

The elderly witnesses became the authors of their own histories. The assembled reflective texts thus elevated former slaves to their proper human status as contemplative adults fully capable of narrating their own life experiences of servitude and faith. At the same time, the resulting documents helped to repudiate the pervasive race-based misrepresentations built into southern history by scholars north and south. They remain the most important contributions of the Radin-Watson and Settle Egypt collections.

Totalitarian institutions such as slavery enforce obedience by easy resort to violence. However, American slave owners preferred compliance to resistance and therefore aimed to quell rebellious sentiments and actions by persuading their human property of the God-sanctioned righteousness of their own captivity. It was an effort to control thought as well as labor. In Gramsci's terms, slave owners extended their cultural hegemony over those in bondage. With the full assent of slave owners, southern white churchmen preached a white version of Christianity that reminded slaves of their duty to submit to God's command that they obey their masters and mistresses.

But white preaching about Christian obedience did not reckon on the human reinterpretive imagination that slaves and black preachers imposed on those exhortations. What they heard in biblical verse, hymns, and even sermons was understood in ways unintended by white proselytizers. Slaves and black clergy, for example, easily identified with powerless and oppressed people of the Old Testament, such as Moses, who led the ancient Israelites out of Egyptian slavery. Other biblical figures also found deliverance in this world rather than in the world to come, inspiring slave songs of yearning and hope for freedom.[1] At the same time an even closer identification joined slaves to Jesus, whose manifest suffering was their suffering and whose death promised them salvation, which of course meant the end of their torment. Eugene Genovese has suggested with considerable justification that for slaves, "Moses had become Jesus, and Jesus, Moses," representing a fusion of the two impassioned goals of slave religion—"collective deliverance as a people and redemption from their terrible sufferings."[2] In times of unreasoned fear on the part of slave owners, white panic singled out black preachers as provocateurs. For example, the baseless alarm about a slave insurrection in 1856 on the Kentucky-Tennessee borderlands along the Cumberland River resulted in the execution of at least five black preachers believed to be leading conspirators.[3]

Feeling the daily injustice of servitude, slaves did not listen passively to white pastoral invocations of the slave owners' God. Captive, denigrated men and women instead found in the Christian message an instrument of opposition in its many possible forms. They ranged from outright violence against the slave owner, to covert actions such as lying or malingering. Slave discontent and the many actions it stimulated exposed the self-interested myth of the obedient slave needing white direction. As to the black narratives of spiritual death and rebirth, they effectively reveal a conversion process, but one in which the slaves converted God to their own human needs.[4] God of the slaves was an all-powerful, benevolent figure demanding only obedience to Himself, not to the earthly concerns of rapacious white people. Conversion constituted a transformed, black-centered conception of salvation and spiritual liberation.

Those converted had achieved, in the face of prior doubt, unqualified certainty about their self-worth, through their direct experience of a redefined Christian God. They found divine love and forgiveness from a God that could not countenance human bondage. The converted individual did not have to prove himself in any way, except through absolute and unwavering faith in God, thus rejecting white Christian preoccupations with hell and eternal damnation. In white churches, an individual's dread and torment sprang from the belief that in choosing salvation he or she had no certainty or foreknowledge of his or her fate. Consequently, people remained in a state of permanent doubt, obsessed by sin and fearing that a punitive God would ultimately consign them to hell.

The pattern of white conversion, particularly the lingering uncertainty and dread about one's spiritual fate, did not rest easily with slaves. They rejected it in favor of a set of beliefs that did not compound their daily anguish with doubt and diffuse threats of damnation. Critical in the Radin-Watson conversion narratives and distinct from white preaching is the lack of individual preparation for salvation; nor did the converted intentionally seek salvation. Also missing is fear or anxiety about reaching heaven. Rather, the Fisk narratives emphasize the futility of preparation because "God chooses His people and God comes at His own time. . . . It is God who does the choosing and the calling." Once the voice is heard, then salvation is assured for those who throw off all doubt about God. He or she, following a heavenly journey, would then come back "to life and human consciousness again, happy and shouting."[5]

Conversion was an intense emotional experience. Many of the narratives describe feelings of despair, often manifested in bodily pain, just prior to hearing a voice and entering a new space between heaven and hell. The despair may be connected to a sense of mourning or personal loss, as in the death of a parent or child, or when Mr. Green describes his desperate and prolonged feelings of depression as a child when he was sold away from his mother. Despondency accompanies the fear and anxiety following the message that one is about to experience death, despite the promise of redemption and rebirth. Gloom may also continue for a time, although God and his angels speak in soft, reassuring voices, addressing the spiritual supplicant, often with such phrases as "My little one." In Radin's words, the slave, facing "personal disintegration . . . and the annihilation of values," sought "a fixed point, and he needed a fixed point, for both within and outside of himself he could see only vacillation and endless shifting."[6] A new conceptualization of the individual in relationship to God, with whom he or she had spoken in death and rebirth, established that fixed point.

The conversion experience reached its climax when the narrators moved beyond their earthly existence to a new world, set in heaven, physically beautiful and welcoming, where they were valued and loved as worthy human beings, fully deserving of an ultimate return. They had seen and conversed with a merciful God or His angelic minions, achieving psychological wholeness and a sense of personal value. Portraying themselves as overwhelmed by the envisioned experience of heaven, they embraced the spiritual journey that established their worthiness and existential legitimacy.

The Fisk research was for Radin more than a historical corrective, vital as that was in pointing the way to a new subject-centered understanding of slavery. The narrative collection also provided psychological insight into slave self-awareness, or ego, and its construction through religious conversion. Unremitting denigration and indifference to or denial of basic human qualities were daily occurrences endured by bondsmen and bondswomen, undoubtedly at great cost to each individual's uncertain sense of self. Those attacks went beyond verbal abuse, physical punishments, and beatings and included sustained affronts to fundamental human feelings and emotions, such as conjugal, parental, and fraternal love. People lived in constant, helpless fear of the slave owner's unchecked power to shatter families through sale; any parent, sibling, or child was vulnerable. Once again, Mr. Green's account of separation from his mother and the psychic damage it inflicted is a case in point. The emotional bonds between family members remained undiminished over the course of decades, even in the face of sale and separation. Newspaper advertisements placed by former slaves seeking reunification with kin who had been sold away continued into the early years of the twentieth century.[7]

Radin was sensitive to the psychological implications of conversion in both research sites. Among the Winnebago, spiritual renewal followed the establishment of a personal connection to God/Earthmaker, induced by peyote. No longer mediated by the spirits of traditional religion, the individual's relationship to divinity was direct and personal. At the same time, consuming peyote in meetings, the equivalent of church services, created or revived social bonds that had been weakened by the decline of clanship. A new sense of community emerged. Radin's accounts of Winnebago and African American conversion, distinctive as they were, suggest that through innovative religion and a direct relationship to God, psychological integration and a sense of personal wholeness were achieved. For Winnebago men especially, traditional religion no longer fit the radically altered circumstances of military defeat and ensuing political and economic dependency. Further, deteriorating social conditions brought on personal depression and antisocial behavior that the peyote religion arrested. The new religion provided an effective means of personal adjustment to radically altered social conditions that could not be turned back. The rapid spread of peyote across the Plains in the two decades on either side of the turn of the twentieth century and its institutionalization within the Native American Church are telling indices of its restorative power in the wake of psychological and social dislocation.

For the elderly African Americans, a personal connection to God also occurred and resolved inner distress. The emotional and cognitive impairment of slavery thus was not irreparable, for black religious inventiveness could create a satisfying sense of self through the ordeal of what was believed to be death and rebirth into heaven. Called by God, individuals described a conversion pattern in which they had personal visions of physical death, soul departure from the body, and moving encounters in heaven with divinity. Unlike the Winnebago, fewer gender distinctions marked the lives narrated in the Radin-Watson collection. The experience of conversion was not stratified by gender; the oppression of slavery equally devastated the lives and selfhood of men and women. Through prior acquaintance with several informants whom he selected as well as his own encounters with Jim Crow, Watson undoubtedly sensitized Radin to this point.

In attending to the reconstructed self—the self made whole—in the narratives, Radin added to a broad anthropological literature that he believed had either denied the existence of a self-conception among ethnographic subjects or provided only the most fragmentary accounts of the self.[8] Although the individual remained the focal point of Radin's research throughout his career, he did not develop anything resembling an analytic understanding of the self. To have done so would have required a sustained comparative framework that Radin had rejected in favor of his forte—the close examination of specific texts drawn from individual narrative accounts of rituals, beliefs, and events. That orientation and his rejection of comparative research aiming for some level of generalization reflected his own strongly held opinions about proper method in anthropology. Radin of course played to his own strengths, as pointed out by Sapir in an incisive assessment of his work shortly after his departure from Fisk. Sapir noted that "everything that Paul has done so far indicates that he is best at an unevaluated descriptive record, whether in ethnology or linguistics. He is not critical enough to do inferential work of any type."[9] Sapir might well have included comparative analysis as a subset of "inferential work."

Radin's interests dovetailed with the insights of more systematic and theoretically inclined psychological anthropologists, such as A. I. Hallowell. Younger than Radin by a decade, Hallowell shared Radin's skepticism about the value of purely cultural descriptions that would meld unique individuals into mere amalgams or ideal types. Ethnographic research in the first half of the twentieth century, prior to the emergence of a distinct psychological anthropology, explored the content of a broadly inclusive culture, including politics, religion, and social organization. Behavior, then, was essentially seen as generic, characteristic of each individual socialized into the rules and values of the culture. Benedict's *Patterns of Culture* is of course emblematic of that preeminent pattern in anthropological writing. Agreeing with Radin, Hallowell argued that even the most systematic and reliable cultural account nonetheless represented the perspective of an observer from outside the culture.

> Presented to us in this form, these cultural data do not easily permit us to apprehend, in an integral fashion, the most significant and meaningful aspects of the world of the individual as experienced by him and in terms of which he thinks, is motivated to act, and satisfies his needs. . . . Because culture can be objectively described and for certain purposes treated as if it were a sui generis phenomenon, it is sometimes implied, or even argued, that it is in fact phenomenologically autonomous. To do so is to misunderstand totally the basic conditions of human psychological adjustment.[10]

Foreshadowing Hallowell's remarks, Radin in 1913 concurred with critiques of ethnological memoirs

> because they represented but the skeleton and bones of the culture they sought to portray; that what was needed, if we were ever to understand the Indian, was an interpretation of his life and emotions from within; which for the most part was what ethnological memoirs did not do.

Accordingly, Radin reported that he met Jasper Blowsnake,

> one of those serious and sedate middle-aged individuals whom one is likely to
> meet in almost every civilization, and who, if they chose to speak in a natural and
> detached manner about the culture to which they belonged, could throw more light
> upon the workings of an Indian brain than any mass of information systematically
> and carefully obtained by an outsider.

As in both the African American collections and the Winnebago life histories, Radin
would have readers believe that he gave very little guidance to his informants. This
seems to have been the case in Nashville, although there is reason to doubt that
claim in his Winnebago work. But in both locales Radin regarded each person as
a unique individual rather than an exemplar of a cultural tradition. He asked his
"sedate middle-aged informant" only for a narration about his beliefs and the people
he met, not the generalized expectations of the culture.[11]

Throughout his career, he implied that beneath the diversity of human cultures
lay a universal psychological substrate that defined the ego and its needs, including
self-respect and personal dignity. Of course, a positive self-conception depends on
seeing oneself in the approving eyes of others. But the people Radin and Watson
encountered could find neither approval nor dignity in the slave regime. They
had to find it for themselves, but not through a religion of passivity and fear as
preached by white clergy. To have adopted white religion as given would simply
have reproduced their earthly degradation on a different plane, where a complicit
God would consider them sinful but offer heavenly reward for unquestioned
subservience to the slave owner. Even a slave's humility and religiosity offered no
protection from denigration and sin-obsessed white preaching.

Radin found that conversion on their own terms brought slaves and former
slaves religious as well as psychological redemption, including a positive self-awareness in a behavioral environment that included relentless abuse diminishing the
person qua person.[12] Redemption began "with a sense of sin and non-realization"
that ultimately gave way to what could only be achieved through a reinterpreted
Christianity, namely, a feeling of "cleanliness, certainty and a re-integration."[13]

In committing his fieldwork to "finding the native," Radin from the outset of his
career cultivated a deep respect for the contemplative musing filling the pages of
Primitive Man as Philosopher. There he argued that intellectual thought in the widest
range of human societies was no less profound than in ancient Greece. He brought

to light what he considered the extraordinary intellectual resources that diverse peoples utilized to create coherent philosophies of life. Radin drew extensively on his Winnebago narratives in establishing that thesis. As a radical humanist, he particularly admired the Winnebago affirmation of practical living recounted in the Medicine Rite because it emphasized earthly existence rather than a spiritual abode after death: "It was life that was to be faced, with all its imperfections, trials, and with all the comedies and tragedies that often played such havoc with ideals of perfection."[14]

Written prior to his Fisk appointment, *Primitive Man as Philosopher* does not consider the thought of liberated American slaves. But in his manuscript "Souls Piled Like Timber," Radin identified ubiquitous creative expressions in the narratives; they rose to the level of literature, indicating that, despite the severest cruelties that human bondage could inflict on body and mind, even slavery could not suppress the quest for meaning, human artistry, and the creative imagination.

Beginning early in the last century, Radin's engagement with unique, historically situated individuals considered their contemplation of philosophical questions such as life and death, slavery and freedom, faith and skepticism. Both on the Plains and in the American South the issues Radin recorded and discussed required an empirical, actor-oriented sensibility grounded in history, culture, and psychology—precisely the strategy mocked by contemporaneous purveyors of biracial fantasies.

The recent revitalization of those fantasies provides the distressing coda for this book, which began with a consideration of Radin's *The Racial Myth*. He meticulously dissected Aryanism and other racial illusions. In that regard, he was very much in the mold of his teacher and sometime antagonist Franz Boas, who set the course of American anthropology for half a century, delineating through empirical study the independence of biology, language, and culture. Still, a residue of scientific racism and biopolitics continued into the post–World War II decades, as the ethnoracial immigration quotas of the 1920s remained in place until 1965, a generation after Boas's death. Until the 1960s, race restrictions in law that denied Americans of African descent their constitutional rights of citizenship as well as their rights as human beings also continued to find their rationale in discredited race theory. Nevertheless, the powerful truths of American anthropology played their role in reforming immigration law and fully enfranchising African Americans. Anthropologists rejected biopolitics and promulgated the idea that cultural behaviors among different groups derive from their varying historical experiences, and that cultural relativism can promote mutual understanding among diverse peoples. Put another way, Franz Boas's posthumous victory contributed to the growth and expansion, however fitful, of an American liberal consciousness that repudiated the racial chimeras of the 1930s.

Or so it appeared, even amid the racial turmoil of the 1960s. Yet as these words are written, the upward trajectory of understanding about race is now confronting countervailing, scientifically discredited forces of denial and ethnoracial hatred. An ominous shadow hangs over the story of intellectual courage and humanism woven through this study. At the end of the second decade of the twenty-first century, the writings of Franz Boas, Paul Radin, and their colleagues, some dating from the late 1800s, have a renewed urgency. In *The Racial Myth,* Radin exposed the pernicious fantasy of Nazism and the delusional belief that race is destiny. He looked forward to a brighter future of universal secular humanism built on mutual loyalties unencumbered by racial allegiance, cultural chauvinism, and jingoistic nationalism. Boas, too, imagined a world made better if people could break "the shackles of tradition," those familiar, emotionally encumbered habits of mind that too often stifle reasonable thought. New nationalisms now emergent in the United States and across Europe, fear of cultural differences, ethnoracial hostility and violence, and the like are the renovated shackles in which too many people remain comfortably bound.

Most people in the United States registered shock at the sight of violent fellow citizens marching in torchlight processions brandishing swastikas and shouting anti-Semitic slogans. The spectacle of public ethnoracial hatred on such a scale recalls the mass rallies of the 1930s in Nazi Germany and even in isolationist America on the eve of World War II. That an American president could find words of praise for these violent reincarnated German American Bundists and Nazi sympathizers is beyond disturbing, for he thereby conferred legitimacy on the racism and anti-Semitism they promote. Approbation of their actions encourages further violence, betrays the highest ideals of the country, and celebrates a willful historical amnesia that would forget the blood and treasure expended in the defeat of their ideological forbears.

The hard-won achievement of American anthropology at the midpoint of the twentieth century is now, if not imperiled, at least under challenge. The new fascism in American streets and at the highest levels of power, the mendacity of racial culpability on which it feeds, and the resurgent xenophobia infecting the

American discourse on race and ethnicity once again remind us that the scientific, humanistic, and moral positions taken by Boas, Radin, and their colleagues have an enduring value that must continue to stand against regression into hate and reason-defying myth.

Notes

INTRODUCTION

1. Paul Radin, *The Racial Myth* (New York: McGraw-Hill, 1934), 119.
2. Ibid., vii.
3. *Pittsburgh Courier,* May 5, 1934, 5.
4. Radin, *The Racial Myth,* 62.
5. Ibid., 118.
6. "Souls Piled Like Timber: The Religious Experience of the Prewar Negro," chap. 8, "The Conversion Experiences: Their Literary Structure" (Paul Radin Papers, Marquette University Special Collections and University Archives, Series 2–2, Box 2, Folder 41), 388.
7. "Blind Spots," editorial in *Opportunity* 2, no. 13 (January 1924): 3.
8. Sidney M. Mintz, "Foreword," in *Afro-American Anthropology: Contemporary Perspectives,* ed. Norman E. Whitten Jr. and John F. Szwed (New York: Free Press, 1970), 13.
9. Lawrence W. Levine, *Black Culture and Black Consciousness: Afro-American Folk Thought from Slavery to Freedom* (New York: Oxford University Press, 2007), 24.
10. Melville J. Herskovits, "The Negro's Americanism," in *The New Negro,* ed. Alain Locke (New York: Simon and Schuster, 1992), 359.
11. Ibid., 353–354.
12. Melville J. Herskovits, "What Has Africa Given America?," *New Republic,* September 4,

1935, 92–94; Herskovits, *The Myth of the Negro Past* (1958; Boston: Beacon, 1990).

13. Bradley W. Hart, *Hitler's American Friends: The Third Reich's Supporters in the United States* (New York: Thomas Dunne, 2018) 31, 44.

14. Jonathan Peter Spiro, *Defending the Master Race: Conservation, Eugenics, and the Legacy of Madison Grant* (Burlington: University of Vermont Press, 2009), 364–368.

15. A. L. Kroeber, "History and Science in Anthropology," *American Anthropologist,* n.s., 37, no. 4, pt. 1 (October–December 1935): 540.

16. Ibid., 541, 566.

17. Franz Boas, "History and Science in Anthropology: A Reply," *American Anthropologist* 38, no. 1 (January–March 1936): 137.

18. Leslie White, *The Social Organization of Ethnological Theory,* Rice University Studies 52, no. 4 (1966): 4.

19. Ibid., 25–26.

20. Boas to Kroeber, February 16, 1931, MUA_PRs01_02–01_1931a, 5; Boas to Kroeber and Sapir, February 17, 1931, MUA_PRs01_02–01_1931a, 6–7; Boas to Kroeber and Sapir, February 18, 1931, MUA_PRs01_02–01_1931a, 8; Theodora Kroeber, *Alfred Kroeber: A Personal Configuration* (Berkeley: University of California Press, 1970), 155.

21. Radin seems to have spoken hardly at all, even informally, about his tenure at Fisk or the research that brought him there. Former Brandeis colleague Maurice Stein, students Richard Werbner, Nancy Kaufman, and Barbara Leons, and acquaintance Herbert Lewis who knew or worked with him in his last years have no recollection of hearing Radin speak of his Fisk appointment, either in class or informally (personal communications with Lewis and Stein, May 28, 2015; Werbner, April 7, 2015; Kaufman, May 16, 2015; and Leons, May 18, 2015).

22. See Herbert S. Lewis, *In Defense of Anthropology: An Investigation of the Critique of Anthropology* (New Brunswick, NJ: Transaction, 2014), 5–7, 12–13. Lewis's masterful essays in this collection expose the errors and historical misrepresentations embedded in the "critique of anthropology." The latter gained considerable influence in the 1980s, when, ironically, critics with little knowledge of the history of anthropology proceeded to castigate that history for imaginary sins. Lewis shares common ground with Mort Sahl, another keen participant-observer, who has remarked, "Those who learn nothing from history are condemned to rewrite it."

23. Stanley Diamond, *Culture in History: Essays in Honor of Paul Radin* (New York: Columbia University Press, 1960).

24. Cora Du Bois, "Paul Radin: An Appreciation," in *Culture in History: Essays in Honor of Paul Radin,* ed. Stanley Diamond (New York: Columbia University Press, 1960), xiii.

25. Stanley Diamond, "Paul Radin," in *Totems and Teachers: Key Figures in the History of Anthropology*, ed. Sydel Silverman (New York: Columbia University Press, 1981), 57.

26. William Y. Adams, "Paul Radin, 1883–1959," in *The Boasians: Founding Fathers and Mothers of American Anthropology* (Lanham, MD: Hamilton, 2016), 161–185.

27. *God Struck Me Dead: Religious Conversion Experiences and Autobiographies of Negro Ex-Slaves*, Social Science Source Documents No. 2 (Nashville, TN: Social Science Institute, Fisk University, 1945).

28. Ralph Linton, "One Hundred Percent American," *American Mercury* 40 (1937): 427–429.

29. Amelia Susman Schultz, "A Tribute to Franz Boas" (presentation at the 71st Annual Meeting of the Society for Applied Anthropology in Seattle, WA, March 29–April 2, 2011), MP3 file, 1:19:21, http://sfaa.net/podcast/index.php/podcasts/2011/tribute-franz-boas/.

30. Zora Neale Hurston, *Dust Tracks on a Road* (Urbana: University of Illinois Press, 1984), 170–171.

31. Jay Miller, "Amelia Louise Susman Schultz, Sam Blowsnake, and the Ho-Chunk Syllabary," *History of Anthropology Newsletter* 42 (2018): http://histanthro.org/clio/amelia-louise-susman-schultz-sam-blowsnake-and-the-ho-chunk-syllabary/.

32. *Unwritten History of Slavery: Autobiographical Account of Negro Ex-Slaves*, Social Science Source Documents No. 1 (Nashville, TN: Social Science Institute, Fisk University, 1945).

33. Lee D. Baker, *Anthropology and the Racial Politics of Culture* (Durham, NC: Duke University Press, 2010), 3–4.

34. Kamala Visweswaran, "Race and the Culture of Anthropology," *American Anthropologist* 100, no. 1 (1998): 70.

35. Baker, *Anthropology and the Racial Politics of Culture*, 165. Lewis's response exposes the presentist political concerns that motivated Visweswaran's article and distorted Boas's record. See Herbert S. Lewis, "Anthropology and Race, Then and Now: Commentary on K. Visweswaran, 'Race and the Culture of Anthropology,'" *American Anthropologist* 100, no. 4 (1998): 979–981.

36. Baker, *Anthropology and the Racial Politics of Culture*, 219.

CHAPTER 1. THE UNSETTLED CAREER OF A RADICAL HUMANIST

1. Paul Radin, *The Road of Life and Death: A Ritual Drama of the American Indians*, Bollingen Series 5 (New York: Pantheon, Inc., 1945), xiii.

2. Ibid., xiii.

3. Paul Radin, *The Italians of San Francisco, Their Adjustment and Acculturation*, abstract from SERA Project 2-F2–98 (3-F2–145), Cultural anthropology (San Francisco: SERA,

1935). Radin indicates that SERA intended the publication of other surveys of San Francisco minorities, including the Chinese and Japanese. Only the Italian survey was published during Radin's lifetime. His work on behalf of SERA provided him much-needed income in the depths of the Depression. On research into the Chinese of San Francisco, see Anthony Bak Buccitelli, "The Reluctant Folklorist: Jon Y. Lee, Paul Radin, and the Fieldwork Process," *Journal of American Folklore* 127, no. 506 (Fall 2014); John Y. Lee, *The Golden Mountain: Chinese Tales Told in California,* collected by John Lee, ed. Paul Radin (Taipei: Oriental Cultural Service, 1971).

4. John Crowe Ransom, "The Idea of a Literary Anthropologist: And What He Might Say of the 'Paradise Lost' of Milton: A Speech with a Prologue," *Kenyon Review* 21, no. 1 (1959).

5. Max Radin memoir, n.d., Robert D. Farber University Archives and Special Collections Department, Brandeis University Libraries, 3–4.

6. Richard Werbner, a student at Brandeis during Radin's appointment, indicated that Radin sometimes spoke of Croce's work (Personal communication, April 9, 2015). No entries for Croce appear in any of Radin's bibliographies.

7. Benedetto Croce, *History, Its Theory and Practice,* trans. Douglas Ainslie (New York: Harcourt, Brace, 1921), 19.

8. Paul Radin, *The Method and Theory of Ethnology: An Essay in Criticism* (New York: McGraw-Hill, 1933), 184.

9. George W. Stocking Jr., review of *The Method and Theory of Ethnology,* 2nd ed., by Paul Radin, *American Anthropologist,* n.s., 70, no. 2 (1968): 371.

10. Gabriel Alejandro Torres Colón and Charles A. Hobbs, "The Intertwining of Culture and Nature: Franz Boas, John Dewey, and Deweyan Strands of American Anthropology," *Journal of the History of Ideas* 76, no. 1 (2015): 140; Herbert S. Lewis, "Boas, Darwin, Science and Anthropology," *Current Anthropology* 42 (2001): 384.

11. Paul Radin, *Primitive Man as Philosopher* (New York: Dover Publications, 1957), 36.

12. Ibid., 53.

13. Ibid., xvii–xviii.

14. Ibid., 5.

15. Ibid., 231–233.

16. Regna Darnell, "Philosophizing with the 'Other,'" in *Invisible Genealogies: A History of Americanist Anthropology* (Lincoln: University of Nebraska Press, 2001), 146.

17. C. G. Jung, "The Type Problem in Modern Philosophy," in *Psychological Types,* Bollingen Series 20 (Princeton, NJ: Princeton University Press, 1971), 300–315.

18. See, for example, Victor Turner, "Muchona the Hornet, Interpreter of Religion," in *The Forest of Symbols: Aspects of Ndembu Ritual* (Ithaca, NY: Cornell University Press, 1967).

19. Radin was likely working on what would become his first publication, "Auf Netztechnik der Sudamerikanischer Indianer" [The Net Technique of South American Indians], *Zeitschrift für Ethnologie,* no. 388 (1906): 926–938.

20. Radin to Lowie, June 1, 1905, Paul Radin Papers, Marquette University Special Collections and University Archives (hereafter MUA), PRs01_01–01_1901a.

21. James Harvey Robinson, *The New History* (New York: Macmillan, 1912), 20–25.

22. James Harvey Robinson, *The Human Comedy* (New York: Harper and Bros., 1937), 42–48.

23. James Harvey Robinson, *An Outline of the History of the Intellectual Class in Europe* (New York: n.p., 1911), 1.

24. Robinson to Boas, May 18, 1926. Franz Boas Papers, American Philosophical Society Archives (hereafter Boas Papers).

25. Radin, *The Racial Myth* (New York: McGraw-Hill Book Co., 1934), 140.

26. Kenneth Burke, review of *Primitive Man as Philosopher,* by Paul Radin, *The Dial* 53, no. 5 (November 1927): 439.

27. Radin, *Method and Theory,* 11–12.

28. Arthur J. Vidich, "Paul Radin and Contemporary Anthropology," *Social Research* 32, no. 4 (Winter 1965): 378. The postmodern movement within American anthropology, accelerating in the 1980s, gave little credit to earlier figures, such as Radin, who anticipated several issues that came to dominate the field. See, for example, Melford Spiro, "Postmodernist Anthropology, Subjectivity, and Science: A Modernist Critique," *Comparative Studies in Society and History* 38, no. 4 (1996): 759–780.

29. Ibid., 383.

30. Arnold Krupat, *For Those Who Come After: A Study of Native American Autobiography* (Berkeley: University of California Press, 1985); Michelle Burnham, "'I Lied All the Time': Trickster Discourse and Ethnographic Authority in *Crashing Thunder,*" *American Indian Quarterly* 22, no. 4 (1998): 469–484.

31. Radin, *Method and Theory,* 177–178.

32. J. David Sapir, "Paul Radin, 1883–1959," *Journal of American Folklore* 74, no. 291 (1961): 65.

33. A. L. Kroeber, review of *The Method and Theory of Ethnology,* by Paul Radin, *American Anthropologist,* n.s., 35, no. 4 (1933): 765.

34. A. L. Kroeber, "The Superorganic," *American Anthropologist,* n.s., 19, no. 2 (1917): 163–213.

35. A. L. Kroeber, "Eighteen Professions," *American Anthropologist,* n.s., 17, no. 2 (1915): 283–288.

36. Franz Boas, "The Study of Geography," in *Race, Language and Culture* (New York: Free Press, 1966).

37. Radin, *Method and Theory,* 28–30.

38. In "Souls," Radin makes this point in relation to his Nashville informants providing autobiographies. Only a few aged former slaves were sufficiently reflective to narrate their life histories. "Souls Piled Like Timber: The Religious Experience of the Prewar Negro" (unpublished manuscript, MUA, n.d.), 8.

39. Paul Radin, *Primitive Religion: Its Nature and Origin* (New York: Dover Publications, 1957), vii.

40. Paul Radin, "Boas and 'The Mind of Primitive Man,'" in *Books That Changed Our Minds,* ed. Malcolm Cowley and Bernard Smith (New York: Doubleday, Doran, 1939), 142.

41. Radin, *Primitive Religion,* vii, 45–48.

42. Ibid., 40–41.

43. "The Nature of Primitive Religion," MUA Series 2-1. This unpublished and undated manuscript written after the 1937 publication of *Primitive Religion* reiterates this point. The manuscript is unconcerned with material or economic factors but rather "the religious experience proper." Radin argues that the latter has been badly misunderstood by theorists of religion, "all of them fundamentally disqualified for the task of interpreting aboriginal religion" because they bring their own cultural preconceptions to the task. Equally debilitating, Radin continues, theorists of religion "do not know enough" since the requisite knowledge can only be gained by long-term residence in an aboriginal community.

44. Radin, *Primitive Man as Philosopher,* 6.

45. Regna Darnell, *And Along Came Boas: Continuity and Revolution in Americanist Anthropology* (Amsterdam: John Benjamins, 1998), 6.

46. Herbert S. Lewis, "Franz Boas: Boon or Bane?," *Reviews in Anthropology* 37, no. 2–3 (2008): 172–176.

47. Darnell, *And Along Came Boas,* 5; Franz Boas, "The Limitations of the Comparative Method of Anthropology," *Science* 4, no. 103 (1896): 901–908.

48. George W. Stocking Jr., *Race, Culture and Evolution: Essays in the History of Anthropology* (New York: Free Press, 1968), 282–286.

49. Radin, *Method and Theory,* 118n.

50. Paul Radin, *The Winnebago Tribe* (Lincoln: University of Nebraska Press, 1990), xv.

51. Radin, *Method and Theory,* 117.

52. Radin, *The Winnebago Tribe,* xvi.

53. Radin, *Method and Theory,* 8–9.

54. J. Owen Dorsey, *Omaha Sociology* (Washington, DC: U.S. Government Printing Office, 1884), 227, 229, 247.

55. Edward Sapir, "Why Cultural Anthropology Needs the Psychiatrist," in *Selected Writings of*

Edward Sapir in Language, Culture and Personality, ed. David G. Mandelbaum (Berkeley: University of California Press, 1985), 569–570.

56. Ibid., 570.
57. Radin, *Method and Theory,* 42–43.
58. Ibid., 238.
59. Sapir, "Why Cultural Anthropology Needs the Psychiatrist," 572.
60. Regna Darnell, *Invisible Genealogies: A History of Americanist Anthropology* (Lincoln: University of Nebraska Press, 2001), 138–139.
61. Radin, *Method and Theory,* 3.
62. Ibid., 261–266.
63. Paul Radin, *The World of Primitive Man,* ix–xi.
64. Robert Redfield, "The Folk Society," *American Journal of Sociology* 52, no. 4 (1947).
65. Edward Sapir, "Culture, Genuine and Spurious" *American Journal of Sociology* 29, no. 4 (1924).
66. Radin, *The World of Primitive Man,* 7, 11–13.
67. F. W. Hodge (Ethnologist-in-Charge) to Charles D. Walcott, Secretary of the Smithsonian Institution, November 16, 1911, MUA_PRs01_01–02_1911c.
68. Radin to Boas, November 1, 1911, Boas Papers.
69. George W. Stocking Jr., "The Scientific Reaction against Cultural Anthropology, 1917–1920," in *Race, Culture, and Evolution* (New York: Free Press, 1968), 270–307.
70. Boas to Kroeber, August 23, 1912, MUA_PRs01_01–02_1912d.
71. Alexander Goldenweiser to Boas, February 18, 1912, Boas Papers.
72. Sapir to Kroeber, May 15, 1913, MUA_PRs01_01–02_1913b.
73. Boas to Kroeber, November 26, 1911, MUA_PRs01_01–02_1911d.
74. Radin to Boas, January 7, 1915, Boas Papers.
75. Boas to Kroeber, January 19, 1917, Boas Papers.
76. Cora Du Bois, "Paul Radin: An Appreciation," in *Culture in History: Essays in Honor of Paul Radin* (New York: Columbia University Press, 1960), xii–xiv.
77. Radin to Boas, October 20, 1920, Boas Papers.
78. Boas to Kroeber and Sapir, February 17, 1931, MUA-PRs01_02–01_1931a.
79. Helen Sarason to Mary Sacharoff, April 11, 1983, MUA_PRs01–02–08_1983–04.
80. Radin to Sapir, December 9, 1916, MUA_PRs01_01–04_1916d.
81. Sapir to Kroeber, November 28, 1930, MUA_PRs01_01–07_1929_Nov-1930_Nov.pdf., 6–7.
82. Radin to Boas, May 3, 1929, Boas Papers.
83. Radin to Boas, April 19, 1932, Boas Papers.
84. Radin, *Method and Theory,* 24–25.

85. Boas to Amelia Susman, July 20, 1937, Boas Papers.

86. Japanese American World War II Evacuation Oral History Project, Interview with Robert Spencer, Calisphere, University of California, http://www.oac.cdlib.org/view?docId=ft0p30026h&brand=calisphere&doc.view=entire_text.

87. Christer Lindberg, "Paul Radin: The Anthropological Trickster," *European Review of Native American Studies* 14, no. 1 (2000).

88. Susman to Boas, August 4, 1937, Boas Papers.

89. Walter Goldschmidt to Mary Sacharoff, April 8, 1983, MUA_PRs01_03–01_1983–04, 6.

90. A. M. Halpern to Mary Sacharoff, October 6, 1982, MUA_PRs01_02–08_1982a, 2–3.

91. Omer C. Stewart to Mary Sacharoff, March 29, 1982, MUA_PRs01_02–06_1982i, 15–18.

92. Nancy Lurie to Mary Sacharoff, November 2, 1981, MUA_PRs01_02–05_1981h.

93. Nancy Lurie to Mary Sacharoff, April 12, 1982, MUA_PRs01_02–07_1982a.

94. Alexander Lesser to Mary Sacharoff, April 9, 1982, MUA_PRs01_02_07_1982a, 2.

95. Paul Radin, *Social Anthropology* (New York: McGraw-Hill, 1932), ix.

96. Paul Radin, "Personal Reminiscences of a Winnebago Indian," *Journal of American Folklore* 26, no. 102 (1913); Paul Radin, *The Autobiography of a Winnebago Indian* (Berkeley: University of California Press, 1920).

97. Susman to Boas, May 23, 1938, Boas Papers; George W. Stocking, "Review of Esther Goldfrank, *Notes on an Undirected Life: As One Anthropologist Tells It,*" *American Ethnologist* 7, no. 1 (1980): 211–212; Amelia Susman Schultz, "A Tribute to Franz Boas," Society for Applied Anthropology, podcast, 2018, http://sfaa.net/podcast/index.php/podcasts/2011/tribute-franz-boas/.

98. Grant Arndt, *Ho-Chunk Powwows and the Politics of Tradition* (Lincoln: University of Nebraska Press, 2016), 107.

99. Joy S. Kasson, *Buffalo Bill's Wild West* (New York: Hill and Wang, 2000), 245; Nancy Lurie, *Mountain Wolf Woman* (Ann Arbor: University of Michigan Press, 1961), 129n10.

100. Arndt, *Ho-Chunk Powwows,* 243–251.

101. Commentary by Doris Radin on Mary Sacharoff's unpublished paper "Paul Radin: The Man and His Work: An Overview," MUA_PRs4, 23. Doris Radin mistakenly thought that her guest was Jasper Blowsnake, the brother of Sam Blowsnake, the autobiographer. Jasper had died in 1926.

102. Paul Radin, *The Autobiography of a Winnebago Indian,* University of California Publications in American Archeology and Ethnology, vol. 16, no. 7 (1920): 417–418.

103. Radin to Kroeber, November 11, 1932, MUA_PRs01_02_01 1932, 9–10.

104. San Francisco Field Office, FBI, 100-18676, MUA_ PRs1-FBI. Radin FBI file. All cited FBI documents are part of the same Freedom of Information Act requests filed by Helene

Hagan. See David H. Price, *Threatening Anthropology: McCarthyism and the FBI's Surveillance of Activist Anthropologists* (Durham, NC: Duke University Press, 2004), 203.

105. William McGuire, *Bollingen: An Adventure in Collecting the Past* (Princeton, NJ: Princeton University Press, 1982), 168–170.

106. Fred Rosenbaum, *Cosmopolitans: A Social and Cultural History of the Jews of the San Francisco Bay Area* (Berkeley: University of California Press, 2009), 289–290; Ray Monk, *Robert Oppenheimer: A Life inside the Center* (New York: Doubleday, 2012), 247.

107. Sidney Cowell to Mary Sacharoff, October 6, 1982, MUA_PRs01_02–08_1982a, 9–11.

108. Price, *Threatening Anthropology,* 199–206. Price provides a detailed examination of the FBI's interest in Radin.

109. San Francisco Field Office of the FBI, February 24, 1945, File 100-51471, MUA_PRs1-FBI.

110. "Dr. Radin Will Teach Two Classes Beginning June 11," flyer, California Labor School, Oakland, June 1935, MUA_PRs01–02–01_1935, pdf., 11.

111. McGuire, *Bollingen,* 96.

112. *San Bernardino County Sun,* September 20, 1946, 1.

113. *Los Angeles Times,* December 16, 1950, 3.

114. G. Eleanor Kimble, "Restrictive Covenants," *Common Ground* (Autumn 1945): 50–51.

115. Mark Brilliant, *The Color of America Has Changed: How Racial Diversity Shaped Civil Rights Reform in California, 1941–1978* (Oxford: Oxford University Press, 2010), 99–101.

116. Ibid., 112–113.

117. Letter of transmittal, California Senate Fact-Finding Committee on Un-American Activities to Senate Chamber, June 18, 1965, 12, University of California, California Digital Library, http://texts.cdlib.org/view?docId=kt4w1003q8&brand=calisphere&doc.view=entire text_.

118. Ibid.

119. *Oakland Tribune,* February 29, 1936, 10; *Los Angeles Times,* August 1, 1940, 1.

120. FBI Agent Report, San Francisco, February 24, 1945, File No. 100-51471, MUA_PRs1-FBI.

121. Ibid.

122. FBI Agent Report, San Francisco, August 7, 1945, File No. 100-51471, MUA-PRs1-FBI.

123. FBI Agent Report, San Francisco, October 2, 1945, File No. 100-51471, MUA-PRs1-FBI.

124. Paul Radin, ed. *African Folktales* (Princeton, NJ: Princeton University Press, 1970), 3.

125. Stanley Diamond, "Paul Radin," in *Totems and Teachers: Key Figures in the History of Anthropology,* ed. Sydel Silverman (Walnut Creek, CA: Altamira, 2004), 64.

CHAPTER 2. OUR SCIENCE AND ITS WHOLESOME INFLUENCE: ANTHROPOLOGY AGAINST RACISM

1. Stanley Edgar Hyman, "Freud and Boas: Secular Rabbis?," *Commentary* (January 1954): 264.

2. George Stocking, "The Scientific Reaction against Cultural Anthropology, 1917–1920," in *Race, Culture, and Evolution: Essays in the History of Anthropology* (New York: Free Press, 1968), 284.

3. Franz Boas to Robert H. Lowie, June 7, 1928, Paul Radin Papers, Marquette University Special Collections and University Archives, PRs01_01–07_1928_Apr–Jun, 9.

4. J. Milton Yinger, "Breaking the Vicious Circle," *Common Ground* 7, no. 1 (Autumn 1946): 3.

5. E. A. Ross, *The Old World in the New: The Significance of Past and Present Immigration to the American People* (New York: Century Co., 1914); John R. Commons, *Races and Immigrants in America* (New York: Macmillan, 1908).

6. Franz Boas, "The Race Problem in Modern Society," in *The Mind of Primitive Man,* rev. ed. (New York: Macmillan, 1938), 235.

7. Stocking, "The Scientific Reaction against Cultural Anthropology," 288.

8. Franz Boas, "Scientists as Spies," *The Nation,* December 20, 1919, 797.

9. Stocking, "The Scientific Reaction against Cultural Anthropology," 287–289.

10. Quoted in Paul Radin, *The Racial Myth* (New York: McGraw-Hill, 1934), 60.

11. Erwin Baur, Eugen Fischer, and Fritz Lenz, *Human Heredity,* trans. Eden and Cedar Paul (New York: Macmillan, 1931), 121.

12. Eugen Fischer to Franz Boas, June 24, 1934, Franz Boas Papers, American Philosophical Society Archives (hereafter Boas Papers).

13. Julia Liss, "Franz Boas on War and Empire: The Making of a Public Intellectual," in *The Franz Boas Papers,* vol. 1, ed. Regna Darnell, Michelle Hamilton, Robert L. A. Hancock, and Joshua Smith (Lincoln: University of Nebraska Press, 2015), 295.

14. *Time,* May 11, 1936, 38–39.

15. Ibid., 37.

16. Paul Radin, "Boas and 'The Mind of Primitive Man,'" in *Books That Changed Our Minds,* ed. Malcolm Cowley and Bernard Smith (New York: Doubleday, Doran, 1939), 130–132.

17. Boas, *The Race Problem in Modern Society,* 226–227.

18. Jonathan Peter Spiro, *Defending the Master Race: Conservation, Eugenics, and the Legacy of Madison Grant* (Burlington: University of Vermont Press, 2009), 366.

19. Radin, "Boas and 'The Mind of Primitive Man,'" 142.

20. Franz Boas, *The Mind of Primitive Man,* rev. ed. (New York: Free Press, 1965), 226. In his review of Howard Odum's *Race and Rumors of Race,* focused on the American South, M.

F. Ashley Montagu remarks that "the South has always fully subscribed to what is today known as the Nazi concept of 'race.'" *American Anthropologist,* n.s., 46, no. 2 (1944): 255.

21. Franz Boas, "The Problem of the American Negro," *Yale Review* 10, no. 2 (January 1921): 394.

22. Ibid., 395.

23. Julia E. Liss, "German Culture and German Science in the *Bildung* of Franz Boas," in *Volkgeist as Method and Ethic: Essays on Boasian Ethnography and the German Anthropological Tradition,* ed. George W. Stocking Jr. (Madison: University of Wisconsin Press, 1996), 157.

24. Franz Boas, "Patriotism," in *Race and Democratic Society* (New York: Biblo and Tannen, 1969), 156.

25. Boas to Dewey, November 6, 1939, Boas Papers. This letter begins with Boas's "exasperation" at unidentified sources seeking to "make it appear as though you and I in our public activities had fundamentally different objectives." He continued: "I believe this is absolutely untrue." Boas was undoubtedly mending fences as a result of tensions with Dewey over the Committee on Cultural Freedom, founded by Dewey and resolute anti-Communist Sidney Hook, to oppose the Popular Front. Dewey and Hook condemned the Popular Front and its apologies for Stalinism and Communist actions in the United States. Boas's commitment to freedom of thought and individual expression was so unwavering that he did not consider how those principles might be turned to cynical and totalitarian purposes by a segment of the Left. Dewey responded to Boas in the same friendly spirit: "I share fully your resentment against efforts put forth to make it appear that our aims are different or that there is any significant opposition between our respective social or economic beliefs." Dewey to Boas, November 12, 1939. Boas Papers. See Gary B. Bullert, "The Committee for Cultural Freedom and the Roots of McCarthyism," *Education and Culture* 29, no. 2 (2013): 25–28.

26. Boas, "Patriotism," 157.

27. Franz Boas, "An Anthropologist's Credo," *The Nation,* August 27, 1938, 202.

28. Ibid., 201.

29. Franz Boas, "On Alternating Sounds," *American Anthropologist* 2, no. 1 (1889).

30. George Stocking, *Race, Culture, and Evolution,* 159.

31. Edward Sapir, "The Psychological Reality of Phonemes," in *Selected Writings of Edward Sapir in Language, Culture and Personality,* ed. David G. Mandelbaum (Berkeley: University of California Press, 1949), 46–60.

32. Boas's "On Alternating Sounds" delivered a death blow to the evolutionary view that language development brings greater sound precision. Noting sound variation

unperceived by speakers in some American Indian languages, Daniel Brinton concluded that this putative imprecision objectively indicated rudimentary language development among early humans rather than a single sound perceived differently through the filter of distinct phonemic systems. See Daniel G. Brinton, "The Earliest Form of Human Speech as Revealed by American Tongues," in *Essays of an Americanist* (Philadelphia: Porter and Coates, 1890), 393, 398.

33. Melville Herskovits, *Cultural Dynamics* (New York: Alfred A. Knopf, 1967), 190.

34. Ruth Benedict and Gene Weltfish, "The Races of Mankind," in *Race: Science and Politics,* ed. Ruth Benedict (New York: Viking, 1945), 167.

35. Roi Ottley, *Roi Ottley's World War II: The Lost Diary of an African American Journalist* (Lawrence: University Press of Kansas, 2011).

36. Walter White, *A Rising Wind* (New York: Doubleday, Doran, 1945), 12.

37. Ruth Landes to Charles S. Johnson, March 6, 1944, Fisk University Archives, Charles S. Johnson Papers, 1866–1965, Box 7, Folder 15.

38. Franz Boas, "The Outlook for the American Negro," in *The Shaping of American Anthropology, 1883–1911,* ed. George W. Stocking Jr. (New York: Basic, 1974), 315.

39. Ibid., 313.

40. W. E. B. Du Bois, *Black Folk Then and Now: An Essay in the History and Sociology of the Negro Race* (New York: Oxford University Press, 2007), xxxi.

41. W. E. B. Du Bois, *The Conservation of Races* (Washington, DC: American Negro Academy Occasional Papers, No. 2, 1897), 9.

42. Quoted in Kwame Anthony Appiah, *Lines of Descent: W. E. B. Du Bois and the Emergence of Identity* (Cambridge, MA: Harvard University Press, 2014), 121.

43. Franz Boas to Andrew Carnegie, November 30, 1906, Boas Papers.

44. Franz Boas to Booker T. Washington, November 8, 1908, Boas Papers.

45. Otto Klineberg, *Race Differences* (New York: Harper and Brothers, 1935), 348.

46. W. E. B. Du Bois, "My Evolving Program for Negro Freedom," in *What the Negro Wants,* ed. Rayford W. Logan (Chapel Hill: University of North Carolina Press, 1944), 70.

47. W. T. Couch, "Publisher's Introduction," in Logan, *What the Negro Wants,* ix.

48. Langston Hughes, "What the Negro Wants," *Common Ground* (Autumn 1941): 54.

49. Couch, "Publisher's Introduction," xiii–xvii, xxii–xxiii.

50. Charles S. Johnson, Review of *What the Negro Wants,* by Rayford W. Logan, *American Sociological Review* 11, no. 2 (1946): 244–245.

51. See especially Robert E. Hemenway, *Zora Neale Hurston: A Literary Biography* (Urbana: University of Illinois Press, 1977). This biography remains the definitive treatment of the life of Zora Neale Hurston.

52. Zora Neale Hurston, *Dust Tracks on a Road* (Urbana: University of Illinois Press, 1984), 170.

53. Hemenway, *Zora Neale Hurston,* 63.

54. Ibid.

55. Langston Hughes, *The Big Sea: An Autobiography* (New York: Thunder's Mouth, 1986), 239.

56. Ibid.

57. Boas to Otto Klineberg, November 25, 1929, Boas Papers.

58. Carter Woodson to Boas, May 15, 1923; Woodson to Boas, November 16, 1926; Boas to Woodson, November 18, 1926; Boas to Woodson, November 22, 1926; Woodson to Boas, December 7, 1926. Boas Papers.

59. Boas to Woodson, November 6, 1926, Boas Papers.

60. For a biography of Parsons, see Rosemary Lévy Zumwalt, *Wealth and Rebellion: Elsie Clews Parsons, Anthropologist and Folklorist* (Urbana: University of Illinois Press, 1992).

61. Woodson to Boas, November 23, 1926, Boas Papers.

62. Hurston to Boas, March 29, 1927, Boas Papers.

63. Hurston, *Dust Tracks,* 174–175.

64. Boas to Hurston, May 3, 1927, Boas Papers.

65. Robert Redfield, Ralph Linton, and Melville J. Herskovits, "Memorandum for the Study of Acculturation," *American Anthropologist,* n.s., 38, no. 1 (1936): 149–152.

66. Melville J. Herskovits, *The Myth of the Negro Past* (Boston: Beacon, 1990), 231.

67. Hurston, *Dust Tracks,* 175.

68. Arthur Huff Fauset, "American Negro Folk Literature," in *The New Negro,* ed. Alain Locke (New York: Simon and Schuster, 1997), 238–244.

69. Zora Neale Hurston, *Mules and Men* (New York: HarperCollins, 1990), xiii.

70. Hurston to Boas, December 27, 1928, Boas Papers.

71. Nell Battle Lewis, Review of *The Negro and His Songs,* by Howard W. Odum and Guy Johnson, *North Carolina Historical Review* 2, no. 4 (1925): 541.

72. Hurston, *Mules and Men,* 1–4.

73. Edwin Embree to Boas, March 26, 1935, Boas Papers. For discussion of the withdrawal of the Rosenwald grant, see the following: Hemenway, *Zora Neale Hurston,* 208–212; Carla Kaplan, ed., *Zora Neale Hurston: A Life in Letters* (New York: Random House, 2002), 105–107.

74. Kaplan, *Zora Neale Hurston,* 167–168.

75. Ben N. Azikiwe, Review of *The Racial Myth,* by Paul Radin, *Journal of Negro History* 20, no. 1 (January 1935): 98–99.

76. *Pittsburgh Courier,* January 2, 1943, 6.

77. *Columbia Spectator,* May 10, 1933.

78. *Columbia Spectator,* May 19, 1933; Paul Rivet, "Tribute to Franz Boas," *International Journal of American Linguistics* 14 (October 1958): 251.

79. Robert H. Lowie, *Biographical Memoir of Franz Boas,* National Academy of Sciences, vol. 24, Ninth Memoir (Washington, DC: National Academy of Sciences, 1947), 309–310.

80. Rivet, "Tribute," 252.

81. St. Clair Drake, "Anthropology and the Black Experience," *Black Scholar* 11, no. 7 (1980): 27–28.

82. *Strangers Abroad,* episode 3, "The Shackles of Tradition," video recording, directed by Bruce Dakowski (London: Central Independent Television, 1985–86).

83. Rosemary Lévy Zumwalt and William Shedrick Willis, "Franz Boas and W. E. B. Du Bois at Atlanta University, 1906," *Transactions of the American Philosophical Society* 98, no. 2 (2008): 33.

84. Spiro, *Defending the Master Race,* xi.

85. Andre Gingrich, "German Anthropology during the Nazi Period: Complex Scenarios of Collaboration, Persecution, and Competition," in *One Discipline, Four Ways: British, German, French, and American Anthropology,* Halle Lectures (Chicago: University of Chicago Press, 2005), 118, 128–129.

86. Spiro, *Defending the Master Race,* 380.

87. Robert Proctor, "From *Anthropologie* to *Rassenkunde* in the German Anthropological Tradition," in *Bones, Bodies, Behavior: Essays on Biological Anthropology,* History of Anthropology, vol. 5, ed. George W. Stocking Jr. (Madison: University of Wisconsin Press, 1988), 174.

CHAPTER 3. FROM OBJECT TO SUBJECT: CENTERING AFRICAN AMERICAN LIVES AT FISK UNIVERSITY

1. Johnson's life and career are discussed in Patrick Gilpin and Marybeth Gasman, *Charles S. Johnson: Leadership beyond the Veil in the Age of Jim Crow* (Albany: State University of New York Press, 2003). For a broader consideration of Johnson's role in the civil rights struggle, particularly in the South, see John Egerton, *Speak Now against the Day: The Generation before the Civil Rights Movement in the South* (New York: Alfred A. Knopf, 1994), 54–55, 436–439.

2. Gilpin and Gasman, *Charles S. Johnson,* 98.

3. Marybeth Gasman, "W.E.B. Du Bois and Charles S. Johnson: Differing Views on the Role

of Philanthropy in Higher Education," *History of Education Quarterly* 42, no. 4 (2002): 510–512.

4. Gilpin and Gasman, *Charles S. Johnson,* 97.

5. The Chicago Commission on Race Relations, *The Negro in Chicago: A Study of Race Relations and a Race Riot* (Chicago: University of Chicago Press, 1922), xv, xviii.

6. Gilpin and Gasman, *Charles S. Johnson,* 13.

7. The Chicago Commission, *The Negro in Chicago: : A Study of Race Relations and a Race Riot,* xiv.

8. Ibid., 594, 632.

9. Ibid., xxiv.

10. A brief but telling example of Johnson's carefully chosen words appears in his remarks about "race pride." He recognizes the "propriety and social value of race pride among Negroes," but he admonishes the community to avoid excessive and exclusive talk about race because it would "promote separation of race interests and thereby . . . interfere with racial adjustment." Johnson's remarks reflect both the spirit of his mentor and the political realities of his time and place. He neither ignores nor denigrates the assertion of black self-esteem. *The Negro in Chicago,* 647.

11. Ibid., xv, 4.

12. Ibid., 55–57.

13. Robert Ezra Park, *Race and Culture* (Glencoe, IL: Free Press, 1950), v, viii–ix.

14. Ernest W. Burgess, "Social Planning and Race Relations," in *Race Relations: Problems and Theory,* ed. Jitsuichi Masuoka and Preston Valien (Chapel Hill: University of North Carolina Press, 1961), 17.

15. Zora Neale Hurston, *Dust Tracks on a Road* (Urbana: University of Illinois Press, 1984), 168.

16. Langston Hughes, *The Big Sea: An Autobiography* (New York: Thunder's Mouth, 1986), 218.

17. Johnson's efforts on behalf of African American writers also aimed to bring their creative talents to the attention of white publishers. However, as Ann Douglas has noted, "Virtually none of the black writers could support themselves on their published work alone, as the majority of white writers did." Moreover, despite Johnson's energetic promotion of African American poets and novelists and his insightful sociological articles about race, sales of *Opportunity* peaked at a modest 11,000 copies per month in 1928. White readers accounted for 40 percent of sales. See Ann Douglas, *Terrible Honesty: Mongrel Manhattan in the 1920s* (New York: Noonday, 1995), 85.

18. Charles S. Johnson, ed., *Opportunity: A Journal of Negro Life* 1, no. 1 (January 1923), n.p.

19. Ibid.

20. "The Verdict of 'Common Sense,'" *Opportunity: A Journal of Negro Life* 1, no. 6 (June 1923): 2. Two years later, Johnson published a very forward-looking article by Howard H. Long, a psychologist in the department of research in the Washington, DC, public schools. Long criticized mental testing and its racial interpretations at several levels, including the in-built cultural biases of the test and the insupportable efforts to link IQ to heredity. See Howard H. Long, "On Mental Tests and Racial Psychology: A Critique," *Opportunity* 3, no. 29 (May 1925): 137–138. Shortly before its publication, Johnson wrote to Boas asking for comment on the paper "as thorogoing [*sic*] as it is provocative." Charles S. Johnson to Franz Boas, April 13, 1925, Franz Boas Papers, American Philosophical Society Archives (hereafter Boas Papers).

21. Franz Boas, "The Real Race Problem," *The Crisis* 1, no. 2 (December 1910): 23–24.

22. James B. McKee, *Sociology and the Race Problem: The Failure of a Perspective* (Urbana: University of Illinois Press, 1993), 61, 93–94.

23. W. I. Thomas to Franz Boas, May 14, 1907, Boas Papers. Thomas's interest in Boas's work is discussed in Stephen O. Murray, *American Anthropology and Company* (Lincoln: University of Nebraska Press, 2013), 163–166.

24. Boas to Thomas, May 18, 2017, Boas Papers.

25. Robert E. Park, "The Conflict and Fusion of Cultures with Special Reference to the Negro," *Journal of Negro History* 4 (April 1919): 112.

26. Ibid., 129–130.

27. Robert E. Park, "Education in Its Relation to the Conflict and Fusion of Cultures," in *Race and Culture* (Glencoe, IL: Free Press, 1950), 278.

28. Robert E. Park, "Mentality of Racial Hybrids," *American Journal of Sociology* 36 (January 1931): 546.

29. Gilpin and Gasman, *Charles S. Johnson,* 45. Although the sociologists of the Chicago school and elsewhere wrapped their findings in the language of empiricism and science, the sociology of race relations since Park's time has provoked some blistering critiques. Emphasizing accommodation, assimilation, and continuing integration in their analyses of race relations in the United States up to the 1960s, sociologists on the whole stunningly failed to anticipate the racial turmoil of that decade, especially in the South, ranging from urban riots and black cultural nationalism, to the repudiation of integration. The 1960s upended conventional sociological thinking about race and undermined the intellectual apparatus of race-relations theory that depended on evolutionary models of gradual change and consensus instead of conflict. See McKee, *Sociology and the Race Problem,* 4–14; Stephen Steinberg, *Race Relations: A Critique* (Stanford, CA: Stanford University Press, 2007). Steinberg's volume is more than a

critique of the race-relations model in sociology; it is a thoroughgoing indictment of the disengaged, value-free nature of American sociology itself that developed shortly after the turn of the twentieth century.

30. St. Clair Drake and Horace R. Cayton, *Black Metropolis: A Study of Negro Life in a Northern City* (Chicago: University of Chicago Press, 1945).

31. Park, *Race and Culture,* 149–151.

32. Ibid.

33. Richard Alba, *Ethnic Identity: The Transformation of White America* (New Haven, CT: Yale University Press, 1990).

34. Howard W. Odum, *Social and Mental Traits of the Negro: Research into the Conditions of the Negro Race in Southern Towns; A Study in Race Traits, Tendencies and Prospects* (New York: Columbia University, 1910).

35. Ibid., 52.

36. William B. Thomas, "Howard W. Odum's Social Theories in Transition: 1910–1930," *American Sociologist* 16, no. 1 (February 1981): 26, 27.

37. Franz Boas, "Industries of the African Negroes," *Southern Workman* 38 (April 1909): 229. Stephen O. Murray writes that Odum and Boas were "allied . . . in antiracist endeavors," but neglects not only the racism in Odum's early work but the fact that, as a southern liberal, he was unwilling to match Boas's boldness in confronting racial terror. Writing to Boas in 1933 at the time of the infamous Scottsboro Boys case, Odum cautions Boas against pressing the argument against lynching through the Committee for the Defense of Political Prisoners. See Murray, *American Anthropology and Company,* 201; Howard W. Odum to Franz Boas, September 27, 1933, Boas Papers.

38. Gilpin and Gasman, *Charles S. Johnson,* 156.

39. Egerton, *Speak Now against the Day,* 284–285, 437–439.

40. Charles S. Johnson, *Shadow of the Plantation* (New Brunswick, NJ: Transaction, 1966), 4.

41. Aldon D. Morris, *The Scholar Denied: W.E.B. Du Bois and the Birth of Modern Sociology* (Berkeley: University of California Press, 2015).

42. W. E. B. Du Bois, *The Philadelphia Negro: A Social Study* (New York: Schocken, 1967), 1.

43. Morris, *The Scholar Denied,* 46.

44. Du Bois, *The Philadelphia Negro,* 389.

45. Ibid., 394.

46. Eugene D. Genovese, "Race and Class in Southern History: An Appraisal of the Work of Ulrich Bonnell Phillips," *Agricultural History* 41 (1967).

47. Ulrich B. Phillips, *American Negro Slavery* (Baton Rouge: Louisiana State University Press, 1918), 291.

48. Ulrich B. Phillips, *Life and Labor in the Old South* (Boston: Little, Brown, 1929), 199.

49. George Washington Williams, *History of the Negro Race in America from 1618 to 1880* (New York: G. P. Putnam's Sons, 1883); Williams, *A History of Negro Troops in the War of Rebellion, 1861–1865* (New York: Harper and Brothers, 1888).

50. August Meier and Elliott Rudwick, *Black History and the Historical Profession, 1915–1980* (Urbana: University of Illinois Press, 1986), 2.

51. Peter Novick, *That Noble Dream: The "Objectivity Question" and the American Historical Profession* (New York: Cambridge University Press, 1988), 77.

52. William A. Dunning, *Reconstruction, Political and Economic, 1865–1877* (New York: Harper and Row, 1962), n.p.

53. William A. Dunning, *Essays on the Civil War and Reconstruction* (New York: Macmillan Co., 1898), 248.

54. Dunning, *Reconstruction,* 213–214.

55. Novick, *That Noble Dream,* 225.

56. John Hope Franklin, *Reconstruction after the Civil War* (Chicago: University of Chicago Press, 1961); W. E. B. Du Bois, *Black Reconstruction in America, 1860–1880* (Cleveland: World, 1964).

57. Allan Nevins and Henry Steele Commager, *A Short History of the United States* (New York: Modern Library, 1942), 236.

58. Ibid., 236–237.

59. Ibid., 237.

60. August Meier, *A White Scholar and the Black Community, 1945–1965* (Amherst: University of Massachusetts Press, 1992), 11.

61. Arthur M. Schlesinger Sr., *The Rise of the City, 1878–1898* (New York: Macmillan, 1933), 385–386.

62. August Meier and Elliott Rudwick, *Black History and the Historical Profession, 1915–1980* (Urbana: University of Illinois Press, 1986), 46.

63. David Blight, *Race and Reunion: The Civil War in American Memory* (Cambridge, MA: Harvard University Press, 2001), 2–4.

64. Du Bois, *Black Reconstruction,* n.p.

65. Meier and Rudwick, *Black History and the Historical Profession,* 98–100.

66. Carter G. Woodson to Franz Boas, May 7, 1917, Boas Papers.

67. Lawrence D. Reddick, "A New Interpretation of Negro History," *Journal of Negro History* 22 (January 1937): 21, 26–28. Ironically, Reddick declared the study of slavery in the United States "exhausted," unless new materials came to light. Reddick had collected testimonies from many ex-slaves when he was a graduate student. See brief note in *Opportunity:*

Journal of Negro Life 17, no. 8 (August 1939): 247. Reddick's collected narratives were never published.

68. Paul Radin, "Literary Aspects of North American Mythology," *Canada Department of Mines, Museum Bulletin No. 16,* Anthropological Series 6, June 15, 1915.

69. Paul Radin, ed., *African Folktales and Sculpture* (New York: Pantheon, 1952).

70. See for example Franz Boas, "Stylistic Aspects of Primitive Literature," in *Race, Language and Culture* (New York: Free Press, 1966).

71. Richard Hofstadter, "U.B. Phillips and the Plantation Legend," *Journal of Negro History* 29, no. 2 (April 1944): 124.

72. Lawrence W. Levine, *Black Culture and Black Consciousness: Afro-American Folk Thought from Slavery to Freedom* (New York: Oxford University Press, 2007), xxiii.

73. Ibid., xxvii.

74. Jerome W. Wright, "Mark Hanna Watkins, 1903–1976," *American Anthropologist* 78, no. 4 (December 1976): 889.

75. Gilpin and Gasman, *Charles S. Johnson,* 99. An inveterate organizer, Johnson arranged conferences, including various race-relations symposia. For example, a 1943 symposium at Fisk on education in colonial areas brought anthropological luminaries to the campus, including Bronislaw Malinowski, Margaret Mead, Ruth Benedict, Melville J. Herskovits, Robert Redfield, and Hortense Powdermaker, to discuss the highly problematic transmission of culture through education in culturally diverse societies. The case of African Americans in the United States was as germane to the issues at hand as were the colonial cases examined by the anthropologists. See Charles S. Johnson, "Introduction to Symposium," *American Journal of Sociology* 48, no. 6 (May 1943): 632.

76. Powdermaker's fieldwork in Indianola culminated in her book *After Freedom: A Cultural Study in the Deep South* (New York: Viking, 1939).

77. Hortense Powdermaker, *Stranger and Friend: The Way of an Anthropologist* (New York: W.W. Norton, 1966), 134–135.

78. Hortense Powdermaker to Charles S. Johnson, July 16, 1938, Charles S. Johnson Collection (original) 1893–1956, Box 17, Folder 8. Fisk University Archives and Special Collections (hereafter Johnson Collection).

79. Powdermaker to Johnson, February 4, 1938, Johnson Collection (original) 1893–1956, Box 17, Folder 8.

80. Johnson, *Shadow of the Plantation,* 125.

81. Ibid., 3.

82. Ibid., 3, 22.

83. Cudjo Lewis, enslaved in Africa and brought to Alabama long after the slave trade

was outlawed, told Zora Neale Hurston of the mockery the newcomers suffered from American-born bondsmen and women who called them "savage." Hurston had gone to Alabama in 1927 at the instigation of Boas in order to interview Cudjo Lewis, preparatory to submitting a report to Carter Woodson for the *Journal of Negro History.* See Zora Neale Hurston, "Cudjo's Own Story of the Last African Slaver," *Journal of Negro History* 12, no. 4 (October 1927): 648–663; and Zora Neale Hurston, *Barracoon: The Story of the Last "Black Cargo,"* ed. Deborah G. Plant (New York: HarperCollins, 2018), 62.

84. Johnson, *Shadow of the Plantation,* 23.
85. Ibid., ch. 1, n. 12.
86. Melville J. Herskovits, *The Myth of the Negro Past* (Boston: Beacon, 1990), 204.
87. Guy B. Johnson, review of *The Myth of the Negro Past,* by Melville J. Herskovits, *American Sociological Review* 7, no. 2 (April 1942): 290.
88. Melville J. Herskovits, "What Has Africa Given America?," *New Republic,* September 4, 1935, 93–94.
89. Charles S. Johnson to Melville J. Herskovits, February 11, 1935, Charles S. Johnson Papers (original), Box 5, Folder 5.
90. "The Negro in America," Lecture 1, n.d., Charles S. Johnson Papers, Register Q, Box 4, Folder 7.
91. "The Negro in America," Lecture 9, n.d., Charles S. Johnson Papers, Register Q, Box 3, Folder 4.
92. W. E. B. Du Bois, "Review of *The Myth of the Negro Past,*" *Annals of the American Academy of Political and Social Science* 222 (1942): 226.
93. C. G. Woodson, "Review of *The Myth of the Negro Past,*" *Journal of Negro History* 27, no. 1 (1942): 117.
94. Ibid., 115.
95. Ibid., 118.
96. Jerry Gershenhorn, *Melville J. Herskovits and the Racial Politics of Knowledge* (Lincoln: University of Nebraska Press, 2004), 139–155.
97. *Pittsburgh Courier,* February 28, 1942, 6.
98. E. Franklin Frazier, *The Negro Family in the United States* (Chicago: University of Chicago Press, 1939), 21, 487.
99. E. Franklin Frazier, "Durham: Capital of the Black Middle Class," in *The New Negro,* ed. Alain Locke (New York: Simon and Schuster, 1997), 339.
100. E. Franklin Frazier, *Black Bourgeoisie* (Glencoe, IL: Free Press, 1957).
101. Arthur A. Schomburg, "The Negro Digs Up His Past," in Locke, *The New Negro,* 31.

CHAPTER 4. THE RADIN-WATSON COLLECTION: NARRATIVES OF SLAVERY AND TRANSCENDENCE

1. Paul Radin to Robert Lowie, April 7, 1953, Paul Radin Papers, Marquette University Special Collections and University Archives, PRs01_02–03_1953b, 2.

2. *Unwritten History of Slavery: Autobiographical Account of Negro Ex-Slaves,* Social Science Source Documents No. 1 (Nashville, TN: Social Science Institute, Fisk University, 1945); *God Struck Me Dead: Religious Conversion Experiences and Autobiographies of Negro Ex-Slaves,* Social Science Source Documents No. 2 (Nashville, TN: Social Science Institute, Fisk University, 1945).

3. *Unwritten History,* iv.

4. Patrick J. Gilpin and Marybeth Gasman, *Charles S. Johnson: Leadership beyond the Veil in the Age of Jim Crow* (Albany: State University of New York Press, 2003), 97.

5. *Unwritten History,* iv.

6. Ibid., i.

7. Paul Radin, "Souls Piled Like Timber: The Religious Experience of the Prewar Negro" (unpublished manuscript, MUA Series 2–2, Box 2, Folder 41), 1.

8. Unpublished draft introduction to *God Struck Me Dead,* Fisk University, Charles S. Johnson Collection (hereafter Johnson Collection) [original] 1893–1956, Register L, Box 4, File 15.

9. Paul Radin, *The Method and Theory of Ethnology: An Essay in Criticism* (New York: McGraw-Hill, 1933), 8–9.

10. Radin, "Souls," 2nd preface, 11 (handwritten).

11. Bransford Watson, interview, Dayton, Ohio, April 3, 2015.

12. " Souls," 3–4

13. Ibid., 5.

14. Ibid., 2.

15. Ibid., 2–3.

16. Ibid., 3.

17. Ibid., 9 (handwritten).

18. Ibid.,8 (handwritten).

19. Ibid. 9 (handwritten).

20. Ibid.

21. Watson's good friend and Wiley College colleague Melvin Tolson, a poet, Harlem Renaissance scholar, and famed debate coach, also experienced Boas's influence indirectly. Tolson praised Franz Boas in his epic poem "Rendezvous with America," which depicts "Boas translating the oneness in the Rosetta Stone of mankind." *Common Ground*

2, no. 4 (Summer 1942): 3–9.

22. Andrew Polk Watson, "Primitive Religion among Negroes in Tennessee" (master's thesis, Fisk University, 1932), 95.

23. Radin, "Souls," 274.

24. *God Struck Me Dead,* 205–218.

25. Ibid., 165–166.

26. Radin, "Souls," 54.; *God Struck Me Dead,* 74.

27. *Unwritten History,* 2.

28. James C. Scott, *Weapons of the Weak: Everyday Forms of Peasant Resistance* (New Haven, CT: Yale University Press, 1985).

29. Jack Glazier, *Been Coming Through Some Hard Times: Race, History and Memory in Western Kentucky* (Knoxville: University of Tennessee Press, 2012), 42–46.

30. *Unwritten History,* 82.

31. Ibid., 84.

32. Ibid., 197.

33. John B. Cade, "Out of the Mouths of Ex-Slaves," *Journal of Negro History* 20 (July 1935).

34. Ibid., 294.

35. Gilbert Osofsky, ed., *Puttin' On Ole Massa* (New York: Harper and Row, 1969).

36. John W. Blassingame, ed., *Slave Testimony: Two Centuries of Letters, Speeches, Interviews, and Autobiographies* (Baton Rouge: Louisiana State University Press, 1977).

37. Ulrich Bonnell Phillips, *American Negro Slavery* (Baton Rouge: Louisiana State University Press, 1918), n.p.; Phillips, *Life and Labor in the Old South* (Boston: Little, Brown, 1929), 219.

38. Radin, "Souls," 4–5.

39. Robert E. Hemenway, *Zora Neale Hurston: A Literary Biography* (Urbana: University of Illinois Press, 1977), 276.

40. Radin, "Introduction," "Souls," 10.

41. The best, extended critical discussion of slave narratives as historical sources, particularly the WPA collection, appears in Paul D. Escott, *Slavery Remembered: A Record of Twentieth-Century Slave Narratives* (Chapel Hill: University of North Carolina Press, 1979). See also Escott, "The Art and Science of Reading WPA Slave Narratives," in *The Slave's Narrative,* ed. Charles T. Davis and Henry Louis Gates Jr. (New York: Oxford University Press, 1985), 44–45; and C. Vann Woodward, "History from Slave Sources," in *The Slave's Narrative,* 53, 56–58. Both Escott and Woodward agree on the substantial value of the WPA narratives as valid and rich historical sources, if the same critical historiographic sensibilities used in conventional documentary research are brought to bear on the WPA materials. The

long record of underutilization of the WPA collection is itself a product of a deep bias in the history profession exemplified by U. B. Phillips, who exercised an enormous influence on those studying slavery and the American South. Since the mid-twentieth century, criticism of the WPA narratives has done little to diminish the continuing use of these texts, even by the critics. See Donna J. Spindel, "Assessing Memory: Twentieth-Century Slave Narratives Reconsidered," *Journal of Interdisciplinary History* 27 (Autumn 1996).

42. Escott has tabulated the race of WPA interviewers, showing the preponderance of white southerners, although in many instances there is no record of the race of particular interviewers. See Escott, *Slavery Remembered,* 188–191. White southern racial postures are evident in the rendering of black testimony in very pronounced vernacular regarding such stereotypic subject matter as ghosts, hoodoo, conjuring, and other instances of black folk belief. Some interviews are commendable. For example, the Evansville, Indiana, interviews of Moses Slaughter and Mary Elizabeth Patterson, respectfully conducted by Lauana Creel, a white music teacher, are rendered in Standard English and provide some context for the portrayal of Slaughter and Patterson as reflective and sensitive individuals offering candid, unvarnished depictions of the searing cruelty of their enslavement. See George P. Rawick, ed., *The American Slave: A Composite Autobiography* (Indiana and Ohio Narratives), supplement, ser. 1, vol. 5 (Westport, CT: Greenwood, 1972), 193–199; Glazier, *Been Coming Through Some Hard Times,* 89–90; Ronald L. Baker, *Homeless, Friendless, and Penniless: The WPA Interviews with Former Slaves Living in Indiana* (Bloomington: Indiana University Press, 2000), 201–203, 231–234.

43. Paul Radin, "History of Ethnological Theories," *American Anthropologist,* n.s., 31, no. 1 (1929): 32.

44. Paul Radin, "Status, Phantasy, and the Christian Dogma," in *God Struck Me Dead,* iv.

45. Watson, "Primitive Religion."

46. Melville J. Herskovits, *The Myth of the Negro Past* (Boston: Beacon, 1990), 232–233.

47. Zora Neale Hurston, "Cudjo's Own Story of the Last African Slaver," *Journal of Negro History* 12, no. 4 (October 1927): 648–663. Hemenway has reported, based on a discovery in 1972, that Hurston, without attribution, drew heavily on an earlier publication, *Historic Sketches of the Old South,* by Emma Langdon. Hurston, in other words, plagiarized the earlier account of Cudjo Lewis. She was courting academic catastrophe, putting at risk her relationship with Boas and Woodson, who would not have tolerated Hurston's dishonesty. Hemenway, *Zora Neale Hurston,* 96–99. Her long-dormant book manuscript about Cudjo has recently been published. See Hurston, *Barracoon: The Story of the Last "Black Cargo"* (New York: Amistad, 2018). See the Afterword by Deborah G. Plant

for further discussion of Hurston's use of Langdon's work. Plant argues that claims of plagiarism are justified in relation to "Cudjo's Own Story of the Last African Slaver," but do not stand up regarding *Barracoon.*

48. Watson, "Primitive Religion," 26, 27.
49. Herskovits, *The Myth of the Negro Past,* 223–228.
50. Watson, "Primitive Religion," 59.
51. *God Struck Me Dead,* 19–22; Paul Radin, "Three Conversions," *Circle Magazine,* nos. 7–8 (1946): 91–94.
52. Radin, "Souls," 377.
53. Radin, "Three Conversions," 90.
54. Audio recordings were certainly possible. Early recording technology had been used by Frances Densmore and by Kroeber and Sapir in studying the Yahi speech and texts spoken by Kroeber's famed informant, Ishi. And of course, Radin used recording equipment in his Winnebago research. More advanced at the time of the Fisk project, the technology was not used, perhaps because of costs or the desire to minimize any possibility of disturbing the narrators.
55. Watson, "Primitive Religion," 10.
56. Radin, "Status, Phantasy, and the Christian Dogma," v.
57. Radin, "Souls," 191–195 (handwritten); *God Struck Me Dead,* 3–6.
58. Ibid., 23–25.
59. Arnold Van Gennep, *The Rites of Passage,* trans. Monika B. Vizedom and Gabrielle L. Caffee (Chicago: University of Chicago Press, 1960), 10–13.
60. Radin, "Status, Phantasy, and the Christian Dogma," vi.
61. Radin, "Souls," n.p.; *God Struck Me Dead,* 44–46.
62. Radin, "Three Conversions," 91.
63. Radin, "Souls," 336 (handwritten).
64. Ibid., 338 (handwritten).
65. Ibid., 336 (handwritten).
66. Ibid., 64 (handwritten).
67. Watson, "Primitive Religion," 80–81.
68. Ibid., 82.

CHAPTER 5. THE WINNEBAGO NARRATIONS: TRADITION AND TRANSFORMATION

1. Paul Radin, "The Nature of Primitive Religion," 207 (unpublished manuscript), Paul Radin Papers, Series 2-2, African American Folk Literature: Souls Piled Like Timber,

Marquette University Special Collections and University Archives (hereafter MUA).

2. Paul Radin, *The Winnebago Tribe* (Lincoln: University of Nebraska Press, 1970), 237–238.

3. Ibid., 18.

4. Anthony F. C. Wallace, "Revitalization Movements," *American Anthropologist,* n.s., 58, no. 2 (1956): 264.

5. Radin, *The Winnebago Tribe,* 361–362; Paul Radin, *Crashing Thunder: The Autobiography of an American Indian* (New York: D. Appleton, 1926), 195–197.

6. Radin undoubtedly struck locals as someone not accustomed to country life but to someplace very different. Just as anthropologists have their "entry stories," or how fieldwork commences in a new, unfamiliar locale, their informants, too, produce anecdotes about the resident alien. And so Radin related a story that concerned his early foray into the Nebraska hinterlands. Informed he would have to rent a horse and buggy, he was also told that he would have to feed the horse and that horses like corn. Radin, the story goes, then purchased a can of corn. Insisting it was without foundation but amused, Radin retold the anecdote, claiming that it had currency among the Winnebago for the next thirty years.

7. Radin, *The Winnebago Tribe,* xvi.

8. Radin, *Crashing Thunder,* x.

9. Paul Radin, *The Road of Life and Death: A Ritual Drama of the American Indians,* Bollingen Series 5 (New York: Pantheon, 1945), xiii.

10. Ibid., 36.

11. James Mooney, *The Ghost Dance Religion and the Sioux Outbreak of 1890* (Chicago: University of Chicago Press, 1965), xi–xii, 11–17.

12. Ibid., 60.

13. Omer C. Stewart, *Peyote Religion: A History* (Norman: University of Oklahoma Press, 1987), 148.

14. Paul Radin, *The Culture of the Winnebago: As Described by Themselves,* Indiana University Publications in Anthropology and Linguistics, Memoir 2 (Baltimore: Waverly, 1949), 1.

15. Ibid.

16. Omer C. Stewart, *Peyote Religion,* 230.

17. Radin, *The Winnebago Tribe,* xvi.

18. Paul Radin, "The Social Organization of the Winnebago Indians: An Interpretation," *Geological Survey of Canada,* Anthropology Series 5, Museum Bulletin No. 10, May 16, 1915.

19. Radin, *The Winnebago Tribe,* 137–142.

20. Paul Radin, "Personal Reminiscences of a Winnebago Indian," *Journal of American*

Folklore 26, no. 102 (1913): 293–318.

21. Nancy O. Lurie, *Mountain Wolf Woman, Sister of Crashing Thunder* (Ann Arbor: University of Michigan Press, 1961), 97.

22. Paul Radin, *The Autobiography of a Winnebago Indian* (Berkeley: University of California Press, 1920), 383–384.

23. Radin, "Personal Reminiscences of a Winnebago Indian," 293.

24. Radin, *Crashing Thunder,* xv.

25. J. David Sapir, "Paul Radin, 1883–1959," *Journal of American Folklore* 74, no. 291 (1961): 65–67.

26. Radin, *The Culture of the Winnebago,* 2–10.

27. Franz Boas, "Recent Anthropology II," *Science,* n.s., 98 (October 15, 1943): 334–335.

28. Radin, *The Autobiography of a Winnebago Indian,* 384.

29. Radin, *The Culture of the Winnebago,* 5.

30. Radin, *The Winnebago Tribe,* xvi.

31. Radin, *The Culture of the Winnebago,* 1–2.

32. Radin, *The Road of Life and Death,* 42.

33. Claude Lévi-Strauss, "Four Winnebago Myths," in *Culture in History: Essays in Honor of Paul Radin,* ed. Stanley Diamond (New York: Columbia University Press, 1960), 352–362.

34. Radin, *The Culture of the Winnebago,* 73.

35. Nancy Lurie to Mary Sacharoff, April 12, 1982, MUA_PR01_02–07 1972a.pdf, 2.

36. Radin, *The Autobiography of a Winnebago Indian,* 430n123.

37. Radin, *The Winnebago Tribe,* 378; Nancy Lurie, "Two Dollars," in *Crossing Cultural Boundaries: The Anthropological Experience,* ed. Solon T. Kimball and James B. Watson (San Francisco: Chandler, 1972), 159.

38. Omer Stewart to Mary Sacharoff, May 18, 1982, MUA_PR01_02–07_1982c, 2–3.

39. Linda M. Waggoner, *Fire Light: The Life of Angel De Cora, Winnebago Artist* (Norman: University of Oklahoma Press, 2008), 68, 157, 158.

40. Boas to Radin, June 1, 1908, Franz Boas Papers, American Philosophical Society Archives (hereafter Boas Papers).

41. Stewart, *Peyote Religion,* 342–356.

42. Paul Radin, "A Sketch of the Peyote Cult of the Winnebago: A Study in Borrowing," *Journal of Religious Psychology* 7, no. 1 (January 1914): 5. This article is Radin's first extended statement on Winnebago peyotism, concentrating particularly on its acculturative dimensions.

43. Paul Radin, *The Method and Theory of Ethnology: An Essay in Criticism* (New York: McGraw-Hill, 1933), 206–208.

44. Radin, *The Winnebago Tribe,* 341–344.

45. Wallace, "Revitalization Movements," 271–273.

46. Radin, *The Winnebago Tribe,* 372–373.

47. Ibid., 21.

48. Radin, *The Method and Theory,* 208.

49. Wallace, "Revitalization Movements," 265.

50. Radin, *The Winnebago Tribe,* 352.

51. Radin, *The Method and Theory,* 219.

52. Radin, *The Winnebago Tribe,* 376.

53. Ibid., 377.

54. Lurie, *Mountain Wolf Woman,* 100.

55. Ibid., 100–103.

56. Radin, *Crashing Thunder,* 1.

57. Radin, *The Road of Life and Death,* 48–49.

58. Lurie, *Mountain Wolf Woman,* 41–42.

59. L. G. Moses, *The Indian Man* (Lincoln: University of Nebraska Press, 1984), 183–187, 192.

60. Alfred L. Kroeber, *The Arapaho,* Bulletin American Museum of Natural History, vol. 18, part 4 (1907): 320.

61. James S. Slotkin, "The Peyote Way," in *Reader in Comparative Religion,"* 4th ed., ed. William A. Lessa and Evon Z. Vogt (New York: Harper and Row, 1979), 299; Weston La Barre, *The Peyote Cult* (Hamden, CT: Shoe String, 1969), viii; David Aberle, *The Peyote Religion among the Navaho* (Norman: University of Oklahoma Press, 1966), 6–9; Omer Stewart, *Peyote Religion: A History,* xiii–xv.

62. Omer Stewart to Mary Sacharoff, May 18, 1982, MUA_PRs01_02–07_1982c.pdf, 2–3.

63. Robert H. Lowie, *Robert H. Lowie, Ethnologist: A Personal Record* (Berkeley: University of California Press, 1959), 50.

64. Robert H. Lowie, *The Crow Indians* (New York: Farrar and Rinehart, 1935).

65. Robert H. Lowie, *Primitive Religion* (New York: Grosset and Dunlap, 1952), 200–204.

66. Weston La Barre, David P. McAllester, J. S. Slotkin, Omer C. Stewart, and Sol Tax, "Statement on Peyote," *Science* 114 (November 30, 1951): 582–583.

67. Aberle, *The Peyote Religion,* 6. Aberle's italics.

68. Ibid., 6, 9.

69. Slotkin, "The Peyote Way," 299–300.

70. Kroeber, *The Arapaho,* 320.

71. Radin, *Crashing Thunder,* 188–189.

72. Radin, *The Winnebago Tribe,* 358.

73. Radin, *Crashing Thunder,* 190.

74. Ibid., 199.

75. Ibid., 195.

76. Radin, *The Road of Life and Death,* 39–40.

77. Ibid., 40.

78. Radin, *The Autobiography of a Winnebago Indian,* 449n203.

79. Radin, *Crashing Thunder,* 203n32.

80. Arnold Krupat, *For Those Who Come After: A Study of Native American Autobiography* (Berkeley: University of California Press, 1985), 86–89. A more recent view of Crashing Thunder's narration, with its "nesting accounts" of a key event, emphasizes the context and choices that the narrator made in representing a critical event in his life. See Grant Arndt, "Indigenous Autobiography *en Abyme:* Indigenous Reflections on Representational Agency in the Case of *Crashing Thunder,*" *Ethnohistory* 59, no. 1 (Winter 2012): 28–29.

81. Radin, *The Road of Life and Death,* 44–45.

82. Ibid., 47–48.

CONCLUSION

1. Lawrence W. Levine, *Black Culture and Black Consciousness: Afro-American Folk Thought from Slavery to Freedom* (New York: Oxford University Press, 2007), 50. Those identifications remain part of the present. Anthropologist Walter Zenner related to the author his experience at a Passover Seder. As the evening progressed, an African American woman on the kitchen staff, listening to the service, was heard to ask, "Are these Jews white or black?"

2. Eugene D. Genovese, *Roll, Jordan, Roll: The World the Slaves Made* (New York: Vintage, 1976), 253.

3. Jack Glazier, *Been Coming Through Some Hard Times: Race, History, and Memory in Western Kentucky* (Knoxville: University of Tennessee Press, 2012), 42.

4. *God Struck Me Dead: Religious Conversion Experiences and Autobiographies of Negro Ex-Slaves,* Social Science Source Documents No. 2 (Nashville, TN: Social Science Institute, Fisk University, 1945), vi.

5. Ibid.

6. Ibid., vi.

7. Glazier, *Been Coming Through Some Hard Times,* 96–97.

8. Paul Radin, *Primitive Man as Philosopher* (New York: Dover Publications, 1957), 160.

9. Edward Sapir to Alfred Kroeber, February 5, 1931, Paul Radin Papers, Marquette University Special Collections and University Archives.

10. A. I. Hallowell, *Culture and Experience* (Philadelphia: University of Pennsylvania Press, 1955), 88.

11. Paul Radin, "Personal Reminiscences of a Winnebago Indian," *Journal of American Folklore* 26, no. 102 (1913): 293–294.

12. The concept of behavioral environment was developed by Hallowell to center analysis on the individual rather than the cultural system, frequently regarded as autonomous and independent of the person. The behavioral environment directs attention to the inside world of the individual and the impact of exogenous factors on the emergence of self-awareness. Hallowell, *Culture and Experience,* 88–90.

13. *God Struck Me Dead,* v.

14. Paul Radin, *The Road of Life and Death* (New York: Pantheon, 1945), 71.

Bibliography

Archives

American Philosophical Society

Franz Boas Papers

Brandeis University

Robert D. Farber University Archives and Special Collections

Fisk University

Special Collections and Archives

Charles S. Johnson Collection (Original and Registers L and Q)

Marquette University

Special Collections and University Archives (MUA)

Newspapers and Magazines

Circle Magazine

The Columbia Spectator

The Crisis

The Dial

Los Angeles Times

The Nation

New Republic

New York Times
Oakland Tribune
Opportunity
Pittsburgh Courier
San Bernardino County Sun
Time

Books and Articles

Aberle, David F. *The Peyote Religion among the Navaho.* 2nd ed. Norman: University of Oklahoma Press, 1966

Adams, William Y. *The Boasians: Founding Fathers and Mothers of American Anthropology.* Lanham, MD: Hamilton, 2016.

Alba, Richard. *Ethnic Identity: The Transformation of White America.* New Haven, CT: Yale University Press, 1990.

Appiah, Kwame Anthony. *Lines of Descent: W. E. B. Du Bois and the Emergence of Identity.* Cambridge, MA: Harvard University Press, 2014.

Aptheker, Herbert. *American Negro Slave Revolts.* New York: International, 1969. First published 1943.

———. *Essays in the History of the American Negro.* New York: International, 1945.

Arndt, Grant. "Indigenous Autobiography *en Abyme:* Indigenous Reflections on Representational Agency in the Case of *Crashing Thunder. Ethnohistory* 59, no. 1 (Winter 2012): 27–49.

———. *Ho-Chunk Powwows and the Politics of Tradition.* Lincoln: University of Nebraska Press, 2016.

Ashley Montagu, M. F. "Review of *Race and Rumors of Race* by Howard Odum." *American Anthropologist,* n.s., 46, no. 2 (1944): 254–255.

Azikiwe, Ben. "Review of *The Racial Myth,* by Paul Radin." *Journal of Negro History* 20, no. 1 (January 1935): 98–99.

Baker, Lee D. *Anthropology and the Racial Politics of Culture.* Durham, NC: Duke University Press, 2010.

Baker, Ronald L. *Homeless, Friendless, and Penniless: The WPA Interviews with Former Slaves Living in Indiana.* Bloomington: Indiana University Press, 2000.

Baur, Erwin, Eugen Fischer, and Fritz Lenz. *Human Heredity.* Translated by Eden and Cedar Paul. New York: Macmillan, 1931. Originally published as *Menschliche Erblichkeitslehre und Rassenhygiene* (Munich: J. F. Lehmanns Verlag, 1921).

Benedict, Ruth, and Gene Weltfish. "The Races of Mankind." In *Race: Science and Politics,* edited by Ruth Benedict, 169–193. New York: Viking Press, 1945.

Blassingame, John W., ed. *Slave Testimony: Two Centuries of Letters, Speeches, Interviews, and Autobiographies.* Baton Rouge: Louisiana State University Press, 1977.

Blight, David. *Race and Reunion: The Civil War in American Memory.* Cambridge, MA: Harvard University Press, 2001.

Boas, Franz. "The Study of Geography." In *Race, Language and Culture,* 639–647. New York: Free Press, 1966. First published 1887.

———. "An Anthropologist's Credo." *The Nation,* August 27, 1938, 201–204.

———. "History and Science in Anthropology: A Reply." *American Anthropologist,* n.s., 38, no. 1 (January–March 1936): 137–141.

———. "Industries of the African Negroes." *Southern Workman* 38 (April 1909): 217–229.

———. *The Mind of Primitive Man.* Rev. ed. New York: Free Press, 1965. First published 1911.

———. "On Alternating Sounds." *American Anthropologist* 2, no. 1 (1889): 47–54.

———. "The Outlook for the American Negro." In *The Shaping of American Anthropology, 1883–1911,* edited by George W. Stocking Jr., 310–316. New York: Basic, 1974.

———. "Patriotism." In *Race and Democratic Society,* 156–159. New York: Biblo and Tannen, 1969. First published 1945.

———. "The Problem of the American Negro." *Yale Review* 10, no. 2 (January 1921): 384–395.

———. "The Real Race Problem." *The Crisis* 1, no. 2 (December 1910): 22–25.

———. "Recent Anthropology II." *Science,* n.s., 98 (October 15, 1943): 334–337.

———. "Stylistic Aspects of Primitive Literature." In *Race, Language and Culture,* 491–502. New York: Free Press, 1966. First published 1925.

Brilliant, Mark. *The Color of America Has Changed: How Racial Diversity Shaped Civil Rights Reform in California, 1941–1978.* Oxford: Oxford University Press, 2010.

Brinton, Daniel G. "The Earliest Form of Human Speech as Revealed by American Tongues." In *Essays of an Americanist,* 390–409. Philadelphia, 1890.

Buccitelli, Anthony Bak. "The Reluctant Folklorist: Jon Y. Lee, Paul Radin, and the Fieldwork Process." *Journal of American Folklore* 127, no. 506 (Fall 2014): 400–424.

Bullert, Gary. "The Committee for Cultural Freedom and the Roots of McCarthyism." *Education and Culture* 29, no. 2 (2013): 25–52.

Burgess, Ernest W. "Social Planning and Race Relations." In *Race Relations: Problems and Theory,* edited by Jitsuichi Masuoka and Preston Valien, 13–25. Chapel Hill: University of North Carolina Press, 1961.

Burke, Kenneth. "Review of *Primitive Man as Philosopher* by Paul Radin." *The Dial* 53, no. 5 (November 1927): 439–440.

Burnham, Michelle. "'I Lied All the Time': Trickster Discourse and Ethnographic Authority in

Crashing Thunder." *American Indian Quarterly* 22, no. 4 (1998): 469–484.

Cade, John B. "Out of the Mouths of Ex-Slaves." *Journal of Negro History* 20 (July 1935): 294–337.

Chicago Commission on Race Relations. *The Negro in Chicago: a Study of Race Relations and a Race Riot.* Chicago: University of Chicago Press, 1922.

Colón, Gabriel Alejandro Torres, and Charles A. Hobbs. "The Intertwining of Culture and Nature: Franz Boas, John Dewey, and Deweyan Strands of American Anthropology." *Journal of the History of Ideas* 76, no. 1 (2015): 139–162.

Commons, John R. *Races and Immigrants in America.* New York: Macmillan, 1908.

Couch, W. T. "Publisher's Introduction." In *What the Negro Wants,* edited by Rayford Whittingham Logan. Chapel Hill: University of North Carolina Press, 1944.

Cowley, Malcolm, and Bernard Smith, eds. *Books That Changed Our Minds.* New York: Doubleday, Doran, 1939.

Croce, Benedetto. *History, Its Theory and Practice.* Translated by Douglas Ainslie. New York: Harcourt, Brace, 1921.

Darnell, Regna. *And Along Came Boas: Continuity and Revolution in Americanist Anthropology.* Amsterdam: John Benjamins, 1998.

———. *Edward Sapir: Linguist, Anthropologist, Humanist.* Berkeley: University of California Press, 1990.

———. "Philosophizing with the 'Other.'" In *Invisible Genealogies: A History of Americanist Anthropology*, 137–170. Lincoln: University of Nebraska Press, 2001.

Darnell, Regna, Michelle Hamilton, Robert L. A. Hancock, and Joshua Smith. *The Franz Boas Papers.* Vol. 1, *Franz Boas as Public Intellectual: Theory, Ethnography, Activism.* Lincoln: University of Nebraska Press, 2015.

Diamond, Stanley. *Culture in History: Essays in Honor of Paul Radin.* New York: Columbia University Press, 1960.

———. *In Search of the Primitive: A Critique of Civilization.* New Brunswick, NJ: Transaction, 1974.

———. "Paul Radin." In *Totems and Teachers: Key Figures in the History of Anthropology,* edited by Sydel Silverman, 51–71. New York: Columbia University Press, 1981.

Dorsey, J. Owen. *Omaha Sociology.* Washington, DC, 1884.

Douglas, Ann. *Terrible Honesty: Mongrel Manhattan in the 1920s.* New York: Noonday Press, 1995.

Drake, St. Clair. "Anthropology and the Black Experience." *The Black Scholar* 11, no. 7 (1980): 2–31.

Drake, St. Clair, and Horace R. Cayton. *Black Metropolis: A Study of Negro Life in a Northern City.*

New York: Harper & Row, 1962. First published 1945.

Du Bois, Cora. "Paul Radin: An Appreciation." In *Culture in History: Essays in Honor of Paul Radin,* edited by Stanley Diamond, ix–xvi. New York: Columbia University Press, 1960.

Du Bois, W. E. B. *Black Folk Then and Now: An Essay in the History and Sociology of the Negro Race.* New York: Oxford University Press, 2007. First published 1939.

———. *Black Reconstruction in America, 1860–1880.* Cleveland: World, 1964. First published 1935.

———. *The Conservation of Races.* Washington, DC, 1897.

———. "My Evolving Program for Negro Freedom." In *What the Negro Wants,* edited by Rayford W. Logan, 31–70. Chapel Hill: University of North Carolina Press, 1944.

———. *The Philadelphia Negro: A Social Study.* New York: Schocken, 1967. First published 1899.

———. "Review of Melville J. Herskovits, *The Myth of the Negro Past.*" *Annals of the American Academy of Political and Social Science* 222 (1942): 226–227.

Dunning, William A. *Essays on the Civil War and Reconstruction.* New York, 1898.

———. *Reconstruction, Political and Economic, 1865–1877.* New York: Harper and Row, 1962. First published 1907.

Egerton, John. *Speak Now against the Day: The Generation before the Civil Rights Movement in the South.* New York: Alfred A. Knopf, 1994.

Escott, Paul D. "The Art and Science of Reading WPA Slave Narratives." In *The Slave's Narrative,* edited by Charles T. Davis and Henry Louis Gates Jr., 40–48. New York: Oxford University Press, 1985.

———. *Slavery Remembered: A Record of Twentieth-Century Slave Narratives.* Chapel Hill: University of North Carolina Press, 1979.

Fauset, Arthur Huff. "American Negro Folk Literature." In *The New Negro,* edited by Alain Locke, 238–244. New York: Simon and Schuster, 1997. First published 1925.

Franklin, John Hope. *Reconstruction after the Civil War.* Chicago: University of Chicago Press, 1961.

Frazier, E. Franklin. *Black Bourgeoisie.* Glencoe, IL: Free Press, 1957.

———. "Durham: Capital of the Black Middle Class." In *The New Negro,* edited by Alain Locke, 333–340. New York: Simon and Schuster, 1997. First published 1925.

———. *The Negro Family in the United States.* Chicago: University of Chicago Press, 1939.

Gasman, Marybeth. "W.E.B. Du Bois and Charles S. Johnson: Differing Views on the Role of Philanthropy in Higher Education." *History of Education Quarterly* 42, no. 4 (2002): 493–516.

Genovese, Eugene D. "Race and Class in Southern History: An Appraisal of the Work of Ulrich Bonnell Phillips." *Agricultural History* 41 (1967): 345–358.

————. *Roll, Jordan, Roll: The World the Slaves Made.* New York: Vintage, 1976. First published 1974.

Gershenhorn, Jerry. *Melville J. Herskovits and the Racial Politics of Knowledge.* Lincoln: University of Nebraska Press, 2004.

Gilpin, Patrick J., and Marybeth Gasman. *Charles S. Johnson: Leadership beyond the Veil in the Age of Jim Crow.* Albany: State University of New York Press, 2003.

Gingrich, Andre. "German Anthropology during the Nazi Period: Complex Scenarios of Collaboration, Persecution, and Competition." In *One Discipline, Four Ways: British, German, French, and American Anthropology,* 111–136. Chicago: University of Chicago Press, 2005.

Glazier, Jack. *Been Coming Through Some Hard Times: Race, History, and Memory in Western Kentucky.* Knoxville: University of Tennessee Press, 2012.

Glick, Leonard B. "Types Distinct from Our Own: Franz Boas on Jewish Identity and Assimilation." *American Anthropologist* 84, no. 3 (1982): 545–565.

God Struck Me Dead: Religious Conversion Experiences and Autobiographies of Negro Ex-Slaves. Social Science Source Documents No. 2. Nashville, TN: Social Science Institute, Fisk University, 1945.

Goldenweiser, Alexander. "Review of *Social Anthropology* by Paul Radin." *American Anthropologist* 35 (1933): 345–349.

Hallowell, A. I. *Culture and Experience.* Philadelphia: University of Pennsylvania Press, 1955.

Harrison, Ira E., and Faye Venetia Harrison. *African-American Pioneers in Anthropology.* Urbana: University of Illinois Press, 1999.

Hart, Bradley W. *Hitler's American Friends: The Third Reich's Supporters in the United States.* New York: Thomas Dunne, 2018.

Hemenway, Robert E. *Zora Neale Hurston: A Literary Biography.* Urbana: University of Illinois Press, 1977.

Herskovits, Melville J. *Cultural Dynamics.* New York: Alfred A. Knopf, 1967.

————. *The Myth of the Negro Past.* Boston: Beacon, 1990. First published 1941.

————. "The Negro's Americanism." In *The New Negro,* edited by Alain Locke, 353–360. New York: Simon and Schuster, 1992. First published 1925.

————. "What Has Africa Given America?" *New Republic,* September 4, 1935, 92–94.

Hofstadter, Richard. "U. B. Phillips and the Plantation Legend." *Journal of Negro History* 29, no. 2 (April 1944): 109–124.

Hughes, Langston. *The Big Sea: An Autobiography.* New York: Thunder's Mouth, 1986. First published 1940.

————. "What the Negro Wants." *Common Ground* (Autumn 1941): 52–54.

Hurston, Zora Neale. *Barracoon: The Story of the Last "Black Cargo."* Edited by Deborah G. Plant. New York: HarperCollins, 2018.

———. "Cudjo's Own Story of the Last African Slaver." *Journal of Negro History* 12, no. 4 (October 1927): 648–663.

———. *Dust Tracks on a Road: An Autobiography.* Urbana: University of Illinois Press, 1984. First published 1942.

———. *Mules and Men.* New York: HarperCollins, 1990. First published 1935.

Hyman, Stanley Edgar. "Freud and Boas: Secular Rabbis?" *Commentary,* 17 (January 1954): 264–267.

Hymes, Dell H. *Reinventing Anthropology.* New York: Pantheon, 1972.

Johnson, Charles S., ed. *Ebony and Topaz.* New York: National Urban League, 1927.

———. "Introduction to Symposium." *American Journal of Sociology* 48, no. 6 (May 1943): 629–632.

———. "Review of *What the Negro Wants,* by Rayford W. Logan." *American Sociological Review* 11, no. 2 (1946): 244–245.

———. *Shadow of the Plantation.* New Brunswick, NJ: Transaction, 1996. First published 1934.

———. "The Verdict of 'Common Sense.'" *Opportunity: A Journal of Negro Life* 1, no. 6 (June 1923): 2.

Johnson, Guy. "Review of *The Myth of the Negro Past,* by Melville J. Herskovits." *American Sociological Review* 7, no. 2 (April 1942): 289–290.

Jung, C. G. "The Type Problem in Modern Philosophy." In *Psychological Types.* Bollingen Series 20, edited by R. F. C. Hull, 300–321. Princeton, NJ: Princeton University Press, 1979.

Kaplan, Carla, ed. *Zora Neale Hurston: A Life in Letters.* New York: Random House, 2002.

Kasson, Joy S. *Buffalo Bill's Wild West.* New York: Hill and Wang, 2000.

Kimble, G. Eleanor. "Restrictive Covenants." *Common Ground* (Autumn 1945): 45–52.

Klineberg, Otto. *Race Differences.* New York: Harper and Brothers, 1935.

Kroeber, A. L. *The Arapaho.* Bulletin American Museum of Natural History, vol. 18, pt. 4 (1907): 279–454.

———. "Eighteen Professions." *American Anthropologist,* n.s., 17, no. 2 (1915): 283–288.

———. "History and Science in Anthropology." *American Anthropologist,* n.s., 37, no. 4 (October–December 1935): 539–569.

———. "Review of *The Method and Theory of Ethnology* by Paul Radin." *American Anthropologist,* n.s., 35, no. 4 (1933): 765–766.

———. "The Superorganic." *American Anthropologist,* n.s., 19, no. 2 (1917): 163–213.

Kroeber, Theodora. *Alfred Kroeber: A Personal Configuration.* Berkeley: University of California Press, 1970.

Krupat, Arnold. *For Those Who Come After: A Study of Native American Autobiography.* Berkeley: University of California Press, 1985.

La Barre, Weston. *The Peyote Cult.* New York: Shoe String, 1970.

La Barre, Weston, David P. McAllester, J. S. Slotkin, Omer C. Stewart, and Sol Tax. "Statement on Peyote." *Science* 114 (November 30, 1951): 582–583.

Langdon, Emma. *Historic Sketches of the Old South.* New York: Knickerbocker, 1914.

Lee, John Y. *The Golden Mountain: Chinese Tales Told in California.* Collected by John Lee, edited by Paul Radin. Taipei: Oriental Cultural Service, 1971.

Lesser, Alexander, and Sidney W. Mintz. *History, Evolution, and the Concept of Culture: Selected Papers by Alexander Lesser.* Cambridge: Cambridge University Press, 1985.

Lévi-Strauss, Claude. "Four Winnebago Myths." In *Culture in History: Essays in Honor of Paul Radin,* edited by Stanley Diamond, 352–362. New York: Columbia University Press, 1960.

Levine, Lawrence W. *Black Culture and Black Consciousness: Afro-American Folk Thought from Slavery to Freedom.* New York: Oxford University Press, 2007. First published 1977.

Lewis, Herbert S. "Anthropology and Race, Then and Now: Commentary on K. Visweswaran, 'Race and the Culture of Anthropology.'" *American Anthropologist* 100, no. 4 (1998): 979–981.

———. "Boas, Darwin, Science, and Anthropology." *Current Anthropology* 42, no. 3 (2001): 381–406.

———. "Franz Boas: Boon or Bane?" *Reviews in Anthropology* 37, nos. 2–3 (2008): 169–200.

———. *In Defense of Anthropology: An Investigation of the Critique of Anthropology.* New Brunswick, NJ: Transaction, 2014.

———. "The Passion of Franz Boas." *American Anthropologist* 103, no. 2 (2001): 447–467.

Lewis, Nell Battle. "Review of *The Negro and His Songs,* by Howard W. Odum and Guy Johnson." *North Carolina Historical Review* 2, no. 4 (1925): 541–543.

Lindberg, Christer. "Paul Radin: The Anthropological Trickster." *European Review of Native American Studies* 14, no. 1 (2000). http://www.indis.se/?p=78.

Linton, Ralph. "One Hundred Percent American." *American Mercury* 40 (1937): 427–429.

Liss, Julia E. "Franz Boas on War and Empire: The Making of a Public Intellectual." In *The Franz Boas Papers,* vol. 1, edited by Regna Darnell, Michelle Hamilton, Robert L. A. Hancock, and Joshua Smith, 293–328. Lincoln: University of Nebraska Press, 2015.

———. "German Culture and German Science in the *Bildung* of Franz Boas." In *Volkgeist as Method and Ethic: Essays on Boasian Ethnography and the German Anthropological Tradition,* edited by George W. Stocking Jr., 155–184. Madison: University of Wisconsin Press, 1996.

Locke, Alain. *The New Negro.* New York: Simon and Schuster, 1992. First published 1925.

Logan, Rayford Whittingham. *What the Negro Wants*. Chapel Hill: University of North Carolina Press, 1944.

Long, Howard H. "On Mental Tests and Racial Psychology: A Critique." *Opportunity* 3, no. 29 (May 1925): 137–138.

Lowie, Robert H. *Biographical Memoir of Franz Boas*. National Academy of Sciences, vol. 24, Ninth Memoir. Washington, DC: National Academy of Sciences, 1947.

———. *The Crow Indians*. New York: Farrar and Rinehart, 1935.

———. *Primitive Religion*. New York: Grosset and Dunlap, 1952.

———. *Robert H. Lowie, Ethnologist: A Personal Record*. Berkeley: University of California Press, 1959.

Lurie, Nancy O. *Mountain Wolf Woman, Sister of Crashing Thunder: The Autobiography of a Winnebago Indian*. Ann Arbor: University of Michigan Press, 1961.

———. "Two Dollars." In *Crossing Cultural Boundaries: The Anthropological Experience*, edited by Solon T. Kimball and James B. Watson. 151–163. San Francisco: Chandler, 1972.

Mangione, Jerre. *The Dream and the Deal: The Federal Writers' Project, 1935–1943*. Philadelphia: University of Pennsylvania Press, 1983.

McGuire, William. *Bollingen: An Adventure in Collecting the Past*. Princeton, NJ: Princeton University Press, 1982.

McKee, James B. *Sociology and the Race Problem: The Failure of a Perspective*. Urbana: University of Illinois Press, 1993.

Meier, August. *Negro Thought in America, 1880–1915: Racial Ideologies in the Age of Booker T. Washington*. Ann Arbor: University of Michigan Press, 1963.

———. *A White Scholar and the Black Community, 1945–1965: Essays and Reflections*. Amherst: University of Massachusetts Press, 1992.

Meier, August, and Elliott M. Rudwick. *Black History and the Historical Profession, 1915–1980*. Urbana: University of Illinois Press, 1986.

Miller, Jay. "Amelia Louise Susman Schultz, Sam Blowsnake, and the Ho-Chunk Syllabary." *History of Anthropology Newsletter* 42 (2018). http://histanthro.org/clio/amelia-louise-susman-schultz-sam-blowsnake-and-the-ho-chunk-syllabary/.

Mintz, Sidney M. "Foreword." In *Afro-American Anthropology: Contemporary Perspectives*, edited by Norman E. Whitten Jr. and John F. Szwed, 1–16. New York: Free Press, 1970.

Monk, Ray. *Robert Oppenheimer: A Life inside the Center*. New York: Doubleday, 2012.

Mooney, James. *The Ghost Dance Religion and the Sioux Outbreak of 1890*. Chicago: University of Chicago Press, 1965.

Morgan, Lewis Henry. *Ancient Society*. Cleveland: World, 1963. First published 1877.

Morris, Aldon D. *The Scholar Denied: W.E.B. Du Bois and the Birth of Modern Sociology*. Berkeley:

University of California Press, 2015.

Moses, L. G. *The Indian Man: A Biography of James Mooney.* Lincoln: University of Nebraska Press, 1984.

Murray, Stephen O. *American Anthropology and Company.* Lincoln: University of Nebraska Press, 2013.

Nevins, Allan, and Henry Steele Commager. *A Short History of the United States.* New York: Modern Library, 1942.

Novick, Peter. *That Noble Dream: The "Objectivity Question" and the American Historical Profession.* New York: Cambridge University Press, 1988.

Odum, Howard W. *American Masters of Social Science: An Approach to the Study of the Social Sciences through a Neglected Field of Biography.* New York: Henry Holt, 1927.

———. *Social and Mental Traits of the Negro: Research into the Conditions of the Negro Race in Southern Towns: A Study in Race Traits, Tendencies and Prospects.* New York: Columbia University, 1910.

Odum, Howard Washington, and Guy Benton Johnson. *The Negro and His Songs: A Study of Typical Negro Songs in the South.* New York: Negro Universities Press, 1968.

Osofsky, Gilbert, ed. *Puttin' On Ole Massa.* New York: Harper and Row, 1969.

Ottley, Roi. *Roi Ottley's World War II: The Lost Diary of an African American Journalist.* Lawrence: University Press of Kansas, 2011.

Park, Robert E. "The Conflict and Fusion of Cultures with Special Reference to the Negro." *Journal of Negro History* 4 (April 1919): 111–133.

———. "Mentality of Racial Hybrids." *American Journal of Sociology* 36, no. 4 (January 1931): 534–551.

———. *Race and Culture.* Glencoe, IL: Free Press, 1950.

Phillips, Ulrich B. *American Negro Slavery.* Baton Rouge: Louisiana State University Press, 1918.

———. *Life and Labor in the Old South.* Boston: Little, Brown, 1929.

Powdermaker, Hortense. *After Freedom: A Cultural Study in the Deep South.* New York: Viking, 1939.

———. *Stranger and Friend: The Way of an Anthropologist.* New York: W.W. Norton, 1966.

Price, David H. *Threatening Anthropology: McCarthyism and the FBI's Surveillance of Activist Anthropologists.* Durham, NC: Duke University Press, 2004.

Proctor, Robert. "From *Anthropologie* to *Rassenkunde* in the German Anthropological Tradition." In *Bones, Bodies, Behavior: Essays on Biological Anthropology.* History of Anthropology 5, edited by George W. Stocking Jr., 138–179. Madison: University of Wisconsin Press, 1988.

Raboteau, Albert J. *Slave Religion: The "Invisible Institution" in the Antebellum South.* New York:

Oxford University Press, 2004. First published 1978.

"The Race Question." Paris: UNESCO, 1950.

Radin, Paul. *African Folktales and Sculpture.* Princeton, NJ: Princeton University Press, 1970.
First published 1952 for the Bollingen Foundation.

———. "Auf Netztechnik der Sudamerikanischer Indianer" [The net technique of South
American Indians]. *Zeitschrift für Ethnologie* 388 (1906): 926–938.

———. *The Autobiography of a Winnebago Indian.* (Berkeley: University of California Press,
1920).

———. "Boas and 'The Mind of Primitive Man.'" In *Books That Changed Our Minds,* edited by
Malcolm Cowley and Bernard Smith, 127–142. New York: Doubleday, Doran, 1939.

———. *Crashing Thunder: The Autobiography of an American Indian.* New York: D. Appleton,
1926.

———. *The Culture of the Winnebago: As Described by Themselves.* Baltimore: Waverly, 1949.

———. "History of Ethnological Theories." *American Anthropologist,* n.s., 31, no. 1 (1929):
9–33.

———. *The Italians of San Francisco, Their Adjustment and Acculturation.* State Emergency
Relief Association (SERA Project 2-F2–98, 3-F2–145). San Francisco: SERA, 1935.

———. "Literary Aspects of North American Mythology." *Canada Department of Mines,
Museum Bulletin No. 16,* Anthropological Series 6, June 15, 1915.

———. *The Method and Theory of Ethnology: An Essay in Criticism.* New York: McGraw-Hill
Book Co., 1933.

———. "The Nature of Primitive Religion." Unpublished manuscript, n.d., Paul Radin Papers,
Series 2-1, Marquette University Special Collections and University Archives.

———. "Personal Reminiscences of a Winnebago Indian." *Journal of American Folklore* 26, no.
102 (1913): 293–318.

———. *Primitive Man as Philosopher.* New York: Dover Publications, 1957. First published
1927.

———. *Primitive Religion: Its Nature and Origin.* New York: Dover Publications, 1957. First
published 1937.

———. *Racial Myth.* New York: McGraw-Hill Book Co., 1934.

———. *The Road of Life and Death: A Ritual Drama of the American Indians.* New York:
Pantheon, 1945.

———. "A Sketch of the Peyote Cult of the Winnebago: A Study in Borrowing." *Journal of
Religious Psychology* 7, no. 1 (1914): 1–22.

———. *Social Anthropology.* New York: McGraw-Hill Book Co., 1932.

———. "The Social Organization of the Winnebago Indians: An Interpretation." *Geological*

Survey of Canada, Anthropology Series 5, Museum Bulletin No. 10, May 16, 1915.

———. "Souls Piled Like Timber: The Religious Experience of the Prewar Negro." Unpublished manuscript, n.d., Paul Radin Papers, Series 2-2, African American Folk Literature, Marquette University Special Collections and University Archives.

———. "Status, Phantasy, and the Christian Dogma: A Note about the Conversion Experiences of Negro Ex-Slaves." In *God Struck Me Dead: Religious Conversion Experiences and Autobiographies of Negro Ex-Slaves.* Social Science Source Documents No. 2, iv–xi. Nashville, TN: Social Science Institute, Fisk University, 1945.

———. "Three Conversions." *Circle Magazine,* nos. 7–8 (1946): 90–96.

———. *The Winnebago Tribe.* Lincoln: University of Nebraska Press, 1970. First published as part of the *Thirty-Seventh Annual Report of the Bureau of American Ethnology.* Washington, DC: Smithsonian Institution, 1923.

———. *The World of Primitive Man.* New York: H. Schuman, 1953.

Ransom, John Crowe. "The Idea of a Literary Anthropologist: And What He Might Say of the 'Paradise Lost' of Milton; A Speech with a Prologue." *Kenyon Review* 21, no. 1 (1959): 121–140.

Rawick, George P., ed. *The American Slave: A Composite Autobiography* (Indiana and Ohio Narratives). Supplement, ser. 1, vol. 5. Westport, CT: Greenwood, 1972.

Reddick, Lawrence D. "A New Interpretation of Negro History." *Journal of Negro History* 22 (January 1937): 17–28.

Redfield, Robert. "The Folk Society." *American Journal of Sociology* 52, no. 4 (1947): 293–308.

Redfield, Robert, Ralph Linton, and Melville J. Herskovits. "Memorandum for the Study of Acculturation." *American Anthropologist,* n.s., 38, no. 1 (1936): 149–152.

Rivet, Paul. "Tribute to Franz Boas." *International Journal of American Linguistics* 14 (October 1958): 251–252.

Robinson, James Harvey. *The Human Comedy.* New York: Harper and Bros., 1937.

———. *The New History.* New York: Macmillan, 1912.

———. *An Outline of the History of the Intellectual Class in Europe.* New York: n.p., 1911.

Rosenbaum, Fred. *Cosmopolitans: A Social and Cultural History of the Jews of the San Francisco Bay Area.* Berkeley: University of California Press, 2009.

Ross, Edward A. *The Old World in the New: The Significance of Past and Present Immigration to the American People.* New York: Century Co., 1914.

Sapir, Edward. "Culture, Genuine and Spurious." *American Journal of Sociology* 29, no. 4 (1924): 401–429.

———. "The Psychological Reality of Phonemes." In *Selected Writings of Edward Sapir in Language, Culture and Personality,* edited by David G. Mandelbaum, 46–60. Berkeley:

University of California Press, 1949. Essay first published 1933.

———. "Why Cultural Anthropology Needs the Psychiatrist." In *Selected Writings of Edward Sapir in Language, Culture and Personality,* edited by David G. Mandelbaum, 569–577. Berkeley: University of California Press, 1985. Essay first published 1938.

Sapir, J. David. "Paul Radin, 1883–1956." *Journal of American Folklore* 74, no. 291 (1961): 65–67.

Schlesinger, Arthur M., Sr. *The Rise of the City, 1878–1965.* New York: Macmillan, 1933.

Schomburg, Arthur A. "The Negro Digs Up His Past." In *The New Negro,* edited by Alain Locke, 231–237. New York: Simon and Schuster, 1992. First published 1925.

Scott, James C. *Weapons of the Weak: Everyday Forms of Peasant Resistance.* New Haven, CT: Yale University Press, 1985.

Schultz, Amelia Susman. "A Tribute to Franz Boas." Presented at the 71st Annual Meeting of the Society for Applied Anthropology in Seattle, WA, March 29–April 2, 2011. MP3 file, 1:19:21. http://sfaa.net/podcast/index.php/podcasts/2011/tribute-franz-boas/.

Shamdasani, Sonu. *Jung and the Making of Modern Psychology.* Cambridge: Cambridge University Press, 2003.

Slotkin, James S. *The Peyote Religion: A Study in Indian-White Relations.* Glencoe, IL: Free Press, 1956.

———. "The Peyote Way." In *Reader in Comparative Religion,"* edited by William A. Lessa and Evon Z. Vogt, 296–300. New York: Harper and Row, 1979.

Spindel, Donna J. "Assessing Memory: Twentieth-Century Slave Narratives Reconsidered." *Journal of Interdisciplinary History* 27 (Autumn 1996): 247–261.

Spiro, Jonathan Peter. *Defending the Master Race: Conservation, Eugenics, and the Legacy of Madison Grant.* Burlington: University of Vermont Press, 2009.

Spiro, Melford E. "Postmodernist Anthropology, Subjectivity, and Science: A Modernist Critique." *Comparative Studies in Society and History* 38, no. 4 (1996): 759–780.

Steinberg, Stephen. *Race Relations: A Critique.* Stanford, CA: Stanford University Press, 2007.

Stewart, Omer C. *Peyote Religion: A History.* Norman: University of Oklahoma Press, 1987.

Stocking, George W., Jr. "Review of *Notes on an Undirected Life: As One Anthropologist Tells It,* by Esther S. Goldfrank." *American Ethnologist* 7, no. 1 (1980): 211–212.

———. "Review of *The Method and Theory of Ethnology,* 2nd ed., by Paul Radin." *American Anthropologist,* n.s., 70, no. 2 (1968): 371.

———. "The Scientific Reaction against Cultural Anthropology, 1917–1920." In *Race, Culture, and Evolution: Essays in the History of Anthropology,* 270–307. New York: Free Press, 1968.

Thomas, William B. "Howard W. Odum's Social Theories in Transition: 1910–1930." *American Sociologist* 16, no. 1 (February 1981): 25–34.

Tolson, Melvin. "Rendezvous with America." *Common Ground* 2, no. 4 (Summer 1942): 3–9.

Turner, Victor W. "Muchona the Hornet, Interpreter of Religion." In *The Forest of Symbols: Aspects of Ndembu Ritual,* 131–150. Ithaca, NY: Cornell University Press, 1967.

Unwritten History of Slavery: Autobiographical Account of Negro Ex-Slaves. Social Science Source Documents No. 1. Nashville, TN: Social Science Institute, Fisk University, 1945.

Van Gennep, Arnold. *The Rites of Passage.* Translated by Monika B. Vizedom and Gabrielle L. Caffee. Chicago: University of Chicago Press, 1960.

Vidich, Arthur J. "Paul Radin and Contemporary Anthropology." *Social Research* 32, no. 4 (1965): 375–407.

Visweswaran, Kamala. "Race and the Culture of Anthropology." *American Anthropologist,* n.s., 100, no. 1 (1998): 70–83.

Waggoner, Linda M. *Fire Light: The Life of Angel De Cora, Winnebago Artist.* Norman: University of Oklahoma Press, 2008.

Wallace, Anthony F. C. "Revitalization Movements." *American Anthropologist,* n.s., 58, no. 2 (1956): 264–281.

Watson, Andrew Polk. "Primitive Religion among Negroes in Tennessee." Master's thesis, Fisk University, 1932.

West, Margaret Genevieve. *Zora Neale Hurston and American Literary Culture.* Gainesville: University Press of Florida, 2005.

White, Leslie. "The Social Organization of Ethnological Theory." *Rice University Studies* 52, no. 4 (1966).

White, Walter. *A Rising Wind.* New York: Doubleday, Doran, 1945.

Williams, George Washington. *A History of Negro Troops in the War of Rebellion, 1861–1865.* New York, 1888.

———. *History of the Negro Race in America from 1618 to 1880.* New York, 1883.

Woodson, C. G. "Review of Melville J. Herskovits, *The Myth of the Negro Past.*" *Journal of Negro History* 27, no. 1 (1942): 115–118.

Woodward, C. Vann. "History from Slave Sources." In *The Slave's Narrative,* edited by Charles T. Davis and Henry Louis Gates Jr., 48–59. New York: Oxford University Press, 1985.

Wright, Jerome W. "Mark Hanna Watkins, 1903–1976." *American Anthropologist,* n.s., 78, no. 4 (December 1976): 889–890.

Yinger, J. Milton. "Breaking the Vicious Circle." *Common Ground* 7, no. 1 (Autumn 1946): 3–8.

Zumwalt, Rosemary Lévy. *Wealth and Rebellion: Elsie Clews Parsons, Anthropologist and Folklorist.* Urbana: University of Illinois Press, 1992.

Zumwalt, Rosemary Lévy, and William Shedrick Willis. "Franz Boas and W. E. B. Du Bois at Atlanta University, 1906." *Transactions of the American Philosophical Society* 98, no. 2 (2008): 1–83.

Index

Aberle, David, 171, 172–74

Abrahams, Roger, 102

accommodation, 90, 91–92

acculturation, 66, 75, 106

African American culture: anthropological approaches to, 66–72; Boas and, 68–70; Christianity and, 4, 66, 129–30, 141, 147, 181–82, 186; folklore and, 75–76, 102; origins of, 4–6, 75, 105–9, 130; value and legitimacy of, 76, 77. *See also* Radin, Paul: African American research by; slavery

African American historians, 3–4, 96, 97–100, 102, 110. *See also* Du Bois, W. E. B.; Woodson, Carter

African American press, 2. *See also Pittsburgh Courier*

American Anthropological Association, 59

American Association for the Advancement of Science, 79–80

American Indian mythology, 36, 101, 155, 160–61

American Indian religion, 149–51, 155–56, 160–62, 172, 183–84; Christianity and, 150–51, 162–63, 167, 170, 174, 177; Native American Church, 162, 171, 172, 184; tobacco and, 150, 160, 166, 174. *See also* peyotism

American Sociological Society, 3–4

Anson, May, 121–22, 124

anthropology: charges against, 10; critiques of race in, 11, 56; observer bias in, 23–24, 76, 125, 185; postmodern movement in, 195 (n. 28); pre-Boasian era of, 29–30, 60; preconceptions in, 21–24, 60–61,

Mason, John Alden, 36

Masuoka, Jitsuichi, 103, 113

McAllester, David, 171

McCarthyism, 48, 51, 54

Mead, Margaret, 8, 12, 32, 77; Radin on, 24–25

Mechling, William H., 36

Meier, August, 99

Mellon, Paul and Mary, 48

Menominee tribe, 149, 172

methodological relativism, 58, 64–65

Mintz, Sidney, 5

Montagu, Ashley, 77, 80–81

morality and science, 56, 89

Mooney, James, 154, 170–71

Mountain Wolf Woman (Stella Stacy), 45, 162, 169

Myrdal, Gunnar, 71, 81

NAACP, 94

nationalism, 3, 63, 188

native intellectuals, 21, 27

native texts, 18, 158

Nazism, 1–2, 22, 53, 57, 59, 61, 63, 66, 67, 70, 71, 78–81, 109, 188; support in U.S. for, 6–7, 80

Negro in Chicago, The (report), 86

"Negro problem," 61, 70, 87, 89, 93, 96

New Negro, The (anthology), 6, 76, 87, 106, 110

Nevins, Allan, 98–99

Northup, Solomon, 125

Novick, Peter, 97–98

Nuremberg trials, 80–81

Odum, Howard W., 76, 84, 89, 92–93, 97, 207 (n. 37)

Ojibwa tribe, 35, 36, 38, 149, 154

Oppenheimer, J. Robert, 48–49, 51

Opportunity (journal), 3, 87–88, 205 (n. 17)

Ottawa tribe, 40

Park, Robert E., 6, 12, 84–87, 89–92, 94–95, 102, 103, 107–10

Parsons, Elsie Clews, 73–74, 102

peyotism, 31, 149–51, 152, 153, 155–56, 160–75, 177, 183–84

Phillips, Ulrich B., 96–98, 101, 125, 126

Pilgrim's Progress, The (Bunyan), 134

Pittsburgh Courier, 2, 9, 77–78, 109

Popenoe, Paul, 88, 99

Powdermaker, Hortense, 14, 103

primitive Christianity, 130

"primitive" concept, 32–34; individuation in primitive peoples, 20–21, 22–27, 31–32

race riots, 85–87, 91–93

race theory, 1–9, 57, 86, 88–89, 187; Boas's critiques of, 55, 59–61, 67–69, 78–80, 88; popular assumptions about, 51–52, 67–68; scientific racism, 14, 57, 59, 69, 78, 80, 187

racial uplift, 85, 101

racism, current surge of, 188–89

Radin, Adolph, 18–19, 45, 62, 176–77

Radin, Doris, 47, 48

Radin, Max, 18, 47–48, 53

Radin, Paul: African American research by, 10, 11, 13–15, 23, 24, 27, 96, 101, 111–19, 125–29, 133–34, 141, 142–43, 148, 153, 179–80; alienation and, 23–24; anthropological (ethnological) approach of, 22–34, 66, 67, 95, 177–78, 179–80, 184–85; background and influences